Early Arianism—A View of Salvation

Early Arianism—A View of Salvation

ROBERT C. GREGG
and
DENNIS E. GROH

FORTRESS PRESS   PHILADELPHIA

Biblical quotations from the Revised Standard Version of the Bible, copyrighted 1946, 1952, © 1971, 1973 by the Division of Christian Education of the National Council of the Churches of Christ in the U.S.A., are used by permission.

The authors wish to acknowledge their gratitude to the following for permission to quote from material previously published:

Catholic University of America Press: A passage from Thomas B. Falls, trans., *Justin Martyr, Fathers of the Church: A New Translation*, vol. 6.

William B. Eerdmans Publishing Company: Quotations from *The Ante-Nicene Fathers*, ed. Alexander Roberts and James Donaldson, vol. 1, *The Apostolic Fathers, Justin Martyr, Irenaeus* and vol. 2, *Fathers of The Second Century*, are used by permission. Quotations from Philip Schaff and Henry Wace, ed., *A Select Library of Nicene and Post-Nicene Fathers of the Christian Church*, second series, vol. 4, *Select Writings and Letters of Athanasius, Bishop of Alexandria*, are used by permission.

Scholars Press: For permission to quote passages from Apostolos N. Athanassakis, trans., *The Life of Pachomius*, Society of Biblical Literature Texts and Translations of Early Christian Literature Series 2.

Peter Smith: A passage from *Origen: On First Principles*, trans. G. W. Butterworth.

The Society for Promoting Christian Knowledge, the publisher, and the author, J. Stevenson: For permission to quote an extract from J. Stevenson, *A New Eusebius.*

Westminster Press: The quotes from *Christology of the Later Fathers*, vol. 3, The Library of Christian Classics, edited by Edward Rochie Hardy and Cyril C. Richardson, published in the U.S.A. by the Westminster Press, 1954, are used by permission, as are the quotes from *Western Asceticism*, vol. 12, The Library of Christian Classics, edited by Owen Chadwick, published simultaneously by S.C.M. Press, Ltd., London, and the Westminster Press, Philadelphia. First published in 1958.

Library of Congress Cataloging in Publication Data

Gregg, Robert C
   Early Arianism—a view of salvation.

   Includes index.
   1. Arianism. 2. Jesus Christ—History of doctrines
—Early church, ca. 30-600. 3. Salvation—History of
doctrines—Early church, ca. 30-600. I. Groh, Dennis,
joint author. II. Title.
BT1350.G64 1981   273'.4   79–7379
ISBN 0–8006–0576–4

7700D80   Printed in the United States of America   1–576

To
Mary Layne Gregg
and
Ed, Anne, and Pat Groh

Contents

Preface

A certain stalemate seems to have been reached in discussions of the early stages of the Arian controversy. The first Arian spokesmen are repeatedly portrayed in the scholarly literature as philosophical cosmologians whose thought, because of a vague similarity to some earlier theological statements, was able to befuddle and beguile unsuspecting Christians and intellectually inexperienced emperors in the opening decades of the fourth century. The three most influential early Arians—Arius (256–336), Asterius the Sophist (d. ca. 341), and Eusebius of Nicomedia (d. ca. 342)—raised a controversy about the nature of God and his essential Son which could only be quelled by the first ecumenical council of the church and by the lonely courage reflected in the writings of Bishops Alexander and Athanasius.

How this small band of intellectual leaders, preoccupied with supposedly obtuse points involving the fracturing of the Godhead, could hoodwink the ecclesiastical East and command its corridors of power from the outbreak of the controversy (ca. 318) to the Synod of Antioch (341) is left to scholarly speculation and hence imagination.

The size of this little group has been expanded frequently to include Arians of the next generations (the neo-Arians), and the thought of these three progenitors has been expounded in terms of the succeeding generation of heretics (notably Aëtius and Eunomius). This has happened despite the fact that Athanasius' three authentic *Orations against the Arians* seem to be occupied entirely by ideas traceable to the thought of Arius, Asterius, and Eusebius of Nicomedia. In fact, the gulf between early Arian and neo-Arian was even greater than that which separated Nicene from neo-Nicene (and hence theologians of the Council of Nicaea from those of the Council of Constantinople in 381).

This book is offered as an attempt to break the scholarly stalemate—to suggest an account of the early Arian movement that is less enigmatic both in its own setting and to historians who study it. We are advancing a new interpretation of the movement's center and substance. This interpretation is based upon a reexamination of the extant primary sources—the letters and fragments of these three early Arians and the writings of those who sought to combat their doctrine. Criticism may be leveled at the use of materials preserved, transmitted, and reported by the Arians' most bitter antagonists. A careful scrutiny of both Arian and anti-Arian materials (particularly Athanasius' writings) has convinced us that orthodox polemicists do battle by distortion rather than by bald fabrication. We formulated our major conclusions from the Arians' own assertions, testing and corroborating Alexander's and Athanasius' reports of Arian teaching against those assertions and accepting from their reports only what was consonant with the emerging profile of early Arianism. Assessment of Athanasius as a source for the Arians needs to continue, giving attention to his rhetorical methods of argument. But we think that our thesis is supported by all the strata of the evidence.

We contend that early Arianism is most intelligible when viewed as a scheme of salvation. Soteriological concerns dominate the texts and inform every major aspect of the controversy. At the center of the Arian soteriology was a redeemer, obedient to his Creator's will, whose life of virtue modeled perfect creaturehood and hence the path of salvation for all Christians. For this reason our inquiry begins with Christology (chapter 1), treats the salvation of believers secondly (chapter 2), and proceeds to examine the problematic cosmology of the Arians from this christological and soteriological perspective (chapter 3). *The Life of Antony* constitutes a test case in the battle between competing soteriologies for the allegiance of fourth-century Christians (chapter 4), and our final chapter contrasts the two major salvific options hammered out in this debate.

A word is required about the terms *orthodox* and *Alexandrian episcopal theology,* which are employed throughout this book. We use the term *orthodox* anachronistically to signify that particular theology (and its proponents) which will ultimately carry the day. From our point of view as historians the term implies no value judgment. The phrase *Alexandrian episcopal theology* refers in this volume to the thought of Alexander and Athanasius (bishops of Alexandria from 312–328 and 328–373, respectively); their ideas differ in some respects, but on major points that concern us, they voice the same general and specific lines of argumentation and exegesis.

Although the primary responsibility for the writing of chapters 1 and 5 rests with Groh, and of chapters 2–4 with Gregg, both the research and authorship have been collaborative throughout, and we consider this close cooperation to have been richly rewarding.

We have benefited from the encouragement and criticisms of a number of scholars who attended readings of parts of this study at the Mid-West Patristics Seminar (1973), the Seventh International Conference on Patristic Studies (Oxford, England, in 1975), the American Society of Church History (1976), and the American Academy of Religion (1977). We are indebted to Dr. W. Taylor Stevenson and the *Anglican Theological Review* for publishing the first results of our research in 1977.

To Professors Glenn F. Chesnut, William R. Schoedel, Thomas Kopecek, Elizabeth Clark, Elaine Pagels, Robert M. Grant, Maurice F. Wiles, G. Christopher Stead, and Peter Brown we extend thanks for helpful questions and suggestions. We would like to acknowledge especially the interest and encouragement we have received from our faculty colleagues in Evanston and in Durham: Albert C. Sundberg, Jr., Ernest W. Saunders, Franklin W. Young, and David C. Steinmetz. The Reverend John L. Schreiber prepared the index.

Finally, this work would not have been possible without the cooperation and generosity of the administrations and staffs of the Divinity School at Duke University and Garrett-Evangelical Theological Seminary.

ROBERT C. GREGG
Durham, North Carolina

DENNIS E. GROH
Evanston, Illinois

Abbreviations

ANF
: *The Ante-Nicene Fathers: Translations of the Writings of the Fathers Down to 325 A.D.*, 10 vols., Alexander Roberts and James Donaldson (Grand Rapids: William B. Eerdmans Publishing Co., 1951–53).

Bright
: William Bright, ed., *The Orations of St. Athanasius against the Arians according to the Benedictine Text* (Oxford: Clarendon Press, 1873).

GCS
: Die griechischen christlichen Schriftsteller der ersten drei Jahrhunderte (Berlin: Akadamie-Verlag, 1897–).

Gregg and Groh
: Robert C. Gregg and Dennis E. Groh, "The Centrality of Soteriology in Early Arianism," *Anglican Theological Review* 59 (1977): 260–78.

JThS
: *Journal of Theological Studies* (London, vols. 1–50, 1899–1949; n.s. vol. 1, 1950–).

LCC¹²
: Owen Chadwick, ed. and trans., *Western Asceticism: Selected Translations with Introductions and Notes,* The Library of Christian Classics, vol. 12 (Philadelphia: Westminster Press, 1958).

Migne PG
: Jacque Paul Migne, ed., *Patrologiae Cursus Completus,* series graeca, 161 vols. (Paris: J. P. Migne, 1857–87).

NPNF
: *A Select Library of the Nicene and post-Nicene Fathers of the Christian Church,* second series, 14 vols., ed. Philip Schaff and Henry Wace (Grand Rapids: William B. Eerdmans Publishing Co., 1956).

Opitz²
: Hans-Georg Opitz, ed., *Athanasius: Werke,* fasc. 2 (Berlin: Walter de Gruyter, 1935).

Opitz³
: Hans-Georg Opitz, ed., *Athanasius: Werke,* fasc. 3, *Urkunden zur Geschichte des arianischen Streits: 318–328* (Berlin: Walter de Gruyter, 1935).

SC   Sources chrétiennes, série grecque, ed. Henri de Lubac and
            Jean Daniélou (Paris: Éditions du Cerf, 1945–).

SVF   Ioannis ab Arnim, ed., *Stoicorum Veterum Fragmenta,* 4 vols.
            (Stuttgart: B. G. Teubner, 1968).

TU   Texte und Untersuchungen zur Geschichte der altchristlichen
            Literatur (Berlin: Akademie-Verlag, 1883–).

VC   *Vigiliae Christianae: A Review of Early Christian Life and
            Language* (Amsterdam: North Holland Publishing Co.,
            1947–).

1

The Arian Christ

Everyone familiar with the early Arian writings knows the large claims made by them for the redeemer. He is *monogenēs theos* (μονογενὴς θεός)[1] or just *monogenēs;*[2] he is a "strong god" (ἰσχυρὸς θεός),[3] a god from above (ἄνωθεν θεός),[4] unchangeable (ἄτρεπτος) and unalterable,[5] the "power"[6] of God, the word of God, wisdom of God,[7] and so forth. But if all the criticism leveled at the Arian representation of Christ by Bishops Alexander and Athanasius, both of Alexandria, could be reduced to a single line, it would read like this: no matter how the Arians huff and puff, what they preach is a creature promoted to the status of a god. The Alexandrian bishops had it exactly right. The Arian Christ was a "creature" or a "work" of God the Creator who had been promoted to the rank of a divine son and redeemer.[8] Many scholars have noted this; few have thought about it; and none has given it the full weight and the systematic treatment that such an arresting christological option deserves.[9]

There are reasons for the scholarly oversight. The lucidity of Athanasius' arguments and his compelling command of rhetoric, the solemn authority of the Council of Nicaea, the momentum of a victorious orthodoxy—all have shaped our scholarly tastes and habits of thinking to the biases of Arius' enemies. Implicitly or explicitly we all play Arius' songs in an Athanasian key.[10] Yet one of the best attested and most ignored aspects of early Arian Christology has to do precisely with the chronicling of the creaturely limitations of their redeemer. The creaturehood of the Son was the pin which swung their christological door, and the portrayal of their redeemer's contingent existence constituted their most unanimous and telling blow against the newly developing Alexandrian episcopal orthodoxy. It is to the picture of this creaturely Christ, this promoted and adopted Son, this savior who is to be saved, that we must turn directly.

1

THE LIMITATIONS OF THE SON

At some point in the year A.D. 324, Bishop Alexander of Alexandria sent a letter to his namesake bishop of Constantinople which the later historian Theodoret preserved for us.[11] In that letter informing Alexander of the nature, progress, and synodal results of Arius' heresy in Egypt, the then bishop of Alexandria made an important charge, passed over by most modern scholars:

> [The Arians] remember all the passages concerning the Savior's passion, both the humiliation and the emptying [Phil. 2:5–11], and what is called his impoverishment [2 Cor. 2:9], and what acquired things [that is, the opposite of essential or natural things] the savior took to himself for our sakes, as a demurrer of his sublime and eternal divinity; but of those sayings [in the scriptures] which are indicative of his nature and glory and nobility and union with the Father, they are forgetful.[12]

The notice alerts us to the special sensitivity which the Arians had for those passages of Scripture that emphasized the suffering and creaturely characteristics to be drawn from the ministry of Jesus on earth. That the Arians turned the very human characteristics of the savior in the Gospels and Epistles to what they thought were their logical cosmological conclusions does not mean that cosmology or the doctrine of God was their starting point, as almost all modern scholars have contended.[13] Dr. Robert Sample has shown, in a fine dissertation on Paul of Samosata, that one of the major results of the Synod of Antioch of A.D. 268 was to render automatically suspect any theological system without a preexistent cosmological Christ.[14] All subsequent late third- and early fourth-century Christologies had to incorporate a preexistent Christ. But the early Arians seem to have proceeded from their exegesis of the scriptures to the conclusion that even the preexistent Christ was, and had to be, a creature, no matter how exalted were the results of his creaturehood. For this very reason Athanasius complained,

> for looking at the human characteristics (τὰ ἀνθρώπινα) of the Savior, they have considered him to be a creature (κτίσμα).[15]

The passage of Alexander's cited earlier gives us only a little information as to the specific passages of scripture used by the Arians. It alludes to 2 Cor. 2:9 and to Phil. 2:5–11, which was one of the most important of the Arian proof texts. Philippians 2 was the first scriptural passage which Athanasius treated systematically in his *Orations against the Arians,* and its themes persisted throughout the work. But a number of years later, safely embedded deep in his masterful attack on the Arians (where it would have less impact on the uninformed), Athanasius introduces a series of Gospel texts used by the Arians to highlight the human characteristics of their redeemer.[16] He announces this section in words almost identical to Alexander's decades before. Like Pharaoh, says Athanasius, the Arians' hearts are hardened, for

> while they hear and see the Savior's human attributes (τὰ ἀνθρώπινα) in the Gospels, they have utterly (τελεῖον) forgotten, like the Samosatene, the Son's paternal Godhead.

Then follows a series of texts drawn from Matthew, Luke, and John employed by the Arians to contend for the creaturehood of the Son and to break the essentialist linkage between the Son and the Father which was being newly developed in Alexandrian episcopal circles.

We will examine the prime characteristics of the earthly Jesus as exegeted and promulgated by Arius and his circle in a moment. But a brief word needs to be said about Arius as a scriptural exegete.

So firmly entrenched in all of our minds has been the picture of Arius as a logician and dialectician that our tendency has been to underrate and overlook his concern for biblical exactitude, especially as we become caught up in the rich scriptural citation of his gifted orthodox enemies. Yet a Latin translation of a fragment from a fourth-century Alexandrian "Jubilee" book carries an interesting notice of Arius' presbyterial days in Alexandria. It refers to him as a person who instructed the laity from scripture, who

> began under the fiction of teaching to exegete the doctrines of scripture, making an assembly in church on Wednesday and Friday as if for hearing the word of God.[17]

The orthodox author, to be sure, portrays Arius as dissembling his heretical thoughts under the guise of promulgating scriptural doctrines; but the import of the reference should not be lost. It acknowledges openly Arius' concern for doctrine based in exegesis of scripture.[18]

From the orthodox citations already given above, we know the Arians pieced together a picture of the earthly Christ which emphasized the existential and psychological aspects of creaturely existence in the ministry of Jesus. Athanasius has cast the Arian exegetical perspective in such a light

3

as to make it appear that they were simply responding to the strong scriptural proof texts of his party, but we have tried to indicate there is good reason to suppose that the Arians did far more than simply return orthodox texts with their own incidental scriptural reference.

The reality of the physical body of Jesus loomed large for the early Arians. In Arius' earliest "confession" to Alexander of Alexandria, he had protested against any christological formula that would bring the divine essence into contact with the human suffering incumbent upon bearing a body.[19] What exegetical conclusions and examples Arius held in the background at this point in 320 we can only surmise from Alexander's letter already cited. But Athanasius ascribes to the early Arians in the third book of his *Orations* a rather impressive list of Gospel texts from which they concluded that Christ had to be a creature. Among them were those texts which emphasized bodily humiliation even to the point of death on the cross. The Arians, reports Athanasius, ask,

> How do you dare to say that the one having a body is the proper Word of the Father's essence, so that he endured such a thing as this [that is, the cross]?[20]

When confronted with texts like John 6:42 and 8:58 emphasizing the Christ's eternality, the Arians stressed the human characteristics of the savior:

> How is he able to be Logos or God who slept as a man, wept, and had to learn by inquiry?[21]

Thus to the physical limitations of the body the Arians added the full range of psychological and spiritual limitations of a creature, buttressing each of their contentions with a Gospel reference. Jesus' fear and uncertainty in the face of the Passion was supported by appeals to John 12:27–28, Matt. 26:30, and John 13:21. These proved to the Arians, as did numerous other passages, that the savior was not the essential *dynamis* of the Father.[22] Nor was the Logos proper (Λόγος ἴδιος) the Christ who cries from the cross and utters in his life the words of Matt. 27:46, John 12:28, John 17:5, Matt. 26:41, and Mark 13:32. After listing the texts on which they made their point, Athanasius quotes their conclusions directly:

> If the Son were, according to your [that is, the orthodox] interpretation, eternally existent with God (ἀϊδίως ὑπάρχων ὁ Υἱὸς πρὸς τὸν Θεὸν), he had not been ignorant of the day [Mark 13:32] but had known as word; nor had been forsaken as being coexistent (συνάρχων) [Matt. 27:46]; nor had asked to receive glory, having it in the Father [John 12:28; 17:5]; nor would he have

4

prayed at all [Matt. 26:41], for being the word, he had needed nothing; but since he is a creature and one of the things generated, on account of this he said such things and he needed what he did not have; for it is proper for creatures to require and ask for what they do not have.[23]

Two aspects of this Arian picture of the biblical Jesus are important enough to their christological and soteriological scheme to require some expansion—the "derived" or "received" character of Jesus' power and the ignorance he evidences of divine and human matters.

Jesus' Derivative and Dependent Authority

The Jesus of history and the preexistent "Son" for the Arians were not only twin aspects of the same christological reality;[24] they were two harmonious ways to safeguard their cardinal principle—that all creatures, the redeemer notwithstanding, were ultimately and radically dependent on a Creator whose sole method of relating to his creation was by his will (βούλημα) and pleasure (θέλημα). There is no better-attested Arian principle. It cuts across every tradition of the early Arians which we possess; Arius, Asterius, and Eusebius of Nicomedia maintained the dependency of all things on the gracious will of the Creator. Eusebius of Nicomedia puts it as bluntly and as forthrightly as any of their party:

> There is nothing from his essence, but all things having come into being by his will, each one exists as it was begotten. For on the one hand there is God, but on the other are the things which will be like his Word with respect to similarity, and the things which came into being according to free will.[25]

This meant to Arius, as to his cohorts, that the very mediator was not an extension of the divine nature but a creation of the divine will.[26] Thus in the early Arian texts ἐκ τοῦ Θεοῦ means, as it does in this letter of Eusebius, "by his will" rather than "out of his substance."[27] Against any notion that the Son possessed his standing and status in the universe by consubstantiality with the Father, the Arians opposed their premise that the redeemer was dependent, as all creatures, on the will of God:

> Unless he has by will come to be, then God had a Son by necessity and against his good pleasure (μὴ θέλων).[28]

We will need to examine with more precision the importance of the Arian doctrine of the will of God when we explicate more exactly the earthly Jesus' relation to the Father; here it will be sufficient to note the dependent nature

5

of the redeemer's very beginning in existence. His existence was fully and uncompromisingly dependent upon the totally free will of the Creator.

The derivative character of the Son's existence was indicated to the Arians by a number of Gospel passages which emphasized the "received" character of the Son's authority and function. Thus Jesus' ἐξουσία is his not by nature but by gift of the Father (Matt. 28:18); his role as judge has the same derivative character (John 5:22). In a similar vein the Arians observed that all things are given (δέδωκεν) into the Son's hand for believing on him (John 3:35). Continuing to select those texts whose verbs and meaning were in the δίδωμι and παραδίδωμι family, the Arians cited also Matt. 11:27 and John 6:37 and concluded from all these texts,

> If he was, as you say, Son according to nature (κατὰ φύσιν), he had no need to receive (λαβεῖν), but he possessed (εἶχε) [these things] according to nature as a Son.[29]

For the Arians the creaturely character of Jesus portrayed in the Gospels even meant that he stood in need of God's empowering Holy Spirit. Therefore, they seemed to have insisted that the Son, as other persons, received the Spirit for empowerment in his life of obedience to the Father.

The argument Athanasius built up, which contains this contention, was constructed to counter the Arian claim to likeness with the Son himself.[30] Athanasius is expounding what it means for us to be "in God" and for the Christ to be "in the Father."[31] The Son dispenses the Spirit to us, he says, rather than receiving it; and in fact, the Spirit draws from the Word rather than the other way around. Thus Christ is "in the Father" essentially; and we are "in God" through Christ:

> . . . except they [the Arians] shall dare, as commonly, so now to say, that the Son also by participation (μετοχῇ) of the Spirit and by improvement of conduct (βελτιώσει πράξεως) came to be himself also in the Father.[32]

Some important themes raised by the above quote—namely, the similarity of the Son's status to ours and the progress of the Son in ethical behavior—will be discussed at length a bit later. What we are trying to emphasize here is the need of the redeemer to receive from the Creator authority, empowerment, and help—even to the extent of receiving the Spirit from God as other human persons had to do.

6

The Limited Knowledge of the Son

An early notice of Arianism carries a charge by Alexander of Alexandria that the Arian redeemer was a creature of limited insight into both God's and his own nature.

> For neither perfectly nor accurately does the Logos know the Father, nor is he able to see him fully (τελείως). And indeed the Son as he is does not even know his own essence.[33]

Almost everything we know of Arius' own thought underscores the accuracy of Alexander's charge. In sight, as in "essential" knowledge, the Son's powers are considerably less than absolute. So Arius testifies in his *Thalia:*

> To speak concisely, God (ὁ Θεός) is invisible to the Son [cf. John 1:18a]; for he is to himself what he is—that is, unspeakable (ἄλεκτος), so that nothing of the things called apprehensible (κατὰ . . . κατάληψιν) does the Son know to declare. For it is impossible for him to investigate the Father who is by himself (ἐφ᾿ ἑαυτοῦ). For the Son himself does not know his own essence, for being a Son he exists truly by the will of the Father.[34]

Here again we see the centrality of the Son's dependence on the divine will; in this case, its corollary is a limited knowledge of the Father and an inability to perceive certainly the essential characteristics of his own essence. This theme apparently ran throughout Arius' *Thalia,* for Athanasius repeats this same point in his report of the document, including the detail of the separate and alien character of the three Persons of the Trinity, which Arius also employed in order to underscore the Son's epistemological limitations.[35] Since the Son is a child of the Father's sovereign will, he has no immediate and natural access into the structures of being. Why Arius takes this position and whence its origins are seldom discussed by scholars. The portions of the *Thalia* quoted to us by Athanasius, as well as Alexander's earlier charge, give no direct scriptural citations by which he reached his conclusions. The orthodox would like us to accept the Arian tenet under the general category of "blaspheming" the Son. But a careful examination of arguments put forward in the *De Decretis* shows that a large portion of the debate was fleshed out by the Arians and orthodox through an examination of models of "sonship" in the scriptures. We shall return to such a method again and again in this study, but here a brief digression is required.

Scholars of the patristic period have a certain right to feel patronized upon being reminded that the unquestioned and universally recognized theological textbook was the Bible. It was the early church's systematic theology, its Kittel *Wörterbuch,* its Greek lexicon. Terms in dispute and debate, phrases which needed explication, and even whole perspectives on soteriology were built up out of a careful examination of systematic and incidental treatments of a given topic by the scriptures. This meant that no matter what nonscriptural elements were added to the pursuit of definitions (for example, elements drawn from philosophy, rhetoric, law), scriptural justification was primary. Thus recent studies have shown that those Fathers considered to be most faithful to exegetical concerns brought to the scriptures hermeneutical baggage from "secular" disciplines which shaped not only the form of doctrine but also its substance.[36] Similarly, heretics who had been charged with amalgamating the scriptures with "pagan" philosophy and myth have in more recent scholarship been considered to be exegetes of some persuasiveness and no little sophistication.[37] It would thus be pedantic and a little high-handed to remind working scholars of the need to penetrate the mist of battle between orthodoxy and heresy to uncover the scriptural hermeneutic of each party before making judgments, were not the mass of the literature on Arianism weighted against precisely such a venture. Arius and his circle are described again and again as philosophers, logicians, demipagans, but only rarely as persons concerned to exegete the scriptures by a careful and self-conscious hermeneutic.[38] Little more has been done to lay bare their opponents' hermeneutical biases. In the case of both Arianism and orthodoxy in the early fourth century, their general biblical hermeneutic exactly corresponds to their soteriological programs. As we have argued elsewhere:

> Salvation, for orthodoxy, is effected by the Son's essential identity with the Father—that which links God and Christ to creation is the divine nature's assumption of flesh. Salvation for Arianism is effected by the Son's identity with the creatures—that which links Christ and creatures to God is conformity of will.[39]

Thus the Arians instinctively gravitated to those scriptural texts and exegetical perspectives which emphasized the empirical commonality of the redeemer's characteristics with those of all other creatures. Athanasius' party from the beginning of the controversy instinctively leaned toward showing the difference or distinction between the redeemer's characteristics and ours. Or, as Alexander so succinctly put it:

> It must be seen that the sonship of our Savior has no community with the sonship of the rest [of people].[40]

In terms then of what the Son could properly know about the Father, both Arian and orthodox scuttled off to their theological textbook, the holy scriptures, to look up passages which spoke about "son" and "sons" and came out precisely where we would expect their respective principles to lead them—on exactly opposite sides of the question. Athanasius accepted the biological definition of "son," in which the "physical" or "natural" relation between Father and Son is primary (for example, Isaac, son of Abraham).[41] This gave him an ontological link between the Son and God which enabled Christ to be God's proper Logos and Wisdom and which invested the Son with the divine omniscience.[42] The Arians located and used an extended sense of "sonship" in the Scriptures by which God was said "to adopt sons" from among his creatures. "Son" in this sense is a circumlocution for "believer," and the term has this meaning in Arian proof texts like Deut. 14:1 and John 1:12.[43] Consequently, whatever properties or powers can be claimed for the Son in the scriptures are read in this extended sense, according to which the Son himself gains these by adoption as a believer; and this point is pressed by the Arians to include even the key realities:

> And Christ is not true God, but by participation (μετοχῇ) even he was made God (ἐθεοποιήθη). The Son does not know the Father exactly, nor does the Logos see the Father perfectly, and neither does he perceive nor the Logos understand the Father exactly; for he is not the true and only Logos of Father, but by a name alone he is called Logos and Sophia and by grace is called Son and Power.[44]

The passage is so laden with import for a picture of early Arianism that we will return to its topics in greater detail a bit later. But a point central to our current discussion emerges: the ontological relation between Father and Son is shattered in Arianism, so that no natural knowledge or perception between Father and Son (indeed, between any father and son) can be presupposed and built upon.[45] The Son is a creature. Just as with all other creatures, no direct *analogia entis* can exist between the sovereignly free Creator whose modus operandi is by his will and the creatures who exist at his pleasure. This is the import of Eusebius of Nicomedia's argumentation denying that God's nature can be deduced from his effects, whether from rebellious sons (Isa. 1:2), inconstant creatures (Deut. 32:18), or drops of dew (Job 38:28).[46]

Numerous passages in the Gospels could show the Arians that according to their lights, they had taken up the proper biblical notion of sonship and

9

drawn the right conclusions about the Son's perceptual limitations. If he were by nature the true and proper Wisdom of the Father, the Arians implied, why do the Gospels preserve passages that show Jesus doesn't know who men say he is (Matt. 16:13), or where Lazarus lay (John 11:34), or how many loaves the disciples had (Mark 6:38)?[47] Nor, they argued, should Jesus be the proper Logos of God; for "of that day and that hour no man knows, no, neither the angels nor the Son" (Mark 13:32).[48]

Athanasius' hermeneutic will lead him to attribute all such passages which speak of the creaturely suffering and limitation of the redeemer to the mortal body borne by the Logos or to a "religious" sense in which Christ asked a question with full knowledge of the matter and of his own imminent response.[49] The Arians took these same passages as obvious proof of the Son's full creaturehood.[50]

We do not know precisely how the various partisans of early Arianism worked out the finer machinery of the Son's limited knowledge. We do possess some lines by Arius that partially reveal his thinking on the subject:

> Let me say clearly how the Invisible is seen by the Son; by the power by which God (ὁ Θεός) is able to see; in his own measure the Son submits (ὑπομένει) to see the Father, as is proper.[51]

What Arius appears to be proposing is a proportionate knowledge vouchsafed to the obedient (that is, ὑπομένει) creature by God the Father.

In this Arius stands closest to a statement found in Irenaeus. Irenaeus argues that the one God is fundamentally invisible (ἀόρατος, *invisibilis*) and yet was seen by the prophets who predicted that God would be seen by men as well. He then quotes Matt. 5:8 to add Christ's support to that testimony and proceeds to explain how it is that the invisible God can be seen.

> But as regards his greatness (τὸ μέγεθος) and his ineffable glory (τὴν ἀνεξήγητον δόξαν), "no one will see God and live" (Exod. 33:20), for the Father is incomprehensible; but as to his love and kindness and his ability to do all things, he gives even this to men who love him, that is, seeing God (τὸ ὁρᾶν Θεόν). . . . And on the one hand, man is not able to see God by himself (ἀφ' ἑαυτοῦ); on the other hand, God when he wishes (βουλόμενος) is seen by men, by whom he wills and when he wills and to the degree that he wills [cf. 1 Cor. 12:11] (καὶ ὁπότε βούλεται καὶ καθὼς βούλεται).[52]

What should be stressed here is the close relationship between dependence on divine will and whatever direct experience of God ("seeing" or "knowing") creatures can have.[53] To be dependent on the will of God is to

10

have proportionate knowledge of him—"to the degree that he wills," says Irenaeus, who echoes the sentiment and language of 1 Cor. 12:11; "in his own measure . . . as is proper," says Arius.[54] What Arius apparently has in mind runs somewhat parallel to an old Christian anthropological scheme of the creature under the Spirit of God (indeed, one who participates in the Spirit)[55] who is not given knowledge of God as he is in himself (Irenaeus says "his greatness" and "his ineffable glory") and whose ability to see depends on the Father's willing self-revelation (Arius: "by the power by which God sees"; Irenaeus: "God gives even this to men who love him, that is, seeing God").

That the Son had a limited or proportionate experience of the Father seems to have indicated to Arius that Christ, like all other creatures, was cast in the role of an obedient servant living by faith in his Father. Athanasius preserves a somewhat extended discussion in his second *Oration* in which he treats Heb. 2:14–18 and 3:2. The announced subject of the discussion is whether the Word "is begotten" or "became."[56] But the major problem is raised by the phrase from Heb. 3:2a ("who is faithful to him that made him"). Debate here focuses on the word "faithful" (πιστόν), which the Arians used to qualify the verbal "made" (lit., "to the one making him," τῷ ποιήσαντι). Thus Athanasius complains:

> Further, if the expression "being faithful" (πιστόν) is a difficulty to them, from the thought that "faithful" is used of him and of all men, because believing (πιστεύων) he receives the reward of faith, it is time also for the same reason on the one hand to accuse Moses, who says, "God is faithful and true,"[57] and on the other hand Paul, who writes, "who will not allow you to be tempted beyond what you are able" (1 Cor. 10:13). But when the saints say such things, they did not think of God in a human way (ἀνθρώπινα); but they recognized there was a double meaning in scripture of the term "faithful" (τοῦ πιστοῦ); the first as "faithful," the second as "trustworthy" (ἀξιόπιστον); the first befits man and the second befits God.[58]

Athanasius then quotes a series of scriptures to make his point—Ps. 145:14 (LXX), 1 Tim. 5:16, Titus 3:8, and so forth—and then concludes,

> "Who is faithful to him that made him" does not imply likeness (τὴν ὁμοιότητα) to other men, nor that *believing,* he *became* well pleasing [emphasis added].[59]

That the divine Son was a "faithful" creature, that is to say, that he exercised faith (believing fidelity) in his Creator, was totally abhorrent to Athanasius.

11

If the Hebrews text was to be understood at all, it could not be taken to refer to the "essence of the Word" but had to be a reference to the Word's incarnation.[60] Nothing could be farther from the Arian picture of the Christ; for Arian and orthodox gravitated to polar opposites in their portrayal of the Son's creaturely limitations, each following his own hermeneutical stance. Though both sides could agree on the major characteristics of the incarnate Christ, each explained them according to his own presuppositions. The Arian seized every opportunity to show that the Jesus of scripture had to be a creature. The orthodox attributed each human characteristic to the "flesh" or to the necessities contingent upon the incarnation for the renewal of our flesh.

We have tried to focus on the Arians' conception of the Son's limitations. So far we have contended that the Arians, proceeding on the basis of their hermeneutic, had drawn forth from the Gospels and Epistles a picture of a creature totally dependent on the will of his Creator. He bore the marks of true humanity—the body's infirmities, the mind's uncertainties, the soul's troublings, the need for divine empowerment through the Spirit. He exhibited obedient trust in his Creator. As presented in several of the sources, the characteristics of the savior stressed by the Arians appear to be advanced with polemical intent. These characteristics are cast by the orthodox as contentious and wrongheaded attacks against the substantial divinity of the Son. The Arians themselves pointed their volleys at their enemies in such a way as to leave the impression with the casual reader that the thrust of their Christology was mainly destructive—it appeared to be aimed at destroying the Alexandrian bishops' position and did not concern itself with positive christological formulations. In fact, this is not the case. Far beyond the clear desire to deflate what the Arians considered to be a disastrously overinflated Christology was the desire to chronicle the savior's creaturely characteristics for a positive soteriology which seemed to the Arians to conform better to scripture and human experience. It is this positive christological concern which goes almost entirely unnoticed in the scholarly and popular literature on Arianism. Writers invariably interpret the movement in its early stages as a conspiracy to "demote" the divine Son to the level of a creature. And indeed, the positive aspects of the christological formulas are at first difficult to see in the sources; but once seen, their ubiquity simply overwhelms the reader. It is to these "constructive" elements of Arian Christology that we now turn.

12

THE OBEDIENT SON

We have seen throughout the first section of this chapter a concerted effort on the part of the Arians to explore and explicate the full creatureliness of the Son. This they did by drawing the closest possible links between Christ and fellow creatures. Alexander and Athanasius took exactly the opposite position by drawing their soteriological and christological boundary in such a way that Christ was set off as far as was possible from all other rational creatures. The closest links were to be drawn between the Father and the Son, and this relationship was given a structural bonding by emphasizing the ontological or essential commonality between Father and Son. Thus for the orthodox the problem of the redeemer's knowing and seeing was solved by the essential divinity of the savior. Nothing of the divine Logos or Sophia could be lost in the process of the Son's becoming incarnate, because divine nature by definition admits of no gains or losses.[61] When the Arians tried to argue for a redeemer that exercised faith, as we have already seen, Athanasius responded with an assertion of the essential unchangeability of the Son and used ἀναλλοίωτος and its verb to interpret and control the πιστός of Heb. 3:2.

> Therefore reasonably the apostle, discoursing concerning the bodily presence of the Word, says, an "apostle and faithful to him that made him," pointing out that even when becoming man, "Jesus Christ" "the same yesterday and today and forever" [Heb. 13:8] is unalterable (ἀναλλοίωτος).[62]

The point was of considerable importance to the orthodox party, for the Son's essential unchangeability removed him ontologically from the realm of moral and ethical choice. *Realm* is not really the correct term to describe the human need to sort out correct from incorrect choices; for Alexander and Athanasius alike regarded it more as a morass than a realm. If the redeemer was allowed to choose between options, they divined, how could anyone be sure that he chose rightly in the face of the stratagems of the devil and the limitations of human life? Therefore, from the very beginning of the Arian controversy, the Alexandrian bishops took the unchangeability of the Son as a fixed plank in their platform against Arius.[63]

From the beginning, the Arians emphasized the Son's free moral choice. When Alexander reports the Arian statements concerning the Son's ethical changeability, he tends to display them in such a way as to preclude the

13

possibility of victorious and proper ethical choice. Thus after telling us that the Arians claimed,

> Wherefore he is both changeable (τρέπτος) and variable (ἀλλοιωτός) as to nature (τὴν φύσιν) as also all rational natures (πάντα τὰ λογικά),[64]

the orthodox will go on to indicate that such a change could mean a change for the worse:

> Someone asked them if the Logos of God is able to be changed, as the devil was, and they were not afraid to say, "Yes, he is able; for being begotten and created, he has a changeable nature."[65]

While the Arians apparently did accept the *theoretical* possibility that Christ would succumb to temptation, this was not the thrust of their position. They were anxious to establish free will in the nature of their redeemer. The God who creates by his sovereign will and who relates to his creation by will alone requires a freely obedient rational creature who responds also by willing. *Thus the redeemer's ability to respond is protected by the doctrine of the changeability of the Son.* For this reason the Arians yoked free will (αὐτεξούσιος) and alterability even in their questions aimed at the man in the street. They asked average folk,

> And has he free will and does not change by his own choosing, being of a changeable nature? For he is not like a stone remaining unalterable by his own power.[66]

One of the biblical texts employed by the Arians to show the Son's alterability was drawn from Ps. 44:7 (LXX). It was one of their most valued proof texts. Athanasius writes in refutation of their exegesis of the verse:

> But the statement "you have loved righteousness and hated iniquity" set forth in the psalm does not show, as you think, the nature of the Logos to be "changeable" (τρεπτήν), but rather it even signifies from this his unchangeability. For since the nature of originate creatures is changeable, and some on the one hand transgressed but others disobeyed, just as was said; and their actions are not steadfast (βεβαία), but often it is possible that one good man presently is changed afterward and becomes another, so that the man now righteous (δίκαιον) is found shortly to be unrighteous; therefore there was need of an unchangeable (ἄτρεπτος) one, in order that men might have as an image (εἰκόνα) and type (τύπον) for virtue the immutability (ἀμετάβλητον) of the righteousness of the Logos.[67]

Athanasius' statement is important in two respects. First, it sets forth

14

categorically the cardinal importance of the concept of the unchange-ability of the Logos to the Alexandrian episcopal soteriology. Free choice implicates the redeemer in the world of ethical instability and provides no ontologically secure model for human behavior.

Secondly, the phrase that the Arians quoted from Ps. 44:7 (LXX), "you have loved righteousness and hated iniquity," shows the link that existed in their minds between "loving" or "affection" on the one hand and free will or choice represented by the changeability of the Logos. The link was a Stoic one that was of basic importance to Arian argumentation over the term ἄτρεπτος at the Council of Nicaea.[68] "Affection" was for them a species of "willing."

It was, as we said, Stoic. Diogenes Laertius preserves a list of the "innocent emotions" (εὐπάθειαι), the third of which is "willing" (βούλησις). *Boulēsis* was defined as "opposite to desire" (τῇ ἐπιθυμίᾳ), being a rational appetency (εὔλογον ὄρεξιν). Diogenes then lists the subcategories of each "innocent emotion," and among the species of *boulēsis* appear benevolence (εὔνοια), goodwill (εὐμένεια), affection (ἀσπασμός), and important for our purposes here, loving (ἀγάπησις).[69] Such a Stoic connection between willing and loving lies behind the interchangeability of the phrases "Son of his love" (cf. Col. 1:13) and "Son of his will" by Origen.[70] Perceiving that the Arians make just such a connection, Athanasius hints strongly that they attributed "human emotions" (ἀνθρωποπαθής) to God by their theories of the Son's generation.[71]

It is in terms of Stoic ethical theory of the Roman period and its critics, modified somewhat in Christian circles, that the Arian statements about the Christ become intelligible.

The Stoics had created and passed down from the classical to the Hellenistic and Roman periods another distinction important for the early stages of the Arian controversy. They distinguished between the sage or wise man (σοφός, *sapiens*) and the fool (φαῦλος, *insipiens*). The sage was a perfected creature. He had arrived at wisdom and so had lost those marks of creaturehood which dogged the rest of humankind—ignorance, error, and especially suffering.[72] In philosophical perspective the term *philosopher*, applied technically to the sage, connoted the apotheosis of human life, which was life as a god. Plutarch recounts as illustrative of this phenomenon that

15

when the youths of Athens were addressed as philosophers, they would quickly demur, saying,

I am no god, I assure you; why think me like the immortals?[73]

In Stoic circles, the primary mark of the sage was his ἀπάθεια or, as it was occasionally termed by a Platonist aiming at the same target, his παντελής ἀπάθεια ("complete indifference").[74] The sages' opposite was as clearly delineated; the presence of the effects of πάθη in a person indicated that one was still a fool.[75]

If, as we think, one of the most important keys to unlocking Arian Christology and soteriology is to be found in Stoic-influenced ethical theory, it becomes important to recapitulate some of Arius' positions already discussed.[76] The Son is pictured as a creature who lacks certain knowledge of his own or his Father's essence. In Stoic terms this meant the Son could not be considered *sophos,* a status which in fact Arius explicitly reserved to the Creator.[77] This did not mean that Arius conceived of God in the traditional Stoic material and somatic sense, at least as Stoic positions were conceived by Greek Christian authors.[78] Arius, like almost all early Christian writers, becomes a biblical Platonist when he has to discuss God's attributes.[79] But the earthly Arian redeemer *emphatically* was not God; he was an embodied creature. Hence Stoic commonplaces about the ethical life in the body could be applied to the redeemer along the lines of Chadwick's general dictim, that for Platonized Christian authors like Clement and Origen, Plato was considered to be right about God but the Stoics right about ethics.[80] Thus the suffering (τό πάθος) of Jesus, as well as his ignorance, would have indicated to Arius that his redeemer was not considered to be a σοφός. Since no πάθη was considered more problematic than fear (φόβος), Christ's Gospel expressions of agitation and fear would further remove him from the corridors of wisdom.[81]

If Jesus was not a wise man, was he then a fool? Technically yes, for the commonplace passed down from the founders of Stoicism continued to hold to the distinction between wise man and fool as the major categories which mattered in classifying humans, and the sources even into late antiquity continue to repeat this old *topos.*[82] But writers of the Roman period grew increasingly dissatisfied with the "all or nothing" quality of this means of classification.

16

Critics and correctors of Stoic understandings like Cicero, Seneca, and even the Platonist Plutarch began to take another line that was already found seminally in Chrysippus[83] by emphasizing the importance of progress toward perfection. The one advancing toward perfection in virtue came to receive increasing stress. Technically one advancing in virtue was still a fool. But Roman pragmatism refused to rest easy with the judgment that all sins were equal and began to focus on the different effects of the sins and on the intentions of those who committed the sins. With that splendid Roman blend of fraternal concern and levelheadedness, writers began to sense that an ignoring of progress in virtue could be tantamount to a discouragement toward virtue. In short, if one emphasized what we would call today the "darkness to light" quality of perfection in virtue, despair of attainment might be the end result (at worst) or ignorance of one's perfected virtue (at best).[84] Hence προκοπή, which had belonged to a kind of ethically neutral zone in earlier thinkers,[85] became *in practice,* if not in theory, a valuable and laudatory avenue to the divine. The person's advance in virtue, complete with pithy instructions to identify and note one's progress, began to be stressed by Roman authors.

With the concern for gradual growth in virtue toward perfection came a new emotionalism in Stoicism. A Stoic of this stripe now emphasized not just ἐπιστήμη *(scientia)* and the mind's tranquil judgment (διάνοια) but *boulēsis (voluntas),* defined by Stoic authors as a rational appetency (εὔλογος ὄρεξις).[86] Thus "willing" (that is, to progress and to perform the good), whose connection to "loving" we have already noted, came to the fore as an important member of a class of emotions called εὐπάθεια.[87] When writers attuned to the new winds of ethical theory took pen in hand, they did so with a pastoral concern which could write lines like Seneca's: "Let *scientia* be absent rather than *voluntas* . . . ," and "A great part of progress to virtue is wanting to progress."[88] Or, criticizing Stoic ethical theory, they could emphasize "emotional" progress of the one who advances, as Plutarch:

> Inasmuch as complete indifference (ἀπάθεια) is a great and divine thing (μέγα καὶ θεῖον), whereas progress, as they say, resembles a sort of abatement and moderation of the emotions (ἡ προκοπή δι᾽ ὡς λέγουσιν ἔοικεν ἐνδόσει τινὶ παθῶν καὶ παρότητι), it is our duty to compare our present emotions (πρὸς αὐτα . . . τὰ πάθη) with their former selves and with one another and thus determine the differences.[89]

17

Just as the Roman writers, particularly the Latins Cicero and Seneca, could take exception to the rigidity of the old Stoic patterns of wise man and fool and emphasize the appetitive aspect of willing the good, so a Christian writer like Origen could state the position,

> But they [the Stoics] say thirdly that to will the good and to run toward the good (τὸ θέλειν τὰ καλά καὶ τὸ τρέχειν ἐπὶ τὰ κάλα) belongs to the middle, and is neither wise (ἀστεῖον) nor foolish (φαῦλον),[90]

and then proceed to demolish it. Origen argued that if willing the good was indifferent, so was willing evil. He then concluded (on Rom. 9:16),

> But it is not in vain when Paul gives all his advice, and when he blames some and approves of others, nor is it vain when we yield ourselves up to willing what is better and to desiring eagerly the things that are excellent.[91]

When Origen returns to this theme some paragraphs later, he comes down firmly on the exercise of will as a key ingredient of προκοπή.[92]

Origen, like Athanasius, knew that human will, if truly free, could also engineer an ethical turn for the worse. This is exactly the impasse in which we left Arius and Athanasius some pages ago in their fight over whether the Logos was changeable. Alexander of Alexandria and Athanasius maintained that "changeable" meant "able to be tempted and fall." And in all fairness to the orthodox, this point the Arians had to grant.[93] But their accent did not fall on the capriciousness of the Son's free will. They stressed not possibility but fact, and the fact was that scripture affirmed, "Jesus *advanced* (προέκοπτε) in wisdom and stature and favor (χάριτι) with God and man" (Luke 2:52). Thus the early Arians put forward a picture of the Christ remarkably like the moderated Stoic advancing one, who possessed the requisite aspiration to perfection and virtue though lacking in perfected knowledge and complete control of his emotions. But as one of the advancing ones, he progressed ever onward toward perfection. Scripture testified both to his advance and to his ultimate perfection which ended in adoption by the Creator as υἱός, understood to mean θεός. It was an old scheme previously used to describe the believer's incorporation into final salvation, as attested in second-century writers like Irenaeus:

> There is none other called God by the scriptures except the Father of all, and the Son, and those who possess the adoption.[94]

The point is that when the Arians said Jesus was changeable, they meant *improvable.* And they described this improvement in virtue along the lines of the Stoic advance, especially as the concept had been modified in pagan and Christian circles to emphasize the positive aspects of the rational appetite termed "willing." In certain Christian circles the interchangeability of terms like *willing* and *loving* and the insistence that willing the good and striving toward the good were themselves worthy (and not merely "indifferent") enabled the Arians to piece together a picture of a Christ advancing through genuine struggle to a triumphant end. It is to a closer look at the Arian description of this advance in virtue that we must now turn.

Improvability and Advance

From the beginning of the controversy the Arians had apparently cited Ps. 44:7 (LXX) as evidence of Jesus' obedient advance in virtue.[95] A major section of Bishop Alexander's *Letter to Alexander* is devoted to combating the Arian statements regarding the Son's advance.[96] In these sections of the letter the changeability of the Son is yoked with advance, showing the connection that existed in the Arians' mind between the changeability of the Son and his moral improvability. The Arians insisted that Jesus,

> having also a changeable nature (τρεπτῆς τυγχάνοντα φύσεως), on account of the diligence and exercise of conduct did not undergo a change for the worse.[97]

Alexander's fight throughout this section of the letter revolves around the differentiation of two kinds of sonship—the natural (φύσει) sonship of his party's Christ whose sonship is unchangeable (ἀμετάπτωτος), and that sonship which devolves on believers by adoption (θέσει) and which is changeable. Thus he contrasts the unchangeability of

> the natural sonship of the paternal endeavor, not by diligence of conduct and practice of moral advancement (οὐ τρόπων ἐπιμέλεια καὶ προκοπῆς ἀσκήσει), but obtaining that [sonship] by a property of nature,

with

> the adoption (υἱοθεσία) of rational creatures which is theirs not according to nature but by fitness of character (τρόπων ἐπιτηδειότητι) and free gift (δωρεᾷ) of God is even changeable (μεταπτώτην).[98]

From such reports as these we discern that the Arians put forward a redeemer by whose free will choices for improvement of character were to be made[99] and the habit of virtue (ἕξις ἀρετῆς) was to be cultivated.[100]

To point toward the progress and wisdom of Jesus which excluded him from being the "proper" Wisdom of God, the Arians cited Luke 2:52.[101] But two of their favorite proof texts were the christological hymn from Philippians 2 and Ps. 44:7 (LXX). Both of these texts set forth a promotional scheme of Christ raised by God to the pinnacle of creaturely exaltation because of his obedient fidelity in the virtuous life. The Arians laid stress on the δίο and διὰ τοῦτο of the respective texts, thus emphasizing the "reward" given to Christ for his life of improvement. Athanasius quotes directly from Arius and Eusebius of Nicomedia to highlight their "heretical" emphasis:

> If on account of this [that is, δίο of Phil. 2:9] he was exalted, and he received grace, and on account of this [that is, διὰ τοῦτο of Ps. 44:7] he was anointed, he received a reward of purpose (μισθὸν τῆς προαιρέσεως ἔλαβε). But having acted from purpose, he is of an entirely changeable nature.[102]

Athanasius draws out his response along the same trajectory as that taken by his predecessor Alexander decades earlier.

> Can anything be plainer and more express? He [Christ] was not from a lower state promoted but humbled himself. Where then is any reward of virtue, or what advancement and promotion in humiliation? For if, being God, he became man, and descending from on high, he is still said to be exalted, where is he exalted, being God?[103]

Orthodoxy draws its firm boundary precisely at this point. Only creatures can improve in virtue and receive God's gracious favor. The redeemer was, and had to be, the very image of God, into whose likeness humans were to be conformed.[104] The Arian position that the very redeemer's likeness to God was to be one of virtuous advance was considered by the Alexandrian bishops to be blasphemous in the extreme. To elaborate on advance to perfection the Arians drew on the same classical notions that their opponents knew; but unlike their opponents, they applied these to the total redeemer, not merely to his human characteristics (τὰ ἀνθρώπινα).[105] Thus Jesus' approach to God was seen as a growth or advance in virtue. A near-contemporary pagan like Porphyry could conceive of ethical conformity to the divine in a similar vein and could counsel an aspirant:

> But the man worthy (ἄξιος) of God is indeed divine (θεῖος). And you honor God best (ἄριστα) when you liken (ὁμοιώσῃς) your own thought (διάνοια) to God. But the likeness will be through virtue alone (διὰ μόνης ἀρετῆς). For virtue alone draws the soul above and toward character (τὸ συγγενές). There is nothing other as great to God as virtue. God is greater (μείζων) than virtue. But God secures (βεβαιοῖ) the man who practices good deeds (καλά).[106]

20

When therefore Arius describes Christ as "God" (θεός) without the article, we have every right to read "divine" (θεῖος); for he has in mind the scheme of a perfected creature who, after progress in virtue, has been raised by the Creator to the status of a υἱός, understood to mean θεός (= θεῖος).[107] Similarly, in the one passage in which Arius terms Christ ἄτρεπτος he means that unchangeability which comes to the perfected creature that holds unswervingly to the love of God.[108] Thus the changeability of the Son meant in Arian strategy "freely improvable"—a Son, as the Arians maintained, who

also by participation (μετοχῇ) of the Spirit and by improvement of conduct (βελτιώσει πράξεως) came to be himself also in the Father (γέγονε καὶ αὐτὸς ἐν τῷ πατρί).[109]

Far more than a borrowing from selected and adapted aspects of Stoic ethical commonplaces buttressed the Arian concern for an improvable redeemer. A number of streams in the biblical tradition seemed to propel the Arians to their conclusion. For example, Prov. 8:22; Heb. 1:4; 3:1–2; Acts 2:36—all directed them toward a promotional christological under- standing.[110] The Arians stressed the phrase "for his works" in the Prov. 8:22 text and linked it to Heb. 1:4:

Being made so much better (κρείττων) than the angels as he had by inheritance obtained a more excellent (διαφορώτερον) name than they.[111]

Thus Arius will write somewhat more perplexingly in his *Thalia:*

One equal to the Son the superior [ὁ κρείττων = God] is able to beget, but not one more excellent (διαφορώτερον), or better (κρείττονα), or greater (μείζονα).[112]

He has in view most probably the Heb. 1:4 text. Again from the same chapter of Athanasius' *Orations* we find the familiar Prov. 8:22b phrase linked to Heb. 3:1–2a:[113]

Wherefore, holy brethren, partakers of the heavenly calling (κλήσεως ἐπουρανίου μέτοχοι), consider the apostle and high priest of our profession, Christ Jesus who was faithful to him that made him.

And the Hebrews text goes on to compare Christ's obedience to that of Moses, a comparison from which the Arians did not shrink.[114] We have already noted how the Arians fitted "who was faithful to him that made him" into their system,[115] so no more needs to be said at this point.

But to the above passages the Arians added Acts 2:36: "Therefore let all

21

the house of Israel assuredly know that God has made the same Jesus whom you crucified both Lord and Christ." Athanasius will argue that the verb "made" refers to the Son's body and therefore to his lordship "toward us."[116] He tells us only that the Arians used this text to argue that Christ was a "creature." But in the light of the promotion of the redeemer which the Arians pressed for with such vigor, we can see some other nuances they drew from the text. "Lord" and "Christ" are titles of achievement—received appellations based on Jesus' life and work.

It might be asked at what point or points Jesus receives his various titles.[117] The New Testament texts cited suggest that the resurrection is the point at which the victorious redeemer has completed his arduous process of obedient improvement; and indeed, the Passion cycle seems to have been the culminating focus of Jesus' development for the Arians. Thus Athanasius will warn them,

> If then they suppose that the Savior was not Lord and King [cf. Acts 2:36] even before he became man and endured the cross, but then began to be Lord, let them know that they are openly reviving the statements of the Samosatene.[118]

Athanasius casts his comment in the form of a condition, in which the reader is meant to equate the Arians' proleptic scheme of titling the redeemer with Paul's denial of any precosmic existence of the Son.[119] Unlike Paul, however, Arius, Asterius, and Eusebius of Nicomedia held to the son's preexistence; what they denied were the "natural" or "essential" prerogatives of that preexistent one.[120] The Arians conceived of all of Christ's major titles, including even "Son," as proleptically given in God's foreknowledge. Thus Christ's titles and his very existence were dependent upon his fulfillment of the path of obedient sonship.

> God, foreknowing him [Christ] to be good, proleptically (προλάβων) gave him this glory (δόξα), *which he had afterward as man from virtue;* so that from his works, which God foreknew, he made such a one as him now to be begotten [emphasis added].[121]

In point of fact it is the end of Christ's ministry that marks the completion of Jesus' growth in virtue. The Arians therefore stressed Christ's endurance of the cross.[122] When they cited texts like "power is given to me" and "glorify your Son" and "power is given to him" in making their point, Athanasius argued that power (ἐξουσία) and glory belong to Jesus both before and after the resurrection.[123] And when it sounds to us as if the redeemer speaks a language of needing "to receive," it is, claimed Athanasius, only from his posture as mediator that he passes on these benefits to human nature:

> So that from these [texts cited] it is clear that what things he possessed as Logos, and such things [as he had] being man, even after the resurrection, he claims (λέγει) to receive humanly (ἀνθρωπίνως), so that men, on the one hand, on earth as "becoming partakers (κοινωνοὶ) of the divine nature" [2 Pet. 1:4], might henceforth have power (ἐξουσία) against demons, and on the other hand, in heaven, as being delivered from corruption, might rule forever.[124]

The Arians, of course, had insisted that their creaturely savior was expressing an exaltation that was granted to one perfected in obedience. *Thus Jesus advanced internally in virtue (προκοπή) so that at the resurrection God could grant him a promotion (βελτίωσις).*[125]

Because of the Arian handling of the doctrine of divine foreknowledge, it is sometimes extremely difficult to know whether they are referring to the earthly, the preexistent, or the postresurrection Son. As we have suggested above, the Arians could read back onto the preexistent one titles and status that he would receive as a recognition from God on the basis of his virtuous earthly life and death. This they did with their most important title for the redeemer, "the Son." Arius uses this appellation throughout fragments of the *Thalia* which have been preserved.[126] Yet we have seen that Christ receives his adoption on the basis of his earthly ministry according to the Arian scheme. How are we to understand the use of the term *son* applied to the preexistent one? For example, Arius wrote in the *Thalia*:

> The Unbegun (ἄναρχος) made (ἔθηκε) the son as a beginning of the creatures (τῶν γενητῶν) [cf. Prov. 8:22a]. And having made this one he advanced (ἔθηκε) [him] for a son (εἰς υἱὸν) to himself.[127]

The text seems to refer to a precosmic son, but elsewhere the Arians have repeatedly stated that Jesus' sonship came by adoption on the basis of his virtuous life. Here again, Arius must have conceived the term as proleptic.

> For even if, as they claim, it having been foreknown (προγνωθείς) that he would be such as was anticipated (προλαμβάνῃ), he receives even from the beginning (καὶ ἅμα τῷ γενέσθαι) the name [Son] and the glory of the name, but he would not differ [Athanasius counters] from the ones receiving (λαμβανόντων) the name after deeds (τὰς πράξεις), even while he is thus attested to be Son.[128]

So the Son stands on a trajectory of accomplishment from his first precosmic generation through his earthly ministry. The cross is a signal point. It marks the end of Jesus' long development in virtue, understood to mean obedience to the Father, since the Arians did not conceive of a perpetual ascent in virtue. But the cross stands as a supreme instance of his existence-long obedience to the Father. The resurrection is the occasion par excellence in which God certifies the quality of the Son's life and promotes him to that position of glory which he held proleptically until then. He is named "Wisdom" and "Word" because he partakes of this aspect of God and participates in it.[129] He is designated "Power" of God because he receives such ἐξουσία from God.[130] He is a son of God by adoption because of participation (μετοχή) in him.[131] This perfected creature is then the Son of God, excelling all others in glory; indeed he is "only-begotten God," understood to mean "beloved Son."[132] Therefore he has even been made God by participation in the God.[133]

But no matter how exalted the Son became, the central Arian model was that of a perfected creature whose nature remained always creaturely and whose position was always subordinate to and dependent upon the Father's will. That meant that whether one described the preexistent instrument of creation, the earthly Jesus, or the regnant Christ of glory, an Arian always had in mind a model of an obedient servant or a favored creature. It is to a closer explication of the redeemer's sonship described in such categories that we must now turn.

Grace and Obedience

The savior whom the early Arians discovered in scripture and promulgated in their writings was never far from an obedient servant who followed God's commands. They seem consciously to have constructed a model of an "underworker"[134] to God, whose basic characteristic was a willing submission to the Father's will.[135]

We have seen already that the Arians insisted their redeemer had to possess free will as represented by a freely changeable (that is, improvable) nature. As a creature who himself was required to exercise faith in God, his fidelity and his changeability were related in Arian understanding. This was reinforced by the interchangeability of *son* (υἱός, παῖς) and *servant* in their biblical exegesis. Thus, in refuting the Arian interpretation of Acts 2:36, Athanasius will insist,

> For even if the Logos existing in the form of God took the form of a servant [Philippians 2], still the assumption of the flesh did not make the Word a servant, being naturally Lord.[136]

24

Similarly, Athanasius reports one of the reasons that the assembled bishops at Nicaea chose the term *homoousios* was to differentiate

the likeness (ὁμοίωσιν) and unchangeability (ἀτρεψίον) of the Son from that which is called "imitation" (μίμησιν) in us, which we receive from virtue on the basis of the keeping of the commandments.[137]

We are not interested in the orthodox opposition except insofar as it transmits the Arian position. And from the two quotations it seems clear that the Arians worked with the model of an obedient servant who kept the commandments. That this is exactly what they promulgated can be seen in Athanasius' objections to their exegesis of Prov. 8:22.

The Arians had laid full stress on the phrase "for his works" meaning "for us," so that the Son's very coming into existence was for our creation.[138] Athanasius will insist that God's Word operates on an entirely different model than human speech.

But God spoke not in order that some underworker (ὑπουργός) might hear, and having learned the will (τὸ βούλημα) of the one might depart and perform it.[139]

One gets a glimpse of how the Arians saw God's Word—it was his *boulēma* for the creation to be obediently followed by the mediator. Thus Athanasius will have to insist that essence is prior both to function and the divine command, so that first Adam and others existed; then they carried out their tasks.[140] This is a subcategory of a general principle Athanasius follows in the second book of the *Orations*—"essences" (αἱ οὐσίαι) are prior to "terms" (αἱ λέξεις).[141] Throughout the second oration this is used in various ways to combat scriptural terms which seem to cast the mediator in the role of a subservient creature. Such was precisely the Arians' contention whether they were engaged in cosmological or anthropological discussions of the redeemer. Thus, Athanasius claimed, because "son" and "servant" are interchangeable terms in scripture, when the Logos is called a son, the relation to his Father should be read as a natural one and not as one contingent upon creation and obedience.[142]

Nothing was more agreeable to the Arians than the interchangeability of "son" and "servant," for we indicated earlier that they preferred the extended scriptural usage of sonship which connotated an adoptive rather than a biological relationship between God the Father and believers.[143] Thus "sons" of God, "servants," "powers," "wisdoms," "words" mentioned in the scriptures were all functionaries of the one God's will. This Arian understanding lies behind their claims that God spoke many words and employed many powers (δύναμεις).[144] Athanasius' countermove against such exegesis will be to return to his general principle enunciated above: essence *precedes* and *interprets* terminology. He will insist that God's Word is no mere "pronunciation" by which his will (command) is made known. His Son and his command are not identical terms.[145] Whether the Arians went so far with their conception of the will of God as to make Jesus the embodiment of that will, as the last cited passages would indicate, may be doubted. They did operate with a scheme of divine command and creaturely response which conceived of the Word of God in voluntaristic rather than hypostasized categories.[146] But that they conceived of a redeemer whose work from creation through crucifixion was the conforming of his life and work to the Creator's will cannot be contested. It is when we turn to their explanation of how Jesus conforms himself to God that this becomes most clear.

The Arians appear to have described the unity of the Son with the Father as an agreement (συμφωνία, σύμφωνος) with God, an agreement in the sense of harmony with him rather than identity; and this is the way they explain John 10:30, "I and the Father are one."

> For they say "since what the Father wills (θέλει), these things the Son also wills (θέλει), and is contrary neither in thoughts (νοήμασιν) nor in judgments, but is in all respects concordant (σύμφωνος) with him, declaring doctrines which are the same and a word consistent and united with the Father's teaching, therefore it is that he and the Father are one [John 10:30]"; and some of them have dared to write as well as say this.[147]

Eusebius in his *Contra Marcellum* quotes Marcellus as attributing this same sentiment and language to Asterius the Sophist.[148] Whether Arius himself ever employed the term συμφωνία or σύμφωνος we cannot say. But as late as the monothelite controversy (ca. A.D. 600), memory preserved under the name of Arius fragments which express not the cooperation between the divine will and the redeemer's but the redeemer's preference for his Father's will. Bardy, who has identified these survivals, points in favor of their authenticity precisely to the fact that their sentiments parallel that of the early fourth-century Arian positions on the will rather than the antimonothelite formulations.[149] So Arius supposedly wrote:

> Thus accordingly one must consider the Gospel passages which say that "I do not seek my own will" (John 5:30), and that "I have been sent from heaven not

in order that I may do my will but the will of the Father who sent me" (John 6:38), so that the willing (τό θέλημα) of the Son does not quite comply with (ἐφέπουμενου) and agree with (συναινοῦντος) the paternal will (τῇ πατρικῇ βουλῇ); fittingly so that he prefers the will of the Father to his own, saying, "Let not my will be done, Father, but yours" (Luke 22:42).[150]

The statement just quoted may not be in disharmony with the Arian exegesis of John 10:30. The latter has to do with how unity and likeness to the divine can be achieved by the savior; and it appears in the context of a discussion on adoption.[151] It therefore does not preclude that the redeemer would not have to bend his will to that of the Creator; in fact, it is precisely potential opposition which makes free choice a reality rather than a simple assent to how things have to be. Such a potential opposition between Jesus' willing and his doing is precisely what Athanasius' doctrine of the consubstantiality of the Son with the Father is designed to avoid. As the very hypostasis of the Father's will, there can be no split in him between hearing and doing.[152]

A second key Arian exegesis underlining more precisely how they conceived Jesus' relation to God can be discerned in their interpretation of John 14:10. Eschewing physical containment of the Creator within the redeemer, they (especially Asterius) yoked the text to Acts 17:28, so that they described the Son as "in the Father" or "in him" not in a unique or essential way but in the sense that other creatures "live and move and have being" in him.[153] This for them was a statement not about the Son's ontology but about the indwelling presence of divine favor, understood here to mean divine empowerment, as we can see from Athanasius' subsequent discussion. Athanasius says that according to Asterius, Christ in speaking the words of John 14:10 was delivering the Father's message like one of the great Old Testament prophets and the apostles who were empowered by grace.[154] Then Athanasius counters,

But if the Lord had said this, his words would not have rightly been, "I in the Father and the Father in me," but rather "I too am in the Father, and the Father is in me too," that he may have nothing of his own and by prerogative (ἐξαίρετον), relatively to the Father as a Son, but the same grace in common with all.[155]

Athanasius' suspicion that what the Arians had in mind was a begraced creature was exactly to the point, though some Arians would admit he had "more than the others."[156] In the same vein, they cited John 17:11, "that they may be one as we are," to underscore that the order in which Jesus was to be ranked was that of the creation and that the unity he shared with his Father was that which Christians also share with God. And this is precisely the direction of their argument—that is, from our experience to Christ's:

> If, *as we* become one in the Father, so also he and the Father are one, and thus he too is in the Father, how pretend you . . . [from John 14:10 and John 17:11] that he is proper and like the Father's essence?[157]

The various ways Arians themselves or their reporters describe the relationship of the redeemer to God—"by participation of the Spirit," "by a participation of grace," "a certain grace and habit of virtue," "by adoption," "by free gift of God," "named Word and Son according to grace," "grace by acquisition," "grace as an accident,"[158] and so on—all these phrases point to a scheme of divine favor which both assists in (though to what degree is uncertain) and acquiesces to Jesus' creative agency, earthly life, and pioneering soteriological work. By grace, says Athanasius, we who are by nature servants have the confidence to call God Father, just as Christ did when he became a servant like us.[159] But Athanasius combats here what was in fact the Arian contention about the redeemer himself—a servant like us by nature who by grace can call God "Father." Servanthood by a creaturely nature freely electing such and divine fatherhood by grace are the twin foundations of the early Arian Christology.

Grace then in the Arian scheme equals the bestowal of divine favor and approval upon obedient (that is, virtuous)[160] creatures. From God's side it is the offer of fatherhood to creatures, represented by adoption beginning at the very creation (so Christ was created "for his works" = for our creation). From the human side it is the opportunity to become a son of God. Thus "grace" from the creature's stance represents something between an opportunity and a privilege. It points to God's victories through his servants and urges us, "Do not reject the favor" (τὴν χάριν).[161] Grace then is related to the revelation of the will and commandment of the Creator and the opportunity to participate in his purpose of saving (= adopting) humankind. There were privileges that accrued, δόξαι. Thus Jesus received ἐπινοίαι (virtually identical with δόξαι): πνεῦμα, δύναμις, σοφία, δόξα θεοῦ, ἀλήθεια, εἰκών, λόγος.[162] Above all, Jesus became υἱός, understood to mean θεός, even μονογενής θεός.

Was grace also an empowering force in the servant's life? Perhaps, for the Arians allude to a participation in the Spirit; and the anonymous Arian homilist points believers to the continuing work of Jesus, understood rather as an "influence for good."[163] Indeed, grace as an empowering force could never be so strong as to overcome the free consent of the creature's will. It could never be so weak as to allow the devil to overcome us.[164] Hence grace, in this sense, implies God's efficient (rather than absolute) power in a freely cooperating world.

Orthodoxy knows a grace which confers sonship on believers; but it never applies this adopting grace to the Christ as did the Arians.[165] Grace which was conferred meant grace which could be withdrawn or lost.[166] Grace is the divine essence brought to human nature *through* the Christ. It is not primarily the revelation of the will of God for the world. It is the communication of the divine knowledge brought by the divine nature to material life. Hence it is the Logos uniting the divine χάρις to human flesh in a way that will ensure that grace will be incorporated irrevocably.[167] It is not so much divine "favor" or divine "approbation" (as in Arianism) as it is the divine condescension—the appearing in history of the true Word, Image, Power, Wisdom, Son. It is not a matter of God's free will, for Athanasius denies that God has free will.[168] Nor does it involve the redeemer's free response, for the presence of the Logos in the body stabilizes and divinizes the will to ensure that corruptibility will be reversed and mutability will be overcome.[169] The life of the redeemer is a χάρις in the sense of a gift, in that it is seen entirely as a divine "condescension" with none of the elements of that transaction which we observed in Arianism.

To modern readers, Arianism looks more appealing since there appears to be more give-and-take and more flexibility in a system of salvation by will. The Athanasian system of a salvation brought by the divine nature seems not to be quite so transactional and risky. But make no mistake about it. The Arian redeemer's mission was every bit as "rigged" as the Athanasian. The Arians never for a moment thought that Jesus actually sinned; only that he *could have* had he so chosen. But God would not have created him in the first place had he been the kind to rebel. He was created precisely because he was of a kind to be obedient and so become a son. The Arians rehearsed God's words, "I have begotten and raised up sons," with full confidence, but with a selectivity that drove the orthodox to fury; for as Alexander pointed out, the rest of the quotation reads, "and they have rebelled against me."[170]

The Arians allowed no such dampening cloud to sail across the sky of human possibility. For the redeemer was not entirely unique. He was *a representative creature.* We are meant to ponder the marvelous fact that another besides Jesus could have been created and sent to do the job. Hence they apply the cardinal number used substantively ("one" or a "certain one") to the redeemer who will be "named" or "called" Son. They employed this terminology to underscore the absoluteness of the Father's sovereign freedom to choose the ground rules for creation and redemption. At one and the same stroke they stated unequivocally the cardinal principle of their soteriology—divine sonship differs in degree but not in kind; therefore the Christ was *representative* Son, but *by no means only possible Son.*[171] It is to this soteriological perspective that we must now turn.

NOTES

1. Athanasius *De Syn.* 15.3 (Opitz[2], p. 243, line 4 [from John 1]). H. M. Gwatkin, *The Arian Controversy*[2] (London: Longman's, Green & Co., 1891), had noted the high Arian Christology but considered it nothing but "the philosophy of the day put into Christian dress" (p. 6).

2. Opitz[3], Urk. 6.2, p. 12, line 7.

3. Athanasius *De Syn.* 15.3 (Opitz[2], p. 243, line 13).

4. From the text of an anonymous Arian homily published by R. P. Casey, "An Early Homily Ascribed to Athanasius of Alexandria," *JThS* 36 (1935): 10, line 28. Cited henceforth as Casey.

5. Opitz[3], Urk. 6.3, p. 12, line 9. For *atreptos, vide* also Athanasius *De Decr.* 5.20.

6. Athanasius *De Decr.* 5.20; Casey 3, p. 6, line 13; Athanasius *De Syn.* 15.3 *(Thalia)* (Opitz[2], p. 243, line 6).

7. Christ as *logos*: Athanasius *De Syn.* 15.3 (Opitz[2], p. 243, line 7); *Or. c. Ar.* 1.5 (Bright, p. 5); 1.6 (Bright, p. 6). Christ as *sophia*: Athanasius *De Syn.* 15.3 (Opitz[2], p. 243, lines 5–6); *Or. c. Ar.* 1.5 (Bright, p. 5).

8. The complaints of the ancients along this line are too numerous to cite, but cf., e.g., Alexander *Ep. ad Alex.* (Opitz[3], Urk. 14.11, lines 15–16; 14.13, lines 19–20; 14.31, lines 21–24, etc.); Athanasius *De Decr.* 6.5; *Or. c. Ar.* 1.5 (Bright, p. 6).

9. J. A. Dorner, *History of the Development of the Person of Christ*, I. II, trans. D. W. Simon (Edinburgh: T. & T. Clark, 1889), pp. 240–41, observed and stressed the promotional aspects of the Arian redeemer. Cf. also the best nineteenth-century study on Arius: Friedrich Böhringer, *Athanasius und Arius oder der erste grosse Kampf der Orthodoxie und Heterodoxie* (Stuttgart: Meyer und Zellers Verlag, 1874), pp. VI, 181–82, 190–92, etc. *Vide* also A. Harnack, *History of Dogma*[3], trans. Neil Buchanan (New York: Dover Publications, 1961), vol. 4, p. 17, item d; p. 19, item g; and p. 39. More recent scholarship has tended to note again these promotional aspects, but only in passing: T. E. Pollard, e.g., *Johannine Christology and the Early Church*, Society for New Testament Studies, Monograph Series 13

(Cambridge: Cambridge University Press, 1970), pp. 160–62. But virtually all recent scholarship has rejected the importance of exploring the ethical progress of this Arian redeemer as an avenue to understanding the Arian position. All take as their starting point Arius' supposedly radical monotheism. Of modern scholars, C. W. Mönnich alone, "De Achtergrond van de Arianse Christologie," *Nederlande Theologisch Tijdschrift* 4 (1950): 378–412, has pointed to the free exercise of the Arian redeemer's will, which brings him to unchangeability and to Stoic ethical backgrounds of this process (p. 406). Mönnich alone contended that the Arian controversy made no sense on formal theological grounds (p. 409). A. Grillmeier, *Christ in Christian Tradition* (London: A. R. Mowbray & Co., 1965), p. 192, n. 2, had at first given Mönnich's position consideration and then promptly banished it from mention in his second edition (London: A. R. Mowbray & Co.; Atlanta: John Knox Press, 1975). For criticisms of Mönnich, *vide* Gregg and Groh, p. 265, n. 14; p. 269, nn. 39–40. Cf. Maurice Wiles, *The Making of Christian Doctrine* (Cambridge: Cambridge University Press, paperback, 1975), pp. 107–8, who pointed to the "god by grace" character of the Arian redeemer and the potential soteriological implications. Wiles, however, thought the evidence for an Arian soteriology was too small and too derivative to posit such a soteriology (but cf. our chap. 2 *infra*). Cf. also D. Ritschl, *Athanasius: Versuch einer Interpretation*, Theologische Studien 76 (Zurich: EVZ-Verlag, 1964), p. 31.

10. *Vide* chap. 5, n. 41, *infra*. The most obvious recent examples of the field's consensus are the various works of T. E. Pollard (*Johannine Christology; Studia Patristica* II.2 [Berlin, 1975]: 287; "The Origins of Arianism," *JThS* 9 [1958]: 106) and the new book by Manlio Simonetti, *La crisi ariana nel IV secolo*, Studia ephemeridas 'Augustinianum' 11 (Rome: Institutum Patristicum 'Augustinianum,' 1975), pp. 46ff.

11. Theodoret *H.E.* 1.4.1 (Opitz³, Urk. 14, p. 19).

12. Opitz³, Urk. 14.37, p. 25. For orthodox strategy concerning these texts, *vide* p. 20 *infra*.

13. Gregg and Groh, pp. 260–63. G. Christopher Stead, *Divine Substance* (Oxford: Oxford University Press, 1977), p. 224, is a happy exception to the unanimity of the field that the doctrine of God was Arius' starting point; Stead points to the way Arius' letters stress the priority of the Father over the Son.

14. Robert L. Sample, "The Messiah as Prophet: The Christology of Paul of Samosata" (Ph.D. diss., Northwestern University, 1977), pp. 181–82; cf. pp. 143–44, 191, 199. *Vide* also idem, "The Christology of the Council of Antioch (268 c.e.) Reconsidered," *Church History* 48 (1979): 18–26.

15. Athanasius *Or. c. Ar.* 3.35 (Bright, p. 190).

16. Athanasius *Or. c. Ar.* 3.26, *NPNF* translation. For the importance of Philippians 2, *vide* Gregg and Groh, p. 274 (contra those scholars who have made Prov. 8:22 the central text and have construed it cosmologically). M. Richard, "Saint Athanase et la psychologie du Christ selon les Ariens," *Mélanges de science religieuse* 4 (1947): 7–9, cited this chapter but did not connect it with Alexander's statement

(*supra*, n. 12). We look forward to the publication of C. Kannengiesser's current study (reported at the Eighth International Conference on Patristic Studies, 1979), which entails a literary analysis of the three *Orations* and a reassessment of their structure, dating, and authorship.

17. "Faciens in ecclesia quarta et sexta feria congregationem quasi ad Dei verbum audiendum"; quoted and critical questions discussed by W. Telfer, "St. Peter of Alexandria and Arius," *Analecta Bollandiana* 67 (1949), *Mélanges Paul Peeters*, I, 117–30.

18. Arius' *Thalia* contained quotations from scripture (cf. p. 21 *infra*); cf. Athanasius *Or. c. Ar.* 1.8; and G. Bardy, *Recherches sur Saint Lucien d'Antioch et son école* (Paris: Gabriel Beauchesne et ses fils, 1936), p. 258. Arius' concern is paralleled by what little we know of the methods of Eusebius of Nicomedia, who, in the one surviving letter from his hand, argues about what can legitimately be inferred about God from texts like Isa. 1:3, Deut. 32:18, Job 38:28: *Ep. ad Paulin.* (Opitz³, Urk. 8.7, p. 17, lines 1–7). Asterius' fragments are laced with biblical citations and allusions, as are his homilies on the Psalms. He also wrote exegetical works: Bardy, *Lucien*, pp. 330–33. For the exegetical hermeneutic of the Arians at Nicaea, *vide* Gregg and Groh, p. 271. See chap. 5, n. 132, *infra*, for two fourth-century Arian commentaries on Job.

19. Arius *Ep. ad Alex.* (Opitz³, Urk. 6, p. 13, line 20).

20. *Or. c. Ar.* 3.27 (Bright, p. 182); for the rejection of God's suffering, *vide* Gelasius frg. X (Bardy, *Lucien*, pp. 240–44).

21. *Or. c. Ar.* 3.27 (Bright, p. 182): "πῶς δύναται λόγος εἶναι ἤ θεός ὁ κοιμώμενος ὡς ἄνθρωπος, καὶ κλαίων καί πυνθανόμενος;"

22. *Or. c. Ar.* 3.26.

23. *Or. c. Ar.* 3.26 (Bright, p. 181), *NPNF* translation, altered.

24. *Vide* chap. 3 *infra* for Arian cosmology.

25. Eusebius of Nicomedia *Ep. ad Paulin.*

26. Arius *Ep. ad. Euseb.* (Opitz³, Urk. 1.4, p. 3): ". . . ὅτι θελήματι καὶ βουλῇ ὑπέστη πρὸ χρόνων καὶ πρὸ αἰώνων . . . ;" Arius *Ep. ad Alex.* (Opitz³, Urk. 6.3, p. 13): ". . . θελήματι τοῦ θεοῦ πρὸ χρόνων καὶ πρὸ αἰώνων κτισθέντα." *Thalia*, in Athanasius *De Syn.* 15 (Opitz², p. 243, lines 5, 11, 19). *Vide* also *infra*, chap. 3 and chap. 5, n. 70.

27. Eusebius of Nicomedia *Ep. ad Paulin.* 8.8.

28. Athanasius *Or. c. Ar.* 3.62 (Bright, p. 215); cf. Gregory of Nazianzus *Or.* 29.6.

29. *Or. c. Ar.* 3.26 (Bright, p. 180). *Vide* Asterius frg. XIII (= *Or. c. Ar.* 3.2) (Bardy, *Lucien*, p. 346) for Christ's *dynamis* as granted by God.

30. *Vide* chap. 2 *infra*.

31. *Or. c. Ar.* 3.24.

32. Ibid. (Bright, p. 179), *NPNF* translation.

33. *Ep. Encycl.* 8 (Opitz³, Urk. 4b, p. 8, lines 4–6).

34. In Athanasius *De Syn.* 15.3 (Opitz², p. 242, lines 14–19).

35. *Or. c. Ar.* 1.6; cf. *Or. c. Ar.* 1.9 (Bright, p. 9). In the *Thalia* (Opitz², p. 242), the ἤγουν of line 24 should be read in conjunction with the preceding lines which speak of the Son's knowledge of the Father (*vide infra* at n. 51).

36. Dennis E. Groh, "Changing Points of View in Patristic Scholarship," *Anglican Theological Review* 60 (1978): 452–55.

37. Ibid., 460–64.

38. Such is the (we think mistaken) consensus of scholarship, of which a few examples may suffice: John Henry Newman, *The Arians of the Fourth Century*⁵ (London: Longmans, Green & Co., 1888), pp. 113–14, 219–20; H. M. Gwatkin, *Studies of Arianism* (Cambridge University Press, 1882), p. 21; and idem, *The Arian Controversy*, p. 6; J. N. D. Kelly, *Early Christian Doctrines*⁴ (London: Adam & Charles Black, 1968), pp. 230–31, 243; É. Boularand, *L'Hérésie d'Arius et la "foi" de Nicée* (Paris: Latouzey & Ané, 1972). *Vide* n. 79 *infra* for specific attributions of philosophical influence.

39. Gregg and Groh, p. 262.

40. *Ep. ad Alex.* (Opitz³, Urk. 14.28, p. 24, lines 6–8); *Ep. Encycl.* (Opitz³, Urk. 4b.8, p. 8, lines 4–6).

41. *De Decr.* 3.6 (Opitz², 6.4, p. 6, lines 12–14); cf. Athanasius *Or. c. Ar.* 2.4.

42. Cf. *Or. c. Ar.* 2.78, where the Son's being the proper *sophia* of God is what guarantees that the Wisdom implanted in us as an image *(eikōn)* will give us knowledge of the Father.

43. *Vide* n. 41 *supra*.

44. Athanasius *Or. c. Ar.* 1.9 (Bright, p. 9).

45. Arius in his *Thalia*, in Athanasius *De Syn.* 15.3 (Opitz², p. 243, lines 20–21), writes: "Accordingly what argument allows the one being from a father to know the one having begotten him with certainty (ἐν καταλήψει). It is clear that that which has a beginning cannot conceive of or grasp the Unbegotten as he is." Cf. lines 19–20, and note the absence of the definite article in the phrase "ἐκ πατρός." Important here is a Stoic distinction (attributed to Zeno and Cleanthes), reported by the second-century writer Sextus Empiricus, which distinguishes among ἐπιστήμι, δόξα, and κατάληψις (*Adv. math.* VII.151, *SVF* 2, pp. 29–30, no. 90). Ἐπιστήμι is the fixed, sure, and immutable (ἀμετάθετον) apprehension (κατάληψις) of the mind; δόξα is the feeble and false assent (συγκατάθεσις); but κατάληψις stands midway between the two. Thus καταληπτικὴ φαντασία contains truth and whatsoever things are not false. Ἐπιστήμη was reserved to the σοφός; δόξα to the Fool; but κατάληψις was common to both. Arius is thinking here not of this latter κατάληψις but of that apprehension (κατάληψις) which the Old Stoics would have called ἐπιστήμη; and this apprehension he denied to the earthly Son. Cf. Plutarch *De Comm. Not.* 7, *SVF* 3, p. 51, no. 213. *Vide* n. 77 *infra*. Thus Jesus was not *Sophos*, for Arius says in the *Thalia*: "γὰρ ἐστι ἴσος, ἀλλ' οὐδε ὁμοούσιος αὐτῷ σοφὸς δὲ ἐστιν ὁ θεός ὅτι τῆς σοφίας διδάσκαλος αὐτός" (Opitz², p. 242, lines 17–18).

46. Gregg and Groh, p. 266, citing *Ep. ad Paulin.* (Opitz³, Urk. 8.7, p. 17, lines 1–7).

47. *Or. c. Ar.* 3.26. The passage also contains an important citation of Lk. 2:52, discussed *infra* (pp. 18, 20).

48. Ibid.

49. *Or. c. Ar.* 3.33 and 3.37, respectively.

50. *Vide* the quotation at n. 23 *supra.*

51. *De Syn.* 15.3 (Opitz², p. 242, lines 21–23).

52. Irenaeus, *Haer.* 4.20.5, in *Irénée de Lyon contre les hérésies,* ed. Adelin Rousseau et al., SC 100 (Paris: Éditions du Cerf, 1965), bk. 4, vol. 11, p. 639. To be sure, the parallel between Irenaeus' statement and Arius' is not exact. Irenaeus, who fights for the unity of the Creator and the Son, would not have portrayed the redeemer as someone being adopted by the Spirit; for Irenaeus goes on to speak about the adoption of believers by God in the Son: cf. Henri Lassiat, *Promotion de l'homme en Jésus-Christ d'après Irénée de Lyon tèmoin de la tradition des apôtres* (Strasbourg: Maison Mame, 1974), p. 286. This section formed a part of Irenaeus' dynamic understanding of human anthropology, according to which persons experience renewed life and growth in the Spirit (Lassiat, *Promotion,* p. 212). The Arian redeemer, as we shall show in the next section, was (on the contrary) an adopted Son.

53. *Vide* Arius' statement at n. 34 of the text, *supra.*

54. *Vide* Arius' statement at n. 51 of the text, *supra.*

55. Cf. Athanasius' report at n. 32 in the text above and *vide* Irenaeus *Haer.* 4.20.5, par. 128 (Gk. frag. 10), Rousseau, *Irénée de Lyon,* p. 642.

56. *Or. c. Ar.* 2.5. The substance of the discussion in chaps. 5–11 concerns itself with this problem.

57. As *NPNF,* vol. 4, p. 351, n. 2 points out, Athanasius has combined Deut. 32:4 and Exod. 34:6 as at Rev. 3:14.

58. *Or. c. Ar.* 2.6 (Bright, p. 74).

59. Ibid.

60. Cf. *Or. c. Ar.* 2.7.

61. E.g., *Or. c. Ar.* 3.51 (Bright, p. 204): "But if he is a God bearing flesh, since indeed he truly is this, and 'the Logos became flesh,' and being God descended to earth, what kind of advance has he who is equal to God?"

62. *Or. c. Ar.* 2.10 (Bright, p. 78), *NPNF* translation, altered. Heb. 13:8 is used already by Alexander, *Ep. Encycl.,* Opitz³, Urk. 4b.14, p. 9, lines 11–12, to counter the changeability of the Son (ca. A.D. 319).

63. *Vide* ibid. and cf. biblical texts cited there. ". . . ὅτι καὶ γενόμενος [λόγος] ἄνθρωπος οὐκ ἠλλοίωται . . ." (Alexander, *Ep. Encycl.,* Opitz³, Urk. 4b.14).

64. Ibid., Urk. 4b.8, lines 2–3.

65. Ibid., Urk. 4b.10, lines 7–10.

66. *Or. c. Ar.* 1.22: "καὶ αὐτεξούσιός ἐστι καὶ ἰδίᾳ προαιρέσει οὐ τρέπεται, τρεπτῆς ὢν φύσεως; Οὐ γὰρ ὡς λίθος ἐστὶν ἀφ' ἑαυτοῦ μένων ἀκίνητος" (Bright, p. 24). Cf. *Or. c. Ar.* 2.18: "αὐτεξούσιός ἐστι, καὶ τρεπτῆς ἐστι φύσεως;" (Bright, p. 87).

67. *Or. c. Ar.* 1.51 (Bright, p. 53); *Or. c. Ar.* 3.20.

68. *Vide, infra,* chap. 2, pp. 67–68. Gregg and Groh, pp. 267 and 271.

69. Diogenes Laertius VII.115, *SVF* 3, p. 103, no. 431. Cf. *SVF* 3, no. 432.

70. *De Prin.* 4.4.1. This passage and the link between "willing" and "affection" were pointed out by H. A. Wolfson, *The Philosophy of the Church Fathers,* 2d ed. (Cambridge, Mass.: Harvard University Press, 1964), p. 226. Wolfson cites also Diogenes Laertius I.116.

71. *De Decr.* 10.5 (Opitz², p. 9, lines 23–25): "ἆρ᾽ οὖν ἀνθρωποπαθὴς ἡ τοῦ υἱοῦ γέννησις; τοῦτο γὰρ ἴσως κατ᾽ ἐκείνους καὶ αὐτοὶ θελήσουσιν ἀντιθεῖναι μὴ γινώσκοντες. οὐδαμῶς. οὐ γὰρ ὡς ἄνθρωπος ὁ θεός, ἐπεὶ μηδέ οἱ ἄνθρωποι ὡς ὁ θεός." For the Stoics a εὐπαθεία such as βούλησις was quite distinct from a πάθη (*SVF* 3, no. 431), but Athanasius here chooses the term ἀνθρωποπαθή to apply to the Arians.

72. Robert C. Gregg, *Consolation Philosophy: Greek and Christian Paideia in Basil and the Two Gregories,* Patristic Monograph Series no. 3 (Cambridge, Mass.: Philadelphia Patristic Foundation, 1975), pp. 103ff.

73. Plutarch *Quomodo quis suos in virtute sentiat profectus* 10: "οὐ τίς θεός εἰμὶ. τὶ μ᾽ ἀθανάτοις εἴσκεις;" Translation and text from Frank Cole Babbit, *Plutarch's Moralia,* 1, Loeb Classical Library (London: William Heinemann Ltd.; New York: G. P. Putnam's Sons, 1927), pp. 432–33.

74. Ibid. 13.

75. Ibid. 12–13. The fool could be considered to be ἀπαθή, but in this usage the term connoted not the tranquility that proceeds from rational judgment but rather from simple obduracy, as at Diogenes Laertius VII.117, *SVF* 3, p. 109, no. 448. Cf. Zeno's definition of suffering (τὸ πάθος) at Diogenes Laertius VII.110, *SVF* 1, p. 50, no. 205.

76. C. W. Mönnich, "Arianse Christologie" (n. 9 *supra*).

77. Athanasius *De Syn.* 15.3 (Opitz², p. 242, line 18). For the sage's knowledge, *vide* Sextus Empiricus *Adv. Math.* VII.432, *SVF* 3, p. 164, no. 657.

78. Cf. Origen *In evang. Ioannis* XIII.21, *SVF* 2, p. 311, no. 1054.

79. Arius' Platonism has been explored by G. C. Stead, "The Platonism of Arius," *JThS* 15 (1964): 16–31; F. Ricken, "Nikaia als Krisis des altchristlichen Platonismus," *Theologie und Philosophie* 44 (1969): 321–41 (especially p. 330 on Arius); and E. P. Meijering, "ΗΝ ΠΟΤΕ ΟΤΕ ΟΥΚ ΗΝ Ο ΥΙΟΣ; A Discussion on Time and Eternity," *VC* 28 (1974): 161–68; reprinted in *God Being History: Studies in Patristic Philosophy* (Amsterdam: North Holland Publishing Co., 1975), pp. 81–88. The Platonism asserts itself primarily in the influence on phrases and formulas from Platonic discussions of time and eternity, which appear in expressions of Arius' like "there was when he was not." There are some major chronological problems in making the case stick, as Meijering has noted ("Discussion on Time," p. 166). The Aristotelianism of Arius and the early Arians, which so many modern scholars have simply presupposed on the basis of notices in the later fourth-century writers, seems to us to be confined to the rejection of the πρὸς τι argument (Stead, "Platonism of

Arius," p. 28), which argument can hardly be confined to Aristotelian circles. J. de Ghellinck, "Quelques appréciations de la dialectique et d'Aristote durant les conflits trinitaires due IVe siècle," *Revue d'histoire ecclésiastique* 26 (1) (1930), improperly lumps Arius and Aëtius together in attributing the use of dialectic to both (pp. 10, 12–14). He points out that the important distinction, used by the early Arians (*De Decr.* 31–32; *Or. c. Ar.* 1.31–32), "ἤ ἀγέννητον πάντως, ἤ γεννητόν," comes from dialectic (p. 24). But dialectic was an integral part of the Stoic school as well, so much so that two important classes of syllogisms (hypothetical and copulative) belong to Stoicism and even to the wider Greek and Latin tradition (pp. 26–28). Do stray Aristotelian elements here, traces of which appear in numerous Fathers, come from Aristotle via the Stoics, or even via the rhetorical tradition (cf. p. 22 for dialectic exercises in the Second Sophistic)? For the unanimity of the heresiographers on Aristotelianism in Arianism as meaning their "argumentation," *vide* H. A. Wolfson, "Philosophical Implications of Arianism and Apollinarianism," *Dumbarton Oaks Papers* 12 (1958): 5.

80. Henry Chadwick, *Early Christian Thought and the Classical Tradition: Studies in Justin, Clement, and Origen* (New York: Oxford University Press, 1966), p. 107.

81. *Or. c. Ar.* 3.26 (Bright, p. 181): "'Ει δύναμις ἦν, οὐκ ἄν ἐδειλίασεν, ἀλλὰ μᾶλλον καὶ ἑτέροις τὸ δύνασθαι παρεῖχεν" (commenting on John 12:27–28, Matt. 26:39, John 13:21). Athanasius shrinks from the Arian attribution of fear to the Word: "εἰ μὲν ἄνθρωπος ψιλός ὁ λαλῶν, κλαιέτω καὶ φοβείσθω τὸν θάνατον ὡς ἄνθρωπος· εἰ δε λόγος ἐστὶν ἐν σαρκὶ . . . τίνα, θεὸς ὤν, εἶχε φοβεῖσθαι;" (*Or. c. Ar.* 3.54, Bright p. 207). Such emotions belong to the flesh, not to the divine nature (*Or. c. Ar.* 3.55). For the importance of the will controlling fear in Roman Stoicism, *vide*, e.g., Epictetus *Disc.* IV.VII.19; IV.I.84. The Stoic substitute for φόβος *(metus)* was εὐλαβεία *(cautio)*: vide *SVF* 3, p. 103, no. 431, and p. 106, no. 437. The *sophos* has no fear—only caution (ibid., no. 431).

82. Plutarch *Quomodo quis in virt. sent. prof.* 2, *SVF* 3, p. 143, no. 535; Diogenes Laertius VII.227, *SVF* 3, p. 143, no. 536; Origen *De Princ.* III, *SVF* 3, p. 145, no. 538.

83. *Vide* Plutarch *De Stoic. repugn.* 20, *SVF* 3, p. 173, no. 691. Cf. J. M. Rist, *Stoic Philosophy* (Cambridge: Cambridge University Press, 1969), pp. 226–28.

84. Plutarch *Quomodo quis in virt. sent. prof.* 1. Note the suddenness of the change from foolishness to wisdom: "ἀκαρεὶ χρόνον καὶ ὥρας . . . μεταβαλὼν ὁ σοφός."

85. Diogenes Laertius VII.107, *SVF* 3, no. 135; and Stobaeus *Ecl.* II.80.22, *SVF* 3, p. 32, no. 136.

86. Diogenes Laertius VII.115, *SVF* 3, p. 103, no. 431. Cicero *Tusc. disp.* IV.12: ". . . eius modi adpetitionem Stoici βούλησιν appellant, nos appellemus voluntatem. Eam illi putant in solo esse sapiente, quam sic definuit: voluntas est, quae quid cum ratione desiderat" (*SVF* 3, p. 107, no. 438).

87. Diogenes Laertius VII.115, *SVF* 3, p. 103, no. 431; cf. no. 432.

88. *Ep.* 81.13 and *Ep.* 71.36 respectively. *Vide* Rist, *Stoic Philosophy*, pp. 225–26. Cf. also Seneca *Ep.* 80.4. Cf. Philo *De Vita Mosis* I.159: "φερέτω γὰρ ἡ διάνοια μάλιστα μὲν τὸ εἶδος τέλειον ἀρετῆς, εἰ δὲ μὴ, τὸ γοῦν ὑπὲρ τοῦ κτήσασθαι τὸ εἶδος ἀνενδοίαστον πόθον" (Loeb Classical Library, ed. and trans. F. H. Colson [Cambridge, Mass., and London: Harvard University Press, 1935]), p. 358. Seneca *Ep.* 95.57, *SVF* 3, p. 139, no. 517: "Actio recta non erit, nisi recta fuerit voluntas: ab hac enim est actio. Rursus voluntas non erit recta, nisi habitus animi rectus fuerit: ab hoc enim est voluntas." For *voluntas* as the Latin equivalent of Arius' term θέλημα in his *Ep. ad Euseb.*, see the ms. (no. 54) found by D. de Bruyne in Cologne Cathedral: text reproduced by Bardy, *Lucien*, p. 228. βουλή is translated here by *consilium*, but a too-precise stability in the meanings of the terms for *will* should not be insisted upon: *vide* the citation in the text below at n. 150 and chap. 5, n. 70.

89. *Quomodo quis in virt. sent. prof.* 13; trans. Babbit, *Plutarch's Moralia*.

90. Origen *De Princ.* 3.1.18, *SVF* 3, p. 143, no. 538.

91. *De Princ.* 3.1.19 (Gr.), trans. G. W. Butterworth, *Origen on First Principles* (New York: Harper & Row, Publishers, Harper Torchbooks, 1966), p. 200.

92. Ibid. 3.1.23.

93. *Vide* n. 65 *supra*.

94. Irenaeus *Haer.* 4, preface; *vide* also 3.6.1–2; 4.1.1.

95. Alexander *Ep. ad Alex.* (Opitz³, Urk. 14.14, pp. 21–22).

96. Ibid. 14.30–34; cf. 14.13–14.

97. Ibid. p. 21, lines 21–22.

98. Opitz³, Urk. 14.34, p. 25, lines 1–5. Cf. Urk. 14.29 for the φύσει/θέσει contrast.

99. *Or. c. Ar.* 1.5 (Bright, p. 6): ". . . οὕτω καὶ αὐτὸς ὁ λόγος ἐστὶ τρεπτός, τῷ δὲ ἰδίῳ αὐτεξουσίῳ, ἕως βούλεται, μένει καλός· ὅτε μέντοι θέλει, δύναται τρέπεσθαι καὶ αὐτὸς ὥσπερ καὶ ἡμεῖς, τρεπτῆς ὤν φύσεως."

100. *Or. c. Ar.* 1.36 (Bright, pp. 37–38). Cf. Philo *Leg. Alleg.* III.210, *SVF* 3, p. 138, no. 512; and Seneca *Ep.* 95.57 (n. 88 *supra*).

101. *Or. c. Ar.* 3.26 (Bright, p. 181): "πῶς οὖν 'φασὶν,' 'οὗτος Σοφία ὁ ἐν σοφίᾳ προκόπτων, . . .' " Note the Stoic technical term ὁ προκόπτων. The distinction between a "proper" Word and Wisdom of God, which remain in God because they are implicit to the divine nature, and the redeemer who is "called" or "named" Word and Wisdom, in the sense that these are bestowed titles, was made by Asterius the Sophist with, says Athanasius, Eusebius of Nicomedia's blessing: *De Decr.* 18; cf. *Or. c. Ar.* 1.32, 2.37. *Vide* also Arius in Athanasius *De Syn.* 15.3 (Opitz², p. 243, line 5).

102. *Or. c. Ar.* 1.37 (Bright, p. 38). Note the Stoic term προαίρεσις.

103. *Or. c. Ar.* 1.40, *NPNF* translation. Cf. *Or. c. Ar.* 3.18–19.

104. *Vide Or. c. Ar.* 2.78–79, 3.10.

105. Athanasius, on the contrary, continually distinguishes between the Son's natural perfection and our acquired perfectability: *Or. c. Ar.* 3.20, 3.22. Hence the Son advances only in his body or his flesh (*Or. c. Ar.* 3.51–52).

106. *Porphyrios* ΠΡΟΣ ΜΑΡΚΕΛΛΑΝ 16, Gr. text ed. and trans. Walter Pötscher (Leiden: Brill, 1969), p. 22, lines 1–6. For the Arians, the rapprochement between Creator and creatures was based upon conformity of will rather than διάνοια (*vide* the material discussed in the text at n. 147 *infra*).

107. Cf. Athanasius' sarcastic application of John 10:33 to the Arians (*De Decr.* 1; cf. *Or. c. Ar.* 3.19–20). Paulinus of Tyre spoke of "many gods" (Opitz³, Urk. 9.3, p. 18, line 7; cf. Pollard, *Johannine Christology*, p. 152). Deification aspects were recognized already by Dorner, *Person of Christ,* pp. 240–41. Maurice Wiles, "In Defence of Arius," *JThS* 13 (1962) and *The Making of Christian Doctrine,* pp. 107–8, pointed to the fact that deification means becoming θεοί κατὰ χάριν rather than οἱ θεοί, but (contra Wiles, p. 108) there is considerable evidence that this soteriological goal was a motivating factor for the Arians (*vide* chap. 2 *infra*).

108. Thus the Arians will allow the term ἄτρεπτος to be applied to the Son at the Council of Nicaea, because it is also written of believers that "nothing shall separate us from the love of Christ": Athanasius, *De Decr.* 5.20. *Vide* Gregg and Groh, p. 271, for the scriptural texts debated at Nicaea. The Arians' point was that Christ's unchangeability would not differ from that of believers.

109. *Or. c. Ar.* 3.24 (Bright, p. 179), *NPNF* translation.

110. Ibid. 1.53.

111. Ibid. Note the appearance of another favorite "promotion" text in Heb. 1:9, Ps. 44:7 (LXX), and the conferred nature of sonship in the texts quoted in Heb. 1:5.

112. Athanasius *De Syn.* 15.3 (Opitz², p. 243, lines 9–10). *Vide Or. c. Ar.* 2.18, where the Arians cite Heb. 1:4 when forced to give up claims to Christ's free will (alterability).

113. Cf. *Or. c. Ar.* 2.1, where Prov. 8:22 and Heb. 3:2a continue to be yoked together.

114. *Or. c. Ar.* 2.27 (Moses). Job was a favorite Arian figure (chap. 5 *infra*, n. 132). Beyond these two *exempla,* it is difficult to know precisely which figures stood in the Arian sources and which represented Athanasius' own *exempla:* cf. *Or. c. Ar.* 1.39 (Moses); 2.51 (with Adam and Noah); 3.52 (Moses here, as Paul, is an *exemplum* of *prokopē*); *De Decr.* 6.6 and *Or. c. Ar.* 3.11 (Adam, Paul, and Enoch; cf. Adam and Paul only at *Or. c. Ar.* 3.18); finally there is a type of listing that begins by mentioning David and then trails off into unspecified saints and prophets (*Or. c. Ar.* 3.2 and 3.10).

115. *Vide* the text *supra* at nn. 57–60.

116. *Or. c. Ar.* 2.11 and 2.11–18, respectively.

117. The Arian term for these titles is δόξαι, employed in the sense of honors given by God for great deeds performed: Asterius, Bardy, *Lucien,* Frg. 33. Cf. Stead, "Platonism of Arius," p. 20. Arius used the term ἐπινοία for these titles. For δόξα as an ἐξουσία conferred by God, *vide* n. 120 *infra*.

118. *Or. c. Ar.* 2.13, *NPNF* translation.

119. For the denial of preexistence to the Christ by Paul of Samosata, *vide*

Sample, "Messiah as Prophet" and "Christology of the Council of Antioch" (n. 14 *supra*); and Stead, "Platonism of Arius" (n. 79 *supra*), p. 21.

120. *Vide* chap. 3 *infra* and cf. Asterius' (frg. XXXIII, Bardy, *Lucien*, p. 353) description of δόξα as an ἐξουσία that is bestowed on Christ, as precosmic δόξα (John 17:5).

121. *Or. c. Ar.* 1.5. Cf. Gregg and Groh, p. 274. Asterius turns the concept of God's foreknowledge a slightly different direction, using it to underscore God's knowledge of how to create, which the mediator then learns (Bardy, *Lucien*, frg. IV = Athanasius *De Syn.* 19). "Foreseen merit" is Chadwick's term (*Early Christian Thought*, n. 80 *supra*).

122. *Or. c. Ar.* 2.13. Cf. the anonymous homilist, "he [Jesus] conquered through the cross (διὰ σταυροῦ νενίκηκεν), and he saved through death, and he released the curse through a curse [cf. Gal. 3:10], and he performed all, and he set us free from the stratagem above": Casey, chap. 10, p. 10. Sample, "Messiah as Prophet," pp. 221–22, overemphasizes the passion of Christ in early Arianism to the exclusion of the resurrection/promotion aspects. The cross is the culmination of the obedience aspect of the Philippians 2 kerygmatic model; but the second half of that model is the resurrection/promotion (cf. *Or. c. Ar.* 1.38, Bright, p. 39). These *twin* aspects form the heart of Arian Christology and its conception of salvific benefits.

123. *Or. c. Ar.* 3.38–40.

124. *Or. c. Ar.* 3.40 (Bright, p. 194).

125. Cf. the argument over the meaning of διό in Phil. 2:9, in which Athanasius opposes the Arian concept of Christ's striving for a prize of virtue (ἆθλον ἀρετῆς) or a promotion of his advance (βελτίωσιν προκοπῆς αὐτοῦ) (*Or. c. Ar.* 1.42; Bright, p. 45). Here προκοπή must refer to the internal strides of the redeemer, as already noted by Robertson (*NPNF*, vol. 4, p. 331, n. 4), and βελτίωσις then designates the promotion of the redeemer by God. The resurrection indicates by means of the διό (though Athanasius denies the validity of this Arian position) this μισθὸν ἀρετῆς or προκοπῆς (*Or. c. Ar.* 1.44, Bright, p. 46). Athanasius maintains the resurrection is simply to indicate the cause (αἰτία) of his resurrection—namely, the incarnation to overcome sin (ibid.)—and is not the occasion of the Son's promotion (*Or. c. Ar.* 1.43; cf. 2.53–54 for his principle of αἰτία). Βελτίωσις also in the sources means simply "improvement." Thus at *Or. c. Ar.* 3.24, Athanasius reports that the Arian Jesus comes to be "in the Father" "βελτιώσει πραξεως." Here it must surely mean "by improvement of conduct." Cf. *Ad Afros* 8 where βελτίωσις also designates moral improvement rather than the promotion God gives at the resurrection (contra *NPNF*, vol. 4, p. 407, n. 6, which stresses the external nature of βελτίωσις in *Or.* 3.24 and *Ad Afros* 8).

126. *De Syn.* 15.3 (Opitz², p. 242, lines, 20, 21, 23, 27; p. 243, lines 2, 3, 9, 11, 14, 16, 18). Cf. Arius *Ep. ad Alex.* 2 and 4 (Opitz³, Urk. 6, p. 12, line 7; and p. 13, line 8).

127. Arius *Thalia*, in Athanasius *De Syn.* 15.3 (Opitz², p. 242, lines 14–15).

128. *De Decr.* 6.5 (Opitz², p. 6, lines 15–18): "κἂν γὰρ, ὥς φασι, προγνωθεὶς ἔσεσθαι τοιοῦτος προλαμβάνῃ καὶ ἅμα τῷ γενέσθαι δέχηται τό τε ὄνομα καὶ

τὴν τοῦ ὀνόματος δόξαν, ἀλλ᾽ οὐδὲν διοίσει τῶν μετὰ τὰς πράξεις λαμβανόντων τὸ ὄνομα, ἕως οὕτω καὶ αὐτὸς υἱὸς εἶναι μεμαρτύρηται." *Vide* n. 120 *supra*.

129. *Or. c. Ar.* 1.9, 1.15.

130. See the text at n. 29 *supra*.

131. *Or. c. Ar.* 1.9, 1.15, 1.16, 1.37; *Or. c. Ar.* 2.37–38.

132. Ibid. 2.21. For the title *monogenēs theos, vide* Gregg and Groh, pp. 276–78.

133. *Or. c. Ar.* 1.15.

134. *Vide* Asterius frg. VIII (Bardy, *Lucien,* p. 344) and chap. 3 *infra*.

135. Note the use of the verb ὑπομένειν to designate both Jesus' endurance of the cross (*Or. c. Ar.* 2.13) and his forbearance to see the Father in the proper measure as befits a creature (*supra,* n. 51). In both texts the notion of "submitting to" is strong. Cf. this to Heb. 12:7 where enduring (*hypomenein*) and sonship are linked. G. Bardy, "Fragments attribués à Arius," *Revue d'histoire ecclésiastique* 26 (1) (1930): 267, had noted the willing submission of the Arian Christ and the emphasis on his obedience.

136. *Or. c. Ar.* 2.14 (Bright, pp. 82–83). For the rendering and meaning of the statement, *vide NPNF,* vol. 4, p. 355, n. 5.

137. Athanasius *De Decr.* 20.3 (Opitz², p. 17, lines 10–11).

138. *Or. c. Ar.* 2.29.

139. *Or. c. Ar.* 2.31 (Bright, p. 100). According to Athanasius, Asterius discovered the idea of the mediator as an underworker, and Arius copied it from him (*De Decr.* 8).

140. *Or. c. Ar.* 2.51; *vide De Decr.* 7.

141. *Or. c. Ar.* 2.3 (Bright, p. 71).

142. Ibid. 3–6.

143. *Supra* at nn. 41–44.

144. Cf. *Or. c. Ar.* 1.5, 2.37; *De Decr.* 9, 16, 20. For the soteriological implications of these texts, *vide* chap. 2 *infra*.

145. *Vide Or. c. Ar.* 2.35, 2.39.

146. Thus the curse which overlies the creation can be released by God's merely speaking the Word without having to unite the divine substance to the human body (*Or. c. Ar.* 2.68). Here the Arians stand remarkably close to Paul of Samosata's understanding as exposited by Sample, "Messiah as Prophet," pp. 170–80. But the parallel has to do with the nonhypostasized nature of God's Word (= his will or command); unlike Paul, the Arians held firmly to a premundane Christ as a distinguishable essence.

147. *Or. c. Ar.* 3.10 (= frg. XIV, Bardy, *Lucien,* p. 346); *NPNF* translation, slightly altered.

148. Frg. XXXII (Bardy, *Lucien,* p. 352) (= Marcellus frg. 72, ed. Kostermann, in Eusebius *Contr. Marcel.* 1.4.55): "ἓν γὰρ εἶναι καὶ ταὐτὸν 'Αστέριος κατὰ τοῦτο ἀπεφήνατο μόνον τὸν πατέρα καὶ τὸν υἱὸν καθ᾽ ὃ ἐν πᾶσιν συμφωνοῦσιν. οὕτω γὰρ ἔφη· καὶ δία τὴν ἐν πᾶσιν λόγοις τε καὶ ἔργοις ἀκριβῆ συμφωνίαν· ἐγὼ καὶ ὁ πατὴρ ἕν ἐσμεν.' " See Bardy, *Lucien,* p. 353, for the

frequency of Marcellus' citation of this fragment. Cf. also the second symbol of the Synod of Antioch (A.D. 341), influenced by Asterian notions (Bardy, *Lucien*, pp. 125–27). Cf. Origen *C. Cels.* 8.12.

149. Bardy, "Fragments attribués à Arius," pp. 266–67.

150. Ibid., p. 265. Contra Pollard, *Johannine Christology*, p. 153, who insisted the Arians did not deal with John 10:30.

151. *Or. c. Ar.* 3.9–11.

152. *Or. c. Ar.* 2.31 and *NPNF*, vol. 4, p. 365, n. 8. Cf. *Or. c. Ar.* 3.57 (Bright, pp. 209–10), where Athanasius locates Jesus' willing principle in the Logos, thereby attributing the agony of Gethsemane to the mutable flesh.

153. *Or. c. Ar.* 3.1–2.

154. *Or. c. Ar.* 3.2.

155. *Or. c. Ar.* 3.3., *NPNF* translation.

156. Eusebius of Nicomedia, *De Decr.* 9.4 = "more favor" along the lines of Ps. 44:7 (LXX): Gregg and Groh, p. 278.

157. *Or. c. Ar.* 3.17, *NPNF* translation.

158. Respectively: *Or. c. Ar.* 3.24; 1.6; 1.36; 1.9; Urk. 14.34; *Or.* 1.37.

159. *Or. c. Ar.* 2.51.

160. Cf. Heb. 1:9–10 and Heb. 5:8. *Vide* Philo, *Vita Mosis* 1.329, where virtuous conduct (ἀρετῆς ἔργα) is defined by the people of Israel who obey (περιθαρχεῖν) Moses.

161. Casey, chap. 10, p. 10, line 27.

162. Arius *Thalia, De Syn.* 15.3 (Opitz², p. 243, lines 6–7).

163. "Jesus does not cease doing good, and yet even now he saves; but he even increases with well-doing, and the well-doing does not cease doing good, in order that we may not cease giving thanks," etc.: *Casey*, p. 10.

164. *Vide* ibid. Thus escape from the devil's evils is "through grace" and the proper response to "the greatness (τὸ μέγεθος) of the one having worked good" is to give thanks "not as much as we owe but as much as we are able" (ibid.).

165. *Vide* G. W. H. Lampe, *A Patristic Greek Lexicon* (Oxford: Clarendon Press, 1961), "χάρις," p. 1517, II.2.1 (Athanasius loc. cit.) and p. 1518, IV.A (Arius loc. cit.).

166. *Or. c. Ar.* 3.38.

167. Ibid.

168. E. P. Meijering, *Orthodoxy and Platonism in Athanasius: Synthesis or Antithesis?* (Leiden: E. J. Brill, 1974), p. 77.

169. *Vide* n. 151 *supra*.

170. Alexander *Ep. ad Alex.* 14.11–12 (Opitz³, p. 21, lines 15–19) (quoting Isa. 1:2).

171. The cardinal number is used in the Arian sources in three basic senses: (1) With the partitive genitive to underline the fact that the Arian redeemer is one of an unspecified number of candidates: Asterius frg. III (Bardy, *Lucien*, p. 343) (= Athanasius *De Syn.* 19), εἷς τῶν πάντων and εἷς τῶν νοητῶν and εἷς . . . τῶν

41

φαινόμενων. Cf. Athanasius' reporting that the Arians considered him to be "μία τῶν γενόμενων δυνάμεων." (2) With the indefinite pronoun which weakens the numerical force: *Or. c. Ar.* 1.5 (*Thalia*), "ἕνα τινά." (3) To emphasize one thing to the exclusion of others; thus God creates the mediator's nature as "*monon hena*" (i.e., from generate natures): *Or. c. Ar.* 2.24 (Bright, p. 94). For this way of classifying εἷς, μία, ἕν, see John Henry Thayer, *A Greek-English Lexicon of the New Testament*⁴ (Edinburgh: T. & T. Clark, 1901 [1958]), pp. 186–87. Cf. the early Arian Athanasius of Anazarba (in Athanasius, *De Syn.* 17) who described Christ as "one of the hundred sheep."

2

The Son:
One of Many Brothers

When Arius and his companions spoke of the Christ, they thought of a being called into existence by the divine will, a creature finite in knowledge and morally changeable. By the steady choice of the good, this "certain one" attained the favor which God, who foreknew his fidelity, conferred upon him, when he "advanced him as a Son to himself by adoption."[1] According to the Arian profession of faith, God's chosen one possessed sonship by virtue of his performance as an obedient creature and by virtue of God's grace, which both anticipated and rewarded his efforts.

The presentation of this Christ in teaching and preaching, which we described in the first chapter, met sharp and hostile resistance in some quarters of the church. For some Christians, the Arian portrait of the Son of God, because the features were so undisguisedly those of a creature, threatened either to erode or to expel the godly power which piety assumed to be his. Although elements of the Christology of Arius had been present in Christian understanding from the movement's beginnings, and though the subordinate status of the Son in relation to the Father had been assumed and taught by theologians honored in the preceding centuries, Arian doctrine was denounced as "novel" and "innovative," hence heretical. The Christian church (and parties within it), like the culture surrounding it, distrusted the new and quickly learned to label "new" what it distrusted.

Why did the early Arians think of Christ in the way they did? The question needs to be considered on more than one level. In their own defense against the charge of inventing doctrine, Arius and Eusebius of Nicomedia were prepared to reveal, immediately and proudly, the source of their teaching. Attempting some five years before the synod in 325 to enlist the

43

uncommitted (or at least silent) bishop of Tyre in the Arian cause, Eusebius urges Paulinus to declare himself "in accordance with the scriptures" and to follow "in the tracks (τοῖς ἴχνεσι) of its words and purposes."[2] The views for which he and others are now persecuted, Eusebius assures his episcopal colleague, are not their own imaginings, but were learned from "the holy scriptures," which testify that the Son is, by his nature, "created, established, and begotten."[3] Similarly, in the earliest days of the dispute Arius is seen to be engaged in a defense of certain interpretations of biblical phrases.[4] A letter of Alexander written prior to Nicaea responds to particular texts which the Arians have presented and reports their practice of collecting passages of scripture to fortify their understanding of Christ.[5]

By the fourth century, however, the bare appeal to scripture served more to agitate than to silence the opposition. In earlier struggles of theological self-definition, Christian groups had learned to point texts at each other like weapons. A teaching which purported to be "in accordance with scriptures" needed the corroboration of authoritative tradition. It needed apostolic pedigree. So a disaffected Arius reminds his episcopal opponent that he teaches none other than the faith of his forebears (ἡ πίστις . . . ἐκ προγόνων), and in the preface of his *Thalia* those champions in whose tracks (again, ἴχνος) he has walked ("suffering much," he says, "for God's glory") are described as "the elect of God, the perceptive . . . ortho-dox . . . partakers of Wisdom."[6] At a first level, the question "Why?" was heard as "By what right?" Arian spokesmen were prepared to give an answer (not at all different from that of the orthodox) which spoke directly to the issues of authority and credentials: their portrait of Christ was derived from and dictated by the holy writings and the hallowed traditions of the church.

At its more intriguing (and more difficult) level, the question is a different one. *To what end did the early Arians portray Christ as they did?* What important purposes were served thereby? What gains were secured by the advocacy of *this* Christology? We meet everywhere the answer accentuated by Bishops Alexander and Athanasius, the answer which holds sway in modern interpretations of Arianism: it was in order to protect the singularity, the monarchy of God, that Arius and his followers came to insist that the Son was not "true God" and was only called God's "Word" and "Wisdom" by a verbal convenience; this Son was in fact a "work" of God whose mode of origination and creaturely limitations marked off his nature from that of God. This portrait of Christ insured an uncompromised monotheism in which the Son did not vie with the Father for prominence and ruled out the possibility of two "First Principles," two eternal and unbegotten beings. We demonstrated in the preceding chapter that far from being a strategy for leaving the stage to God alone, the Arian program presented a Christology which was articulated with considerable care. The inner dynamic of the scheme, whereby the obedient one progresses to full and enduring sonship, indicates a range of concerns more extensive than those previously credited to Arian thinkers.

What significance did this christological scheme hold for Christians of Arius' persuasion? Response to the question at this level depends upon the way in which the primary documents are read. They are works of disputation written under the rules of late antique polemic, which means that a sharp eye is needed to discern serious arguments among the numerous conceits and ploys. The orthodox and the Arians observed the codes and conventions of polemic and were equally adept at argument by insinuation, slander by association, and the deflection and misrepresentation of opponents' assertions.[7] Plain speech is not the style of patristic debate, and it is necessary to proceed with caution even when attempting to discern *primary* issues at stake in a controversy.

The word "polemic" carries connotations which seem to link it both with the Greek verb πολεμεῖν ("to wage war") and the less familiar πάλλειν ("to brandish, wield"). The distinction between earnest combat and menacing gesture is useful in the assessment of early literary attacks upon Arian teaching. Nothing illustrates the point so clearly as the task of defining the chief complaints and contended points in the dispute. To ask Alexander and Athanasius what the Arian purpose is involves asking them to state the charges, to identify the offense which has been committed. If the specific "counts" are considered as in a legal proceeding, and accorded equal weight, the bill of particulars published by the champions of orthodoxy is confusing and self-contradictory.

According to one set of accusations, the "Ariomaniacs" seek to destroy the distinctive revelation by which the Christian community lives. This charge has a double aspect. From one perspective, it is the claim, stated in varying degrees of intensity, that the heresy consists in assaults against the Christ (κατὰ τοῦ Χριστοῦ). Bishop Alexander's sketches are typical and graphic: Arians stand in battle formation against the divinity of the Son of

45

God; they are a cloud-raising pack of brutes howling against the Christ.[8] All of their subtle phrases work for the destruction of the deity of the Word.[9]

Athanasius indulges in a brand of early Christian anti-Semitism in his effort to link the Arian Christology with the Jews' denial of Jesus' messiahship. Labeling Arius and his company the "new Jews of the present day," inspired to their hatred of Christ by their Father, Satan, he likens the Arian "Judaizers" to the Pharisees who challenged Jesus by asking, "Why do you, being a man, make yourself God?"[10] Carrying the comparison to its conclusion, he charges his opponents with being enemies and slayers of Christ.[11] One of the stock charges which G. C. Stead has cautioned is "extremely hazardous to accept," the argument is an anti-Jewish form of the *reductio ad haeresim*—the attribution of guilt by correspondence of erroneous ideas (and in this case, evil actions).[12]

As we saw in the first chapter, the two Alexandrian prelates agree about one of the elements at work in the Arian "blasphemy." Alexander complains that these troublers of the church are obsessed with the biblical passages touching upon Christ's human limitations and passion (reference is made to "humiliation," "self-emptying," and "poverty," suggesting Phil. 2:5–11 and 2 Cor. 8:9) while they disregard texts hymning the Son's eternity and deity. One of Athanasius' festal letters registers the same point: "Because of his coming down . . . and looking upon him as having suffered . . . they do not believe in him as the incorruptible Son of the incorruptible Father."[13] As represented by these orthodox spokesmen, the Arian concentration upon texts treating the ministry and death of Christ has a single objective—it is a tactic for impugning the heavenly dignity of the Son.

In warning against easy acceptance of the stock charges utilized by rhetoricians, G. C. Stead suggested attention to "the connecting link of argumentation."[14] In the case of the two items under discussion—the comparison of Arian and Jew, and the heretics' practice of gathering texts highlighting Christ's human vulnerability—the connecting thread is not difficult to see. Behind the accusation that Arians denied the deity of the Son there stood, no doubt, a series of propositions such as these: Arius and his allies harp upon the humanity of Christ, bolstering their view with selected texts; the Jews could see in Jesus only a man, and they called for his death; since the Arians call Christ a "creature" and "work," they "smite him who is their helper with their tongue," and are not worthy of the name Christians.[15]

46

Arian teachers could be indicted for warring *kata Christou* not only because they denied his divinity but because they insisted upon his status as an originate being. They sought to separate the Father and his image, in order "that they might level the Son with things originated, . . . ranking him among these."[16] This second aspect of the accusation pervades anti-Arian writings, and several unambiguous statements indicate that it was understood as the obverse of the same charge of Christomachy. Alexander refers to an organized gang of Christ-battlers "denying the divinity of our savior and proclaiming that he is equal to all."[17] Arian Christomachy has two aspects, frequently yoked in orthodox polemic: " 'denying the Son' (1 John 2:23) and numbering him among the creatures."[18]

From the viewpoint of the orthodox theologians the inclusion of the Son in the order of creation nullified his special sonship, his identity with the divine nature. How could he be "only-begotten" when numbered among the rest?[19] Furthermore, the Father would be coimplicated in the Son's creatureliness. Because of the Alexandrian episcopal hermeneutic requiring predicates of the Son to be predicates also of the Father, Athanasius argued that if his opponents count Christ as one of the "all" (which Paul in 1 Cor. 8:6 says came into being through him), they will think of the Father in similar terms—that is, as a creature.[20] If Christ is creature, one argument runs, the actions of the church by which the faithful gain redemption lose their effect:

> In thinking to be baptized into the name of one who exists not, they will receive nothing; and ranking (συντασσόμενοι) themselves with a creature, from the creation they will have no help, and believing in one unlike and foreign to the Father in essence, to the Father they will not be joined, not having his Son by nature . . . the wretched men henceforth remain destitute and stripped of the Godhead.[21]

It is the status of the Son which insures sacramental efficacy. By considering Christ a "common man" the Arians make grace into something which is not secure (βέβαιος). A creature receives grace and is capable of forfeiting it. The creature-Christ of the heretics cannot bestow enduring grace, is incapable of dispensing saving help.[22] Such, according to Athanasius, are the consequences of calling the Son κτίσμα and ποίημα. The consequences correspond exactly to the Arian intention, which is to strip the Son of the dignity and power proper to deity. The various assertions that Christ is "equal to," "ranks with," is "leveled" with the creatures are signals of the impious conspiracy against the Son, disguised as efforts to honor and elevate God the Father.

47

To summarize, one prominent charge directed against Arian doctrine has two faces: the divinity of the Son is deprecated, and he is demeaned by being brought to the level of other beings which once did not exist. Alongside this indictment stands an accusation which presumably carries equal force, although it runs in an altogether different direction. Having advanced low and disparaging thoughts about God's Son, the Arians are guilty of overestimating themselves. In Pauline language, they think more highly of themselves than they ought to think. This accusation, while it includes a slap at the temerity of Arius and Eusebius, is aimed ultimately not at arrogance of persons in the Arian camp but at their anthropology, at the estimate of human nature which their Christology assumes. Too much is being claimed for creatures. These dangerous teachers do not fear "to equal servile beings to the nobility of the Triad, and to rank the King, the Lord of Sabaoth, with subjects"—they attempt to mix the unmixable (τὰ ἄμικτα).[23]

In the third of the Athanasian *Orations*, the Arians can be seen arguing that creatures (or better, believers) can enjoy union with the Father in the same fashion which enables the Johannine Christ to say, "I and the Father are one," and "I in the Father and the Father in me." In this contention Athanasius sees audacity and recklessness reminiscent of the satanic presumption recorded in Isa. 14:14—the boast that heaven will be attained and likeness to Christ obtained. This is the Arian offense.

> The things given by grace to men, these they want to make equal to the divinity of the giver. Thus hearing that men are called sons, they hold themselves equal to the true and natural Son. . . . They are so arrogant as to suppose that as the Son is in the Father, and the Father in the Son, so will they be.[24]

Athanasius is appalled by the exegesis and by the assumptions which undergird it: "Neither we shall ever be as he, nor is the Word as we are."[25] Even when believers speak of having life "in God," he notes, it is the Spirit indwelling them which is in God, not they themselves.[26]

Inspection of the two chief indictments brought against the Arians, if both are accurate, leaves us in a quandary. According to orthodox testimony, Arians demean Christ, denying his divine honor; and yet they boldly aspire or claim to be as he is. Is it plausible that Arius and his followers denigrated Christ and simultaneously claimed (in the interest of exalting rather than incriminating themselves) to be like him? This account of the religious scheme of the Arians is at odds with itself. It is, we need to remember, the work of rhetoricians who desire to entrap the foe by an array of arguments which need less to be consistent with one another than they need to be individually effective in damaging the opponent's cause. Nevertheless, the task remains of penetrating rhetorical strategies in order to discover which issues most deeply occupied the disputants. In this instance, it is important to ask whether one of these anti-Arian indictments, or both of them, stripped of polemical interpretation, serve to better illuminate what the Arians were fighting for and why they framed the Christology they did.

Arian insistence that the Son "once was not" and was thus a creature of God is thoroughly attested in preserved fragments of Arius' teaching and in the literature written to combat his doctrines. From the interpretations given by the Arians' opponents the significance which Arius and his following attached to this creaturely sonship is difficult to learn. Because Alexander and Athanasius interweave description and denunciation, extended exposure to their arguments makes it possible to lose sight of some reasonably sure information about the religion of the Arians. Simple questions need to be asked afresh. Is there evidence to support the charge that Arians termed the Son of God a "creature" and "work" *in order to* deny his deity or to deprecate the figure who stood at the center of the Christian community's memory and consciousness? Orthodox descriptions of Arian beliefs and intentions, if taken at face value, would suggest that Arian worship unfolded in a mode and with language altogether different from orthodox, if in fact *Christian* worship were possible to them at all. Such charges are not explicitly made—no doubt because they could not be made. The Arians did not, as Athanasius' own discussion reveals, baptize in the name of the Father alone, nor did they reserve the use of the word "God" to the Father alone.[27] As we have shown in the opening chapter, Arian Christians spoke of an advancing, not a demoted, Son. They understood the divinity of the Son differently from the orthodox. They were adamant in their resistance to a definition of the savior's sonship circumscribed by essentialist categories, by reference to οὐσία shared by Father and Son eternally. Apart from objection to particular understandings and conceptualizations of fatherhood and sonship, we have no substantial evidence of Arian reticence to revere and honor the Son.

To what end did the Arians portray Christ in the way they did? Read with the Arian Christology in view, and with questions about soteriology in the foreground, the early debate of the controversy reflects just how daring, in fact, the Arian view of Christ was. Its audacity and its appeal consisted in the promises held out to those who believed that portrait of God's creature-Son to be true.

ADOPTION AS SALVATION:
"COMMON TO US AND TO THE SON"

The two views of sonship held by orthodox and Arian, which were so important for our understanding of the Christology of the Arians, are crucial to their soteriology as well. The foundational axiom from which the orthodox theology of Alexander and Athanasius proceeded was the conviction that the Son is the "exact and precisely similar image of the Father." All attributes of the Father (except his property as the unbegotten) are located in the Word: eternity, immutability, perfection, all-sufficiency.[28] "The Son is the Father's All," Athanasius writes at the end of his *Orations*, as if summarizing his entire case against the Arians.[29] In accordance with this basic postulate, everything said of the Son had to be predicated of the Father as well.

When the soteriological dimensions of the conflict between orthodoxy and Arianism are perceived, it is evident what idea of sonship this principle and hermeneutic was designed to produce. Christ's sonship could only be of an essentially different order from the sonship bestowed upon believers. Bishop Alexander registers the point with purposeful sharpness:

> It must be seen that the sonship of our savior has no community with the sonship of the rest [of men]. . . . there are no other natural sons besides himself.[30]

Only as natural offspring of the divine paternal *ousia* could the Word, by assuming flesh, renew and deify humanity, securing it in imperishability.[31]

The foundation of Arius' Christianity is both implicit and explicit in the declaration that the Son is creature, one among the beings made and sustained by the will of God.[32] The Arian hermeneutic cannot be misconstrued: what is predicated of the redeemer must be predicated of the redeemed. As will be seen, the central point in the Arian system is that Christ gains and holds his sonship in the same way as other creatures. Arius' doctrine that Christ was advanced to God by adoption contains the ground and definition of the faith and hope of believers. The early Arians portrayed Christ as they did because the advocacy of this Christology gave fullest expression to their understanding of the content and dynamic of salvation.

In an intriguing piece of narrative in *De Decretis* 19–20, portions of the "floor fight" at Nicaea are recounted. Athanasius explains why Arian obstinacy necessitated the fateful designations of the Son as "one in essence" (ὁμοούσιος) and "from the essence of God" (ἐκ τῆς οὐσίας τοῦ θεοῦ). The orthodox (which is to say, those who were to depart from the synod with official but not unchallenged right to be so called) proposed a series of terms and phrases designed to underline the unique and exclusive bond between Son and Father. To their consternation, the Arians (whispering to each other and signaling each other with winks, our narrator reports) were too amenable. They made no objections. Such words and phrases as "always," "in him," "like," and "power" were perfectly acceptable to them. Though Alexander and his allies hoped such terminology would fix a boundary between Father and Son on the one hand and all things originate on the other, the Arians declared that the language was "common to us and the Son." Scripture speaks, they argued, of believers being "in him" (that is, God) and refers to people (and lesser creatures) as "powers" just as it designates Christ God's "power and wisdom" (1 Cor. 1:24). Advocates of the Arian teaching were anxious to demonstrate that such language did not distinguish the Son from creatures but indicated instead their community. Though the strategy of the Arians is depicted as cunning and mischievous, it is not to be doubted that their commitment to what is "common to us and the Son" was central and serious. Nothing demonstrates this so forcefully as the ways in which Arian reasoning drew connecting lines between Christ and the Christian. No properties of the savior, nothing in his character and his works, were beyond the reach of those things Arians proclaimed were common also to his fellow creatures.

Arian insistence upon this commonality was responsible (as seen in chapter one) for the distinction which orthodox thinkers sharpened between "natural" sonship and sonship in a more extended, inclusive sense. The biological sonship of Isaac to Abraham was contrasted with the convenantal sonship by which Israel and those responsive to Christ are called children and sons of God.[33] If the Son of God were understood to be related to his Father in the latter sense, Athanasius observes, "then he would seem to differ from us in nothing . . . having obtained the title of Son, like others, from his virtue."[34] In his view it is imperative to deny that the Word is a son in the manner in which others may claim sonship—as beings dependent upon their Maker and "as all things are from God" (2 Cor. 5:18). The Word of

51

God is and must be, by contrast, a son "natural and authentic from a father," a "true offspring . . . like Joseph was from Jacob, and the radiance from the sun."[35] For orthodoxy, indispensable soteriological interests hinge upon this distinction. They are visible throughout Athanasian writings, and typically so in a comparison he draws between Moses and the Word: whereas the former, like all men, was robed in flesh in order that he might have existence, the Logos became man in order to sanctify the flesh.[36]

Athanasius' objection to thinking of the Word of God as a son "like others" who would "differ from us in nothing" responds directly to Arian teaching, which he represents accurately, even if he distorts its objective. Only the conception of sonship which has applicability to all created beings will be tolerated by Arius and his companions. "No one is son of God by nature (φύσει)," they argue, nor does anyone have a peculiar relationship to God—that is, a kinship unique in kind.[37] The Arian system allowed and employed a single way of speaking of a son. The features of this sonship are recoverable from significant portions of debate between the controversy's antagonists, and notably in the arguments surrounding interpretation of certain biblical texts. The extent to which Arian interest in this filial identity not only embraced the person of the Son but characterized and encouraged a particular form of Christian discipleship and devotion has not been detected in previous scholarship. It was seen in the preceding chapter that a number of distinctive elements coalesced in the Arian understanding of Christ. Ideas of adoption, changeability, the role of virtue, advance and improvement, participation, and estimates of knowledge and volition all contribute to a view of sonship possessing its own logic and dynamic. Because Arian Christians did not attribute one brand of sonship to Christ and another to those who came to say "Abba, Father," it is necessary to examine the manner in which the Arians conceived of these various components (adoption, changeability, participation, and so forth) as being "common to them"—as constitutive of that sonship (and daughtership) which they believed themselves to possess. Though accused of presumption and blasphemy for attempting to be equal to the Son, it is probably safe to assume that from their angle of vision, they were simply taking seriously the obligation to be "imitators" of Christ. Christian belief and action as *imitatio* had already by the fourth century run a colorful (and varied) course. The imitation in which Arian Christians placed great confidence was, as will become evident, an emulation of a very particular and self-conscious kind.

Strategies for salvation which depend upon the imitation of Christ may skirt dangerously close to crude "adoptionism." However, Arian thinkers can be demonstrated to have taught the Son's preincarnate existence even while denying his eternity. Nowhere does Arius, Eusebius, or Asterius suggest that the Son's beginning was marked by the birth (or baptism) of Jesus of Nazareth. According to them, the one called "Word" and "Son" was created before all ages. To the charge which resides in Athanasius' remarks in the first *Oration* the Arians were not really vulnerable:

> He was not man, and then became God, but he was God, and then became man, in order to deify us.[38]

Important aspects of the Arian Christology did nonetheless raise the specter of the primitive forms of adoptionism which had won followings and criticism in former eras (for example, Mark, the Ebionites [as described by Eusebius of Caesarea and Hippolytus], and Hermas, *Sim.* V). On more than one occasion Athanasius complains that as the Arians describe Christ, he is merely a parallel to heroes of the biblical tradition. In reaction, he warns that Christ was not anointed "like Aaron or David or the rest . . . but in another way above all his fellows."[39] And in an effort to break any connection which the impious might want to make between the calling of Christ and that of such persons as Moses and the prophets, Athanasius must interpret the baptismal narratives in a particular way. At the Jordan, he says, the Spirit did not descend upon the Word (who needed no sanctification), but upon us through him.[40]

A passage in one of Bishop Alexander's letters provides clearer indication of Arian interest in these traditions about Jesus. In claiming that God selected Christ on account of his diligent conduct and unswerving choice of the good, the Arians speak "as if, should Paul and Peter also make good with respect to this [life of discipline], nothing would distinguish their sonship from his."[41] Even as Alexander reports it, this is apparently less a hypothesis about where such an idea of sonship would inevitably lead than it is a glimpse of the manner in which Arians actually understood and appropriated to themselves what the Christ represented as fellow creature. This letter, predating Nicaea, contains evidence that Arians argued this view of the election of the Christ from (among other texts) Ps. 44:7 (LXX). As an interpretation of the Son (its application in Heb. 1:9), the passage says that because (διὰ τοῦτο) he "loved righteousness and hated iniquity," he was anointed above his companions (μετόχους). In view of the unwillingness of the Arians to admit different meanings of the word "son," it is legitimate to assume that the "companions" of the psalm passage were considered, as a consequence of their upright behavior, candidates for divine favor of the same kind. Indeed, the fuller context of the passage in Alexander's letter (which will receive more extensive treatment below) demands the conclusion that Arians believed the election by merit to belong to the Christian "just as also [to] that one" (ὥσπερ κἀκεῖνος), the Christ.[42]

In an important section in the third *Oration*, Athanasius deals with the issue in virtually an identical manner. As if to suggest that they are unaware of them, he spells out the consequences of the Arians' claim that the Father and Son enjoy a union on the basis of concordant (σύμφονος) wills. If the Word is like the Father in this way only, the same might be said for angels, powers, dominions, the sun, moon, and stars, all of which "are themselves also sons, as the Son (εἶναι καὶ αὐτοὺς, ὡς τὸν Υἱὸν, υἱούς) . . . [for] neither in judgments nor in doctrines are they discordant, but in all things they are obedient to the one who has made them." The next step in the rebuttal, though presented as a telling proof against fallacious Arian reasoning, would have been welcomed with that frustrating agreeableness Arians reputedly showed at Nicaea. To them, there was no scandal in Athanasius' observation that

> among men too will be found many like the Father [that is, in the same way the Son is ὅμοιος]—the greatest number being martyrs, and before them the apostles and prophets, and again before them the patriarchs, and many even now . . . [43]

It cannot be supposed that Athanasius does not perceive the Arians' reasons for treating the "oneness" between Father and Son (John 10:30 and 14:10 are under debate) as they did. The Arians maintain this doctrine of concordant wills as something common to saints and the Son. Athanasius predictably registers the objection that "none of these is Word or Wisdom or only-begotten Son or Image."[44] Soteriology is pitted against soteriology, and neither adversary thinks otherwise.

The adoptionist Christologies which antedated the Arian controversy drew criticism for failing to distinguish the savior sufficiently from other "greats," from other prophets and holy men. Whether these schemes included not only a Christology but a corollary idea of salvation through imitation it is difficult to know, due to the limited sources and the sketchiness of our knowledge of such groups as the Ebionites. Though our own sources for early Arian thought pose similar problems, the structure of the adoptionism they taught is capable of fuller description.[45] At this point it is not the rationale and "mechanics" of adoption which concern us. Rather, our interest centers in the Arian doctrine that the Son of God was adopted Son *as it affected and shaped Arian Christians' understanding of redemption.*

Fear is expressed that Arians will deceive some of the faithful, causing them to think that in parallel fashion to the inspiration of "saints" of earlier times, the Word visited one man, thus sanctifying (ἁγιάζων) Christ and being manifest in him "as also in the others" (ὥσπερ καὶ ἐν τοῖς ἄλλοις).[46] The conflicting definitions of "son" held by orthodox and Arian thinkers led the former to a discussion of the meaning of Pauline references to adoption (υἱοθεσία), particularly in Romans 8. In order to make his case, Alexander employs the distinction between things such by nature and things such by attribution (φύσει and θέσει). Christ's natural sonship "surpasses by an inexpressible preeminence the sonship of those who have been adopted as sons through his [that is, the Son's] appointment."[47] The Son's possession of the paternal deity, *by nature his*, has nothing in common with the adopted sonship which Paul said belongs to heirs. With the famous election text of Rom. 8:29 explicitly in view, Athanasius commences his rebuttal of the Arian interpretation with an exegetical observation, then proceeds to the argument used by Alexander. Scripture, he says, employs the verbs "create" and "beget" in reference to humans to denote their creation and their adoption respectively.[48] The Creator subsequently becomes Father of those enabled by the Spirit to cry "Abba, Father." According to Athanasius, Paul's words support the distinction between sonships, for adoption belongs to those "who could not become sons, being by nature creatures, otherwise than by receiving the Spirit of the natural (φύσει) and true Son."[49] With these attempts to confine adopted sonship to creatures should be grouped the several similar treatments of sonship "by grace" (κατὰ χάριν), since the ideas are synonymous in the debate.[50] Nothing unfamiliar, therefore, is met in Athanasius' reasoning about heroes like David, Solomon, Elijah, Elisha, and the apostles, who spoke words and worked wonders not by their own might "but in the Lord's grace" (τῇ τοῦ Κυρίου χάριτι). If the divine Word meant to be identified and counted among these, he would have spoken differently in the Fourth Gospel, saying instead, "I *too* am in the Father."[51]

As the Word is natural, not adopted, Son, so also he dispenses grace, not being its recipient.[52]

Efforts of the orthodox theologians to drive a wedge between the Word's natural sonship and the sonship by adoption (encompassing past heroes and present believers) do not combat, nor were they in actuality intended to combat, an Arian desire to demote and degrade the Son. Rather, the attempted distinction is meant to wreck an Arian proposition possessing affirmative soteriological content. Arius and his followers believed that God has and will have many sons—many, in fact, who might be called his "words."[53] Sharing in a single kind of sonship, Christ is one among many brothers. Therefore, as the Son gained his name "by grace" and was "by adoption" raised by God to himself, likewise other creatures, being faithful in the manner of that "certain one" chosen before time, might be recipients of the Father's favor and glory.[54] It is this concept of salvation which stands behind numerous Arian utterances of the sort recorded in *De sententia Dionysii* 23:

> . . . this Lord is foreign and alien to the essence of the Father, and is only called "Word" conceptually, and is not natural and true Son of God, but this one *also* is called Son by adoption, as a creature [emphasis added].[55]

The connection of this kind of proposition with Arius' view that only the Reason intrinsic to God could be properly and "truly" termed Word and Wisdom is not to be denied.[56] What has not been seen with sufficient clarity is its place in a purposeful scheme of salvation, a scheme which illuminates Arius' interest in making the claim that "God speaks many words."[57] Because the character of their relationship to the Creator and Father is not dissimilar to the relationship enjoyed by the "Firstborn," other created beings may share with him designations bestowed through divine favor. Others may be called with him "sons," "words," and "powers." It is difficult to imagine what other meaning and purpose could attach to a little-discussed assertion found in the *Thalia*. Arius grants that God is not able to produce a son more excellent than Christ, but he states,

> One equal to the Son, the Superior is able to beget.[58]

Adoption, he argues, is "common to us and to the Son," and this is the salvation for which Christians hope.

As invoked by early Arian spokesmen, the idea of participation (μετοχή) is very closely aligned with this adoptionist scheme and should be examined for signals of the dynamic by which these Christians believed themselves to be related to God. Prominent in the surviving fragments of the *Thalia* is Arius' contention that because he partakes (μετέχοντα) of God's own Λόγος and Σοφία, the Son is called "Word" and "Wisdom." This is not a participation due to common essence; as alien and dissimilar οὐσίαι, Father, Son, and Spirit cannot have *substantial* participation in each other.[59] The manner in which Arius employs the language of participation gives further evidence of the ethical and voluntarist cast of his thought. When he states that the Word is called God "by participation of grace" (μετοχῇ χάριτος), he has in mind that obedience whereby the Word "remains good by his own free will, while he chooses."[60] From early in the controversy, the meaning which Arians gave to μετέχειν and its derivatives was pressed upon the opposition. Pointing to Ps. 44:7 (LXX) and maintaining that the Christ did not *by nature* possess anything superior to the other sons of God (the companions, or τοὺς μετόχους of the psalm verse), they asserted that "he was elected on account of [his] diligence of conduct and discipline, since he did not incline toward what is inferior."[61] Christ's elevation, then, was a reward for performance. But this performance was not, in principle, beyond the capabilities of "his companions," for they held in common with him the powers (and limitations) of creaturehood.

Arians also made much of the reference (in Heb. 3:2) to Christ as one "who was faithful to him that made him," as we showed earlier. In the course of his extensive reply to Arian interpretation of the passage, Athanasius reveals that they believe "that 'faithful' is used of him as of others, as if he exercises faith and so receives the reward of faith."[62] Connotations of the Arian view of sonship by participation are visible in Athanasius' objection. Christ is, he says, "faithful, not as sharing (μετέχων) faith with us, nor as having faith in anyone as we have, but as deserving to receive faith in all that he says and does. . . ."[63] The early Arians would not have disagreed with the last phrase. As chosen and proven Son of God, the Christ deserved to be trusted and honored for his words and deeds. But Arianism clearly held that Christ's participation in the Father involved fidelity and obedience, and that he was not on account of his nature exempt from this ethically challenging mode of relationship to his Creator-Father.

Elsewhere, Athanasius registers his disapproval of the heretics' doctrine that the Son came to be "in the Father," like others, "by participation of the Spirit and by improvement of conduct" (μετοχῇ τοῦ πνευμάτος καὶ βελτιώσει πράξεως). Rather than partaking of the Spirit, the Son bestows it, Athanasius retorts, marshaling as evidence 1 John 4:13. As provocative as the argumentation itself is the reason which Athanasius gives for quoting John against the Arian view of participation: it "will stop the Arians from any longer thinking they shall be as the Son!"[64] The conclusion seems justified that for Arius and his followers Christ's participation in the Father, entailing as it did the exercise of faithfulness, served as a paradigm for their own relationship of obedience. In this connection, it is striking to observe that Arius himself is capable of using language of participation in reference to Christ and to Christians. As the Son is said to partake of the Father's own Wisdom, so also Arius refers to his own predecessors and teachers as "partakers of Wisdom" (τῶν σοφίας μετεχόντων).[65] It might be added that Arius' designations of his forebears as "God's chosen" and God's "Holy Spirit–receiving" in the *Thalia*'s preface become subjects of greater interest after the structure of his Christology and soteriology is perceived, for these phrases do not distinguish the saved from the savior. They underline attributes of the sonship common to both.

The horror with which orthodox thinkers regarded the Arian assertion of Christ's mutability has been well-documented above. To think the Christ morally free and capable of choice (even, theoretically, of choosing wrongly) was, to them, tantamount to obliterating his capacity to be savior. As Alexander and Athanasius understood the gulf between divine and creaturely natures, the Arian Christology made salvation impossible. Sonship obtained and sustained on the basis of merit, while the acceptable definition of the adoption available to believers and the goal of Christian living, could not be attributed to God's own Son. Athanasius writes that "one assimilated to God by virtue and will is liable also to the purpose of changing."[66] Believers (creatures), being alterable by their very nature and unstable in will, held their status as God's favored ones tentatively. Falls from grace were possible, as scripture attested.[67] What stability and security there was in their condition as redeemed creatures was due solely to the divine nature of the redeemer, whose incarnation worked God's purpose—the reversal of human corruptibility, the renewal and deification of flesh. "The only-begotten Son has the sonship as one incapable of change," and he is therefore empowered to provide the gift which "abides surely for us."[68] Both Alexander and Athanasius are insistent that the Word is the unchangeable Son of God in contrast to adopted sons who, vulnerable to moral fluctuations, depend upon his help if they are to continue in the way of sanctification.[69]

With equal fervency and with soteriological objectives just as clearly in mind, the Arians taught that the savior himself consistently chose the good and was chosen by God as a "reward of his purpose" because of his virtue and his works.[70] This, they argued, was the clear sense of the "wherefore" and "therefore" in such scriptural passages as the hymn in Philippians 2 and the verse in Psalm 44. In consequence of his life of obedience and love of righteousness Christ was the anointed one of God.

There is no disagreement between orthodoxy and Arianism about the existence and propriety of a relationship to God framed and realized through ethical choices, performance of deeds, and improvement and progress. Both parties are capable of speaking of "sons from virtue and grace," as the extended debate illustrates; and both assume this to be the character of the pious life *for creatures*. This sonship of course includes the Arian Christ while it excludes the eternal Logos of orthodoxy.

From the numerous and ubiquitous discussions of sonship in both Alexander's and Athanasius' writings, and from their direct quotations of Arius and Asterius, it cannot reasonably be doubted that Arians saw themselves mirrored in this portrait of the Christ as the one who advanced toward God, winning the prize for works accomplished. All that he is, they are. Reliant upon gospel presentations of Jesus, they concentrated on the creaturely performance of the savior and trusted that by making the "very same advance which he made when he became man" (to use Athanasius' phrase), they too would become the elect of God. We saw in the first chapter the attention the Arians devoted to portions of the Gospels illustrating that Christ's powers were derivative, that he grew in wisdom, prayed, lived in anticipation (but ignorance) of the Day of the Lord, was forsaken, and asked to receive glory. For them the christological conclusion was unambiguous: as creature and originate being he spoke as he did "and needed what he did not have"—such is the condition of humans.[71] Athanasius complains that his opponents, "looking at what is human in the savior . . . , have judged him a creature."[72] Both the texts chosen and the significance given them suggest that the Arians would have stated the matter differently: *seeing redemption in a creature, they beheld the shape of their own redemption*. Athanasius' lengthy response to Arian treatment of favorite Johannine texts (10:30; 17:11, and so forth) reveals his clear awareness of their audacious aims. In claiming that Father and Son are "one" or "like" on account of agreement of will, the Arians arrogantly propose that the union which the Son has with the Father can be theirs as well. Furthermore, they mistake the imitation which enables believers to become virtuous sons for equality with the Word.[73] The aim and movement of Athanasius' rebuttal in *Oration* 3.20–23 is worthy of attention. Equality with the Son is impossible because, he says (reiterating orthodoxy's basic principle), the Word is unlike us and like the Father. The Son is exemplar and teacher only in a certain sense and surely does not invite us to become his peer. When, according to Athanasius, Christ prays (in John 17:11) "that they may be one as we are," he is offering instruction in creaturely harmony, *not* inviting creatures into the same ontological fellowship he shares with the Father. As an exegete Athanasius is straining, but it is crucial for him to deny any idea of unity or likeness between Father and Son which would grant admittance to those who by the exercise of will and the practice of virtue might also claim to be sons and heirs—or more exactly, "co-heirs with Christ."

The care with which Athanasius proceeds to explain proper and improper understanding of the word "as" (καθώς) indicates his same concern. He warns that when the Lord asks "that they may be one *as* we are," he does not proclaim that we have that identity (ταυτότητα) which belongs only to the Word by nature identical with the Father. "As" indicates an image or example, not absolute sameness. Athanasius theorizes that our situation is like that of Jonah, about whom Matthew wrote, "For *as* Jonah was three days and three nights in the whale's belly . . ." and so forth. Jonah was not the savior, to whom the evangelist likened him, but a parallel. The conclusion is inescapable: ". . . if we too become one as (καθώς) the Son in the Father, we shall not be as the Son, nor equal to him, for he and we are but parallel."[74] The entire argument is most intelligible as an answer to an Arian reading of the texts which linked Christ and creatures to God by conformity of will and which saw in this identity of Christ with others who gained their sonship "from virtue" the way of salvation itself.

Arian enthusiasm for Heb. 1:4 is explicable on the same grounds, even if the elaborate Athanasian refutation tends to obscure the most obvious sense it must have held for them.[75] The verse speaks of the Son at God's right hand, after he had made purification for sins, "having become as much superior (κρείττων) to the angels as the name he has obtained is more excellent than theirs." The passage reverberates with precisely that

adoptionist teaching which the Arians had effectively exploited in Phil.
2:9–11 (also Ps. 44:7 and Acts 2:36). The savior and his name (bestowed and
obtained on the basis of his exceptional works) are exalted above other
names. The verse was favored for its Christology—and for its soteriological
implications. This is indicated by the thrust of an Athanasian counterargu-
ment which focuses upon the word "superior" or "better" (κρείττων). The
Alexandrian bishop labors to convince his readers that the word is not a
comparative term but one which contrasts Son and angels as distinct and
different, that is, as divine nature in contradistinction to originate nature.
This fragile argument (not at all strengthened by the example from Prov.
8:11: "wisdom is better than rubies") is advanced in order to make the point
we have encountered in other forms: ". . . there is no kinship (συγγένεια)
between the Son and the angels."⁷⁶ Athanasius knows (and admits) that
comparison applies to subjects of the same kind, not those that differ. He is
resisting once again Arian teaching. The word "superior" or "better" is part
of the language of comparison, they apparently insisted, pushing the
consequent view that "comparison . . . implies oneness of kind."⁷⁷ We
know that the Arians understood the Son's preeminence over other sons as
one of degree, not one of kind. He had "more than the others," they taught,
explaining their assertion that he was creature, but not as one of the
creatures, "because of his excelling them in glory."⁷⁸ Athanasius' protest in
De decretis 6 opposes the Arian affirmation. Even if, as the Arians say, it was
foreknown by God that this particular creature would prove to be the one
who did not falter in his movement toward the good, acting in accordance
with the Father's will,

> still there will be no difference between him and those who receive the name
> after their actions (μετὰ τὰς πράξεις), as this is the ground upon which he also
> has been declared to be Son (υἱὸς εἶναι μεμαρτύρηται).⁷⁹

Two other facets of the Arian portrait of Christ warrant discussion in
terms of their bearing on soteriology. These are the related tenets that (*a*)
the Son's knowledge of the Father is incomplete and (*b*) his relationship to
the Father admits of growth or "advance."

The *Thalia* contains the inflammatory propositions that the Son sees the
Father "in due measure . . . as is proper" and that the Son is incapable of
knowing the Father as he is in himself. A creature cannot comprehend the
Unbegun, who is ineffable.⁸⁰ The orthodox response, built upon texts such

as Matt. 11:27 ("no one knows the Father except the Son"), explains gospel indications of Christ's ignorance along the lines of Athanasius' indispensable theory of the scripture's "double account" of the savior—these are references not to the eternal Word but to the "economy," to his saving incarnation, in which he can be said to possess the properties of the flesh which he assumed as an instrument.[81] As God's Wisdom, however, it is improper and absurd to propose what Arius does, namely that the Son's apprehension of the Father is limited. The proportionate knowledge of the Father which Arians claim for the Son includes, by its definition, other creatures who, though rational, could not be thought to possess power to know the ineffable Deity, nor even their own essences.[82] And Athanasius points out that if the Son knows the Father, being himself a "work," "then the Father must be known by all according to the proportion of the measures of each, for all are works as he is."[83] This estimate of the way in which Arians believe the Son and sons are related to the Father, however, is significantly off target, as we have attempted to demonstrate in preceding pages. Under the influence of the Stoic ethical category of "those who advance" (προκόπτοντες) in wisdom more through what they "will" and "intend" than what they "perceive" and "know," the Arians envision Christ and his fellow creatures on a pilgrimage of this character. Luke's assertion that "Jesus advanced (προέκοπτεν) in wisdom and in stature, and in favor with God and man" served Arian Christians as a description of discipleship. Προκοπή consisted in the endeavor to do the Father's will, to be thoroughly obedient to the one who made them.[84]

This positive idea of "advance," framed along philosophical lines and justified by Luke 2:52, evoked from Athanasius one of his less stunning disputative efforts. He offers a set of alternative interpretations (because he is reacting, rather than initiating, in this instance), suggesting that Christ grew by taking on greater physical size, or the manifestation of the Godhead "advanced" in the awareness of those who recognized who he was, or (finally) that Luke teaches that Christ's manhood advanced in Wisdom—that is, "he advanced in himself."[85] Athanasius is appalled by what he regards as the inevitable result of the Arian idea of προκοπή:

If he advanced when he became man, it is plain that before he became man, he was imperfect, and the flesh became for him a cause of perfection, instead of he for the flesh.[86]

62

The orthodox Christology of descent demanded a Logos in need of nothing, a plenary Wisdom beyond improvement. His utter sufficiency and his eternal perfection distinguished him from heroes like Enoch, Moses, and the apostle, who in each case reached forward, "looking to the step before him."[87] Christ's distinction from other men gave meaning to his merciful condescension into flesh and made him their savior.

Counterposed to this idea of the savior's requisites is the Arian portrait of the creature-redeemer, dependent upon the Father's will for his existence and obedient to the same will in order to obtain his favored status as Son. The Arian soteriology required the savior, that he might be imitable, to be related to the Father on the same terms as other finite beings. This entailed a bond and connection postulated not upon the ability to know and perceive the Father's essence and to enjoy ontic identity, but upon the dynamic (so frequently met in biblical depiction of covenant) of command and obedience, upon the transactions of will which constitute the people—the sons and daughters—of God.

In an important and revealing passage (written prior to Nicaea), the Arians are reported to have made the claim of commonality with the redeemer in direct and unmistakable terms, and to have provided the biblical warrant for their conviction. To his episcopal counterpart in Constantinople, Bishop Alexander writes:

> The accursed ones say, "Certainly we also are able to become sons of God, just like that one [that is, Christ]. For it is written, 'I begot and raised up sons' (Isa. 1:2)."[88]

Alexander proceeds to tell that he called attention to the remainder of the text from Isaiah: ". . . but they rebelled against me." Such rebellion, he comments, is not natural (φυσικόν) to the savior, who is unchangeable. But the Arians respond by saying that God foreknew the savior would not be disobedient, and thus "elected him above all the others." Alexander carefully reports the Arian explanation of why this election is not limited to Christ alone.

> For not as one possessing by nature (φύσει) something compelling selection from the other sons . . . but being also of a changeable nature, he was elected on account of [his] diligence of conduct and discipline (διὰ τρόπων ἐπιμέλειαν καὶ ἄσκησιν), since he did not incline toward what is inferior.[89]

63

At this point Alexander interjects as a hypothesis the point to which the Arians no doubt gave vigorous assent (indeed, their very claim depends upon it): the apostles by a similar effort of behavior and fidelity might possess a sonship no different from Christ's.[90]

The reply which Alexander makes is most provocative in that it illustrates the tendency repeatedly encountered in orthodox argumentation to deflect or divert Arian soteriological assertions in the direction of concerns which might more precisely be called theological or cosmological in character. Invoking passages from the Fourth Gospel, Alexander argues that the Son was not created out of the nonexistent, that there never was when he was not. Alexander apparently sees, or wishes his reader to see, the foregoing Arian assertion in these terms. The Word was not a son as others are sons and daughters of God, and did not come into being *ex nihilo,* nor was there a beginning of his generation. Arian remarks which have a single and transparent thrust—the affirmation of the sonship which they can attain *just as that one* (ὥσπερ κἀκεῖνος)—are challenged on the grounds that the Father and Son are inseparable (ἀχώριστα). As a refutation, it takes for granted and takes as its nonnegotiable starting point the impenetrable boundary of nature (φύσις) which separates the Father and Son from all created beings.

What the Arians assert, however, runs an entirely different course and bespeaks a different concern. This is a quoted assertion, not a deduction or an orthodox *reductio ad absurdum,* and it dominates a letter written well before Nicaea. It is the sonship to be held by believers which is being proclaimed, and in this proclamation there is little ambiguity. What is predicated of the redeemer must be predicated of the redeemed.

It is because of problems raised about the attributes of the Son that Alexander complains (like Athanasius after him) of Arian use of a truncated version of Isa. 1:2.[91] He who is from the essence of the Father, hence immutable and unalterable, cannot be grouped with rebels. But the Arian response is thoroughly consistent with the principles which can be seen to inform their Christology and its correlative soteriology: *just as* Christ (being changeable and free to choose evil as Satan had) persevered in the good by the exercise of his will and was chosen Son, so also, Arian Christians professed, "we are able to become sons."[92]

A positive conviction about the nature of salvation prompts Arian Christians to lay claim to full status as sons of God. Equal to the Son, they are the ones whom the Superior is able to beget, for God's advance of the Son to himself by adoption contains in itself the promise of the adoption of others. As creatures changeable and in that mutability improvable, they can share in the testing and the reward known initially to the firstborn Son, who "was faithful to the one who made him." According to the Arian thinker Asterius, many can say with Jesus, "I am in the Father and the Father in me." The conclusion is properly drawn by his opponent: "As a consequence he is no longer one Son of God and Word and Wisdom, but, as others, is only one out of many."[93] Athanasius pushes the viewpoint of the Arians toward caricature when he hints at military formation, but he does not mistake their basic contention: when they teach, he says, an " 'offspring, but not as one of the offspring,' they bring many sons into line and one of these they determine to be Lord, so that according to them he is . . . one of many brothers."[94] The Son's identity with the creature is critical for the Arian scheme of salvation no less than the orthodox soteriology depends upon the possession of the paternal essence by the Word *alone*. So it becomes clearer what cardinal matters of the faith were at stake in the years preceding and following the council at Nicaea. The character of the savior, the savior's relation to God and to creatures, the process and means by which salvation comes to believers, and (surely implicit in all these) anthropology, the estimate of the limitations and capacities which belong to the human creature—these were the issues which so sharply divided orthodox and Arian Christians in the opening decades of the controversy.

The persistent accusations of the Alexandrian episcopate are best ignored: Arians neither organized a conspiracy against the divinity of the Christian savior nor did they work to diminish his centrality in the consciousness and action of people within the church. Far from it. Elected and adopted as Son, this creature who advanced by moral excellence to God exemplified that walking "in holiness and righteousness" which brings blessing upon all children of God who would do likewise. In this sense, and with this idea of salvation intended, the Arians preached their Christ and in that very preaching summoned believers to hope for and to strive for equality with him.

It remains to be asked what was the range and extent of this equality which Arians celebrated between Christ and Christians. If all that is said of the redeemer could be said also of the redeemed, Arians were in a position to speak of their own sonship in very daring language indeed. In the *Thalia* and in a letter to his ally Eusebius, Arius calls the Son "strong God" and "full God." Other adopted sons, on Arian principles, were entitled (at least potentially) to the same appellations, "just as that one." Athanasius spoke with some accuracy and certainly with full seriousness when he warned that the Arians sought "to ascend to heaven and be like the Most High."[95] Equality with the one chosen Son "superior to the angels" was a legitimate hope, given the axiomatic commonality of Christ and other sons of God. The literature of the controversy contains indications that the Arian spokesmen produced their own version of a doctrine of the deification of believers—one "high" enough to compete with and threaten the Athanasian theory that the incarnation effected the reversal of human corruptibility and enabled persons to become divine. The idea of a common sonship of Christ and creatures stands behind Arius' declaration in the *Thalia* that Christ is not true (ἀληθινός) God, that is, God himself, but possesses the name "God," like others, by participation.[96] In all probability the Arians quoted Ps. 82:6 in support of their right to the title of θεοί: "I said, 'You are gods, sons of the Most High, all of you.'" Athanasius can be supposed to be answering Arian interpretation of this text when he distinguishes the Son as "true God, existing one-in-essence (ὁμοούσιος) with the Father," from other beings to whom he spoke the words of the psalm, those who receive his grace by the agency of the Son and Spirit.[97]

As articulated by Athanasius, the orthodox concept of deification or perfection is rooted in the assumption of bodily substance by divinity. It is maintained that unless the eternal Word had borne the body, no perfection would have occurred, and all would remain trapped in corruptibility. The Father's work of creation and salvation being completed by the Word, however, "men, redeemed from sin, no longer remain dead, being deified (θεοποιηθέντες)."[98] The conjunction of divine and creaturely substances in the incarnate one, according to this view, results in the renewal and transformation of the weaker, perishable nature of creatures by the stronger, imperishable nature of Godhead.[99]

Although the contours of the Arian idea of deification cannot be traced with comparable fullness, we can be certain that a markedly different kind of transaction was visualized. If believers and saints were to become Gods just as Christ, the dynamic of this process would have been conceived along lines congruent with the Arian doctrine of the "practice of moral advancement" (προκοπῆς ἄσκησις). Arius and his followers thought of ethical growth, the completion of a discipleship lived out in terms of willing and obeying. Such a pilgrimage involved imitation of the redeemer's movement from ethical changeability to that unwavering and glory-meriting fidelity which is reflected in the Arian sequential designation of the Christ as both τρεπτός and ἄτρεπτος. Athanasius protests that the reference in Heb. 3:2 to Jesus' faithfulness "implies no parallel to others." [100] Arian Christians surely thought otherwise. Emulation of the savior was compelled by the preceding portion of the verse, which enjoins, "Therefore, holy brothers, partakers (μέτοχοι) of the heavenly calling, consider the apostle and high priest of our profession, who is faithful . . . ."

Indeed, to the ears of those who found Arius' interpretation of the Christian gospel persuasive, the epistle's earlier references to the common origin of the sanctifier and the sanctified, and to the savior's work "in bringing many sons to glory," conveyed a single meaning and message. Like the faithful one, Christians on the way to perfection were challenged to remain good by choices freely made and to look toward the Father's bestowal of glory "attained from virtue." [101] Possessing the name "God" μετοχῇ, the believer's participation, like that of Christ, consisted in doing what the Father wills, in being "in all respects concordant with him . . . [and speaking] a word consistent and united with the Father's teaching." [102] And finally, if Christ the advancing one is the model for the fulfillment of this moral progress, believers, in becoming Gods like him, become "unalterable and unchangeable, perfect creature[s] of God." [103] Presumably in the Arian scheme of salvation, which is controlled by voluntarist rather than substantialist thinking, it is not inconsistent to speak of creatures as Gods. They participate in God's will, and thus warrant the name, though they are not (as Christ is not) "true God." Perfection is understood in terms of the community of will and covenantal obedience, not in terms of the renovation and *metastasis* of creaturely essence.

The central point in the Arian system is that Christ gains and holds his sonship in the same way as other creatures—thus it is asserted that what is predicated of the redeemer can and must be predicated of the redeemed. In claiming for creatures equality with the Son, even to the point of possessing the glory attaching to the title "God," the Arian Christians revealed just how audacious their soteriological ideas were. Though this way of thinking about deification bears the particular stamp of their Christology, Arius and his company were, it seems, in thorough accord with that tendency in early

Christianity to identify the believers as θεοί, a motif fortified by themes from the Psalms and the Fourth Gospel, and given succinct expression by Irenaeus:

> There is none other called God by the scriptures except the Father of all, and the Son, and those who possess the adoption.[104]

Arians scandalized their opponents not only by what they took from the Son of God but by what they assumed for themselves as his companions in testing and triumph.

This bold insistence upon the things "common to us and to the Son," which nettled the champions of orthodoxy from the outset of the dispute, manifests the deepest interests of the followers of Arius. Mention was made earlier of their willingness at Nicaea to have such terms as "eternal," "in him," and "like" applied to the Son. The same could be said of believers, as the Arians proceeded to demonstrate by quotation of scripture. Here it is important to note that when, on that occasion, the orthodox put forward the word "unchangeable" (ἄτρεπτος) as a term which could not describe creatures but only the Son, the Arians present at the synod assented to this term also, confident that it did not damage their case. In defense of the applicability of "unchangeable" to themselves, they paraphrased Paul's utterance in the eighth chapter of Romans. "Nothing will separate *us* from the love of Christ," they declared.[105] By using this text in this way, the Arians made clear that for them unchangeability had to do with constancy of affection, with persistence in willing, with steadfast faith. To be ἄτρεπτος, they held, was not to possess a natural property reserved to Godhead alone but to intend and to do those things which accord with the Father's good purpose. Inseparability from the love of God was that which the chosen one and other adopted sons could be said to share in their perfected state.

Bound in a secure identity and union as originate beings, the redeemer and the redeemed hold in common the limitations, aspirations, abilities, and accomplishments proper to those beings attempting to do the will of the God who framed and sustains all creation. The positive and constructive force of the celebrated Arian watchwords ("there was when he was not," "creature," "work," "changeable") was actually expressed by their full soteriological implications, as epitomized and made explicit in phrases like "even as we," "like us," "as all others." Sounding like a refrain through the preserved Arian teachings are these reminders that statements about the savior include the saved. He had a beginning of his existence, as others. He is called "power" as others, and knows the Father as we also do. He is changeable and wills the good as we can. He carries the title "God" by participation of grace, like others. So run the assertions of the *Thalia,* designed to expound Christian doctrine and experience from this soteriological perspective.[106] And this perspective is what scandalized and outraged Alexander, Athanasius, and their allies—legitimizing their charge that Arians presumed to make themselves equals of the Son of God. Against every Arian argument and piece of exegesis Athanasius thrust an interpretation meant to sever the connection between the eternal, coessential Word of God and creaturely nature. The burden of his polemic and biblical exposition serves this end. He declares: one can find "parallels" but no sameness between Christ and other men; scripture contains a double account of the Son which permits attribution of human qualities to him without compromising his full deity and without making him like the rest; the Word is natural Son of the Father, having no part in that adoption which others gain from virtue. The entire effort attests to the vigor with which Arian thinkers chased their soteriological objectives, for in declaring that they too were able to become sons of God, they served notice that every christological assertion contained the promise which vivified and gave hope to Christ's coheirs. Viewed from this perspective, the Arian desire to say at every turn "we also, just as he" points to their investment in the biblical texts advanced in debate. In imitation of the "one who in every respect has been tested as we are, yet without sinning," the Arian believer perceived his own rewards in the exaltation which Christ received on account of his obedience unto death (Phil. 2:5–11), in the anointing won through love of righteousness (Ps. 44:7), in the more excellent name which he obtained (Heb. 1:4; Phil. 2:9), in the greater glory given him for his fidelity (Heb. 3:1–2), in his advance in wisdom and in God's favor (Luke 2:52), and in the oneness which exists between the Father and Son (John 10:30; 17:11, 21). As these passages in scripture describe Christ's election as Son of God, so do they proclaim the sonship of believers in the same mode—through obedience, through willing God's will. That is the soteriological basis of the religion of Arian Christians, daring enough to appeal and to scandalize.

Believing the Arian picture of salvation blasphemous, orthodox representatives introduced and took battle positions behind the word ὁμοούσιος, judging that this idea of identity of essence could alone differentiate the Son's divine likeness and unchangeability from that imitation (μίμησις) which the faithful appropriate "through virtue from keeping commandments." [107] Believers' identification of themselves with the pioneer and perfecter of their faith, as proclaimed by Arianism, Athanasius hoped to combat with a sharp line of demarcation:

> But if he [Christ] wishes us to call his very own Father "our Father," it is not necessary, on account of this, to equate ourselves (συνεκτείνειν) with the Son according to nature.[108]

The entire campaign of the Arians is waged, however, in order to win just this. Christ's limitations, they declared, are exactly ours (willing, choosing, striving, suffering); and likewise Christ's benefits and glories are exactly ours. The Arians proclaim no demotion of the Son but a promotion of believers to full and equal status as sons—that is, υἱοί, understood to mean θεοί. All the curious Arian exegesis concerning Powers and Words and Wisdoms is designed to underscore this central soteriological claim. Because of this claim's importance to early Arian spokesmen, soteriology never recedes very far into the background, whether attention is being addressed to Christology (as we saw in the previous chapter) or to cosmology, our next concern.

NOTES

1. Athanasius *De Syn*. 15.3 (Opitz², p. 242, line 15).
2. Eusebius of Nicomedia *Ep. ad Paulin*. 2 (Opitz³, Urk. 8.2, p. 15, lines 8–9).
3. Ibid. 4. (Opitz³, Urk. 8.4, lines 8–11). The translation of this passage in the *NPNF*, vol. 3, p. 42 (Theodoret, et al.), is, at best, misleading.
4. Arius *Ep. ad Alex*. (Opitz³, Urk. 6.5).
5. Alexander *Ep. ad Alex*. (Opitz³, Urk. 14.4, 37). In his encyclical (Opitz³, Urk. 4b), Alexander counters the Arian propositions with a series of biblical texts which already indicate an exegetical exchange. The Athanasian homily on Luke 10:22//Matt. 11:27 preserves the flavor of debate over a particular text—this one brought forth, from all appearances, by the Arians. See chap. 1, p. 6 ff.
6. Arius *Ep. ad Alex*. (Opitz³, Urk. 6.2, line 3) and Athanasius *Or. c. Ar*. 1.5 (Bright, p. 5).
7. G. C. Stead, "Rhetorical Method in Athanasius," *VC* 30 (1977): 121–37, has shown the extent to which the strategies of the rhetorician are employed by Athanasius in his apologetic and polemic writings, finding parallels to Aristotle's twenty-eight topics in *Rhetoric* 2.23. Particularly provocative are the questions Stead raises about the cogency and validity of many of the arguments used in the *Orations against the Arians*.

8. Alexander *Ep. ad Alex.* (Opitz³, Urk. 14.41, 44, lines 7–9, 20–22).

9. Alexander *Ep. Encycl.* 5 (Opitz³, Urk. 4b.16).

10. Athanasius *De sent. Dionys.* 3 and *De Decr.* 1.5. The proper question, according to Athanasius, would have been the reverse: Why does God become man?

11. Athanasius *Fest. Ep.* 10.9 (*NPNF,* vol. 4, p. 531).

12. Stead, "Rhetorical Method," 131–32: "[It] has not been sufficiently noticed . . . that there is a whole series of stock charges, some of them reaching back into pre-Christian antiquity, which are turned against theologians of the most widely varying persuasions as the ingenuity of the orator can suggest. In these cases what is important and sometimes original is the connecting link of argumentation; it is extremely hazardous simply to accept the stock charge. Yet this is what has often been done by admirers of Athanasius in his treatment of the Arians."

13. Alexander *Ep. ad Alex.* (Opitz³, Urk. 14.37); and Athanasius *Fest. Ep.* 10.9.

14. Stead, "Rhetorical Method." See n. 12 *supra.*

15. Athanasius *Fest. Ep.* 10.9 and *Or. c. Ar.* 1.3.

16. Athanasius *Or. c. Ar.* 1.22, *NPNF* translation (Bright, p. 24).

17. Alexander *Ep. ad Alex.* (Opitz³, Urk. 14.4, p. 20, lines 7–8).

18. Athanasius *Or. c. Ar.* 1.4 (Bright, p. 5).

19. Alexander *Ep. Encycl.* 12 (Opitz³, Urk. 4b, p. 9, line 1). The orthodox complaint that Arians pull the Christ from the height of deity by "ranking" and "numbering" him among the creatures and by making him their equal is frequently met—e.g., Alexander *Ep. ad Alex.* (Opitz³, Urk. 14.4, p. 20, lines 7–8, and 14.11, p. 21, lines 10–11); and Athanasius *Or. c. Ar.* 1.18, 22, 23; 2.62–63 (Bright, pp. 9, 23–24, 132–33).

20. Athanasius *Or. c. Ar.* 1.19 (Bright, p. 21). *Vide* Stead, "Rhetorical Method," p. 127, on "retorting a dilemma."

21. Athanasius *Or. c. Ar.* 2.43, *NPNF* translation (Bright, p. 111).

22. Athanasius *Or. c. Ar.* 3.38 (Bright, p. 193). *Vide* also *Or. c. Ar.* 3.12–13.

23. Athanasius *Or. c. Ar.* 1.18 (Bright, p. 19).

24. Athanasius *Or. c. Ar.* 3.17 (Bright, pp. 171–72).

25. Athanasius *Or. c. Ar.* 1.39, *NPNF* translation (Bright, p. 179). *Vide* also *Or. c. Ar.* 3.18.

26. Athanasius *Or. c. Ar.* 3.25 (Bright, p. 180).

27. Athanasius *Or. c. Ar.* 2.41–42; 3.16 (Bright, pp. 110–12, 169–70). For Arius' own remarks, see Athanasius *De Syn.* 15 (Opitz², p. 243, lines 3–4, 13) and Arius *Ep. ad Eus.* (Opitz³, Urk. 1.4, line 2). Hence Athanasius' vexation in *Or. c. Ar.* 1.10 (Bright, p. 10): ". . . who is there among men, either Greek or Barbarian, who dares to rank among creatures one whom he meanwhile confesses to be God . . . ?"

28. Alexander *Ep. ad Alex.* (Opitz³, Urk. 14.47, p. 27, lines 13–15).

29. Athanasius *Or. c. Ar.* 3.67 (Bright, p. 220): πάντα γάρ ἐστιν ὁ Υἱὸς τοῦ Πατρός.

30. Alexander *Ep. ad Alex.* (Opitz³, Urk. 14.28, 33, p. 24, lines 6–8 and lines 30–31).

31. Alexander *Ep. ad Alex.* (Opitz³, Urk. 14.13–14, p. 21, lines 19–23) and Athanasius *Or. c. Ar.* 2.47, 70, 74, 77; 3.23, 38 (Bright, pp. 117, 140, 145, 147, 177–78, 192-193).

32. Athanasius *De Syn.* 15 (Opitz², p. 243, lines 11 and 19).

33. Athanasius *De Decr.* 6 (Opitz², pp. 5–6) and *Or. c. Ar.* 1.37 (Bright, pp. 38–39).

34. Athanasius *De Decr.* 6 (Opitz², p. 6, lines 12–15).

35. Athanasius *De Decr.* 22 (Opitz², p. 19, line 5) and *Or. c. Ar.* 1.37 (Bright, p. 38).

36. Athanasius *Or. c. Ar.* 2.10 (Bright, pp. 78–79).

37. Alexander *Ep. ad Alex.* (Opitz³, Urk. 14.13, p. 21, lines 20–21).

38. Athanasius *Or. c. Ar.* 1.39 (Bright, p. 40). *Vide* chap. 1, n. 119.

39. Athanasius *Or. c. Ar.* 1.47 (Bright, p. 49).

40. Ibid.

41. Alexander *Ep. ad Alex.* (Opitz³, Urk. 14.13–14, p. 21, lines 19–24). See also the reference in Athanasius *De Decr.* 6 to the similarity of Christ's sonship (on the Arian definition) to that of Adam, Enoch, Paul, and the penitent thief.

42. *Vide* Alexander *Ep. ad Alex.* (Opitz³, Urk. 14.11, p. 21, lines 15ff.), and treatment *supra,* pp. 63 ff.

43. Athanasius *Or. c. Ar.* 3.10 (Bright, p. 164). The passage continues, "and many even now keep the Savior's command, being merciful 'as their Father which is in heaven.' "

44. Ibid.

45. On the practice and political importance of adoption in Greco-Roman society, *vide* A. Wentzel, "Studien über die Adoption in Griechenland," *Hermes* (1930): 167–76; M. H. Prévost, *Les adoptions politiques à Rome sous la république et le principat* (Paris: Recueil Sirey, 1949); and the remarks in F. Lot, *The End of the Ancient World and the Beginnings of the Middle Ages* (New York: Harper & Row, Publishers, 1961), p. 14; and H. Mattingly, *Roman Imperial Civilization* (New York: W. W. Norton & Co., 1971).

46. Athanasius *Or. c. Ar.* 3.30 (Bright, p. 185).

47. Alexander *Ep. ad Alex.* (Opitz³, Urk. 14.29, p. 24, lines 10–11). In the succeeding section of the epistle, Alexander interprets Rom. 8:14ff. in this way: "Wherefore our Lord, being Son of the Father by nature (φύσει), is worshiped by all; but those who have put off the spirit of bondage through brave deeds and through moral advance, being benefited by the natural Son (τοῦ φύσει υἱοῦ), themselves become sons by adoption (θέσει)."

48. Athanasius argues that the reverse is true for the Son, who was "begotten" first from his Father by nature, then "created" when he assumed flesh: *Or. c. Ar.* 2.61 (Bright, pp. 131–32).

49. Athanasius *Or. c. Ar.* 2.58–59 (Bright, pp. 127–30). The argument leads, predictably, to the celebrated Athanasian soteriological affirmation: " 'The Word became flesh' in order that he might make man capable of divinity."

72

50. *Vide* Athanasius *Or. c. Ar.* 2.61 (Bright, p. 131): ". . . if we become sons by adoption and by grace . . ."

51. Athanasius *Or. c. Ar.* 3.2–3 (Bright, pp. 156–57). *Vide* Asterius' use of this text in chap. 1, pp. 27ff., and in chap. 3, pp. 116–17.

52. Athanasius writes in *Or. c. Ar.* 3.11 (Bright, 164–65): "One and the same grace is from the Father in the Son, as the light of the sun and of the radiance is one, and the sun's illumination is effected through the radiance" (*NPNF* translation). Cf. chap. 1, p. 29.

53. Athanasius *De Decr.* 16 (Opitz², p. 13, lines 29–31). The punctuation given by Opitz is to be preferred to that assumed in the *NPNF* translation; the question belongs to Athanasius, and is not a continuation of the Arian declaration.

54. Athanasius reports the teaching of Arius, in *Or. c. Ar.* 1.5 (Bright, p. 5): ". . . τὸν Υἱὸν ὠνομάσθαι [πάλιν] κατὰ χάριν Λόγον καὶ Υἱὸν αὐτόν," and in *De Syn.* 15 (Opitz², p. 242, line 15): "καὶ ἤνεγκεν εἰς υἱὸν ἑαυτῷ τόνδε τεκνοποιήσας." In *De Decr.* 9 (Opitz², p. 8, lines 26–29), Athanasius summarizes: ". . . in your judgment he will differ not at all, in terms of nature, from others, so long as he too was not, and came to exist, and the grace of the name was united to him in his creation on account of virtue."

55. Athanasius *De Sent. Dionys.* 23 (Opitz², p. 62, line 29, through p. 63, line 2). *Vide* also Alexander *Ep. Encycl.* (Opitz³, Urk. 4b, p. 8, lines 3–4).

56. See the treatment of this doctrine in chap. 3.

57. Athanasius *De Decr.* 16–17 (Opitz², pp. 13–15).

58. Athanasius *De Syn.* 15 (Opitz², p. 243, lines 9–10).

59. Athanasius *De Syn.* 15 (Opitz², p. 242, lines 24–26) and *Or. c. Ar.* 1.5 (Bright, p. 5).

60. Athanasius *Or. c. Ar.* 1.5 (Bright, p. 6).

61. Alexander *Ep. ad Alex.* (Opitz³, Urk. 14.13–14, p. 21, line 19, through p. 22, line 3).

62. Athanasius *Or. c. Ar.* 2.6 (Bright, p. 74).

63. Athanasius *Or. c. Ar.* 2.9 (Bright, p. 77). A passage which falls later in the same work (3.1) shows how Athanasius chooses to speak of participation: "[Not] as God, by coming into the saints, strengthens them, is he thus also in the Son. For he is himself the Father's Power and Wisdom, and by partaking of him things originate are sanctified in the Spirit; however the Son himself is not Son by participation (μετουσίᾳ), but is the Father's own offspring" (*NPNF* translation, altered).

64. Athanasius *Or. c. Ar.* 3.24 (Bright, p. 178). He adds: "What then is our likeness and equality to the Son? Rather, are not the Arians confuted on every side? And especially by John, that the Son is in the Father one way, and we become in him in another, and that neither we shall ever be as he, nor is the Word as we, . . ." (*NPNF* translation).

65. Athanasius *Or. c. Ar.* 1.9 and 1.5 (Bright, p. 9 and p. 5). The Arians, we know, frequently quoted Heb. 3:1, with its address to the "holy brothers, partakers

(μέτοχοι) of the heavenly calling" (*vide Or. c. Ar.* 1.53). Here, as elsewhere, they seem to have been influenced by the ideas and language of the epistle.

66. Athanasius *Ad Afros* 7 (Migne PG, vol. 26, 1041B; *NPNF* translation).

67. Alexander *Ep. ad Alex.* (Opitz[3], Urk. 14.34, p. 25, lines 3–7). *Vide* also Athanasius *Ad Afros* 7: "But that originate things are changeable, no one can deny, seeing that angels transgressed, Adam disobeyed, and all stand in need of the grace of the Word. But a mutable thing cannot be like God who is truly unchangeable, any more than what is created can be like its creator. This is why, with regard to us, the holy man said, 'Lord, who shall be likened unto thee?' and 'who among the gods is like unto thee, Lord?' " (*NPNF* translation, altered).

68. Alexander *Ep. ad Alex.* (Opitz[3], Urk. 14.34, p. 25, lines 2–3) and Athanasius *Or. c. Ar.* 3.40 (Bright, p. 195).

69. Alexander *Ep. ad Alex.* (Opitz[3], Urk. 14.34, p. 25, lines 3–5) and Athanasius *Or. c. Ar.* 3.29ff. and 3.20 (Bright, pp. 184ff. and pp. 174–175).

70. Athanasius *Or. c. Ar.* 1.37 and 1.5 (Bright, pp. 38 and 5).

71. Athanasius *Or. c. Ar.* 3.26 (Bright, pp. 180–81). *Vide* the treatise, probably Athanasian, entitled *In Illud 'Omnia.'*

72. Athanasius *Or. c. Ar.* 3.35 (Bright, p. 190).

73. Athanasius *Or. c. Ar.* 3.10ff. (especially 3.17, 19). *Vide* Bright, pp. 163ff.

74. Athanasius *Or. c. Ar.* 3.23 (Bright, p. 177), *NPNF* translation.

75. Athanasius' treatment in *Or. c. Ar.* 1.53–63 closes upon the term γενόμενος, arguing against the view that it denotes the originate character of the Son. In this, his line of reasoning is parallel to (perhaps influenced by) his view of the crux in Prov. 8:22—"κύριος ἔκτισέ με. . . ."

76. Athanasius *Or. c. Ar.* 1.55 (Bright, p. 58).

77. Athanasius *Or. c. Ar.* 1.56 (Bright, pp. 58–59).

78. Athanasius *De Decr.* 9. (Opitz[2], p. 8, line 34, through p. 9, line 1) and *Or. c. Ar.* 2.23 (Bright, p. 91).

79. Athanasius *De Decr.* 6 (Opitz[2], p. 6, lines 15–18). *Or. c. Ar.* 1.37–38 (Bright, pp. 38–40) shows Athanasius tackling the same problem, with the definition of "son," the Philippian text, and the concept of "advance" all involved in his argumentation. If the savior is not according to his essence true Son and true God but is called Son because of the grace given him, he did not have the name from the first—". . . it was the prize of works done" and "advance" (προκοπῆς), when he became "obedient unto death." Athanasius protests, as his soteriology requires, that this errant view of the Son disallows the flesh's promotion—the flesh (in effect, the career of Jesus) actually promotes the Word. The idea moves finally in the direction of the *Grundprinzip* of orthodoxy: ". . . he himself only is true Son and . . . very God from very God, not receiving these prerogatives as a reward for his virtue, nor being another beside them, but being all these by nature and according to essence . . . so that one cannot doubt that after the resemblance of the unalterable Father, the Word also is unalterable" (*Or. c. Ar.* 1.39, *NPNF* translation, altered). We note once more the orthodox drive toward referring statements about the Son to the

Father's attributes, a contributing factor in the mistaken view that the battle is joined over other than soteriological issues. The passage in question reveals plainly the extent to which Athanasius operates as advocate of a soteriology and engages the Arians as promoters of a different scheme of salvation.

80. Athanasius *De Syn.* 15 (Opitz[2], p. 242, lines 21–23), *Or. c. Ar.* 1.6 (Bright, p. 6), and *Ad episc. Aegypti* 12 (Migne PG 25, 565B–C).

81. Athanasius *Or. c. Ar.* 3.29–31 (Bright, pp. 184–86). On treatment of Matt. 11:27 in the anti-Arian discourses, see *Or. c. Ar.* 2.22; 3.26–41, 44.

82. It is striking that the Arian argument against knowledge of οὐσία becomes a strategy of the orthodox theologians (notably the Cappadocian Fathers) when the doctrines of Aëtius and Eunomius must be answered in the latter half of the fourth century.

83. Athanasius *Or. c. Ar.* 2.22 (Bright, pp. 90–91).

84. Luke 2:52. *Vide* chap. 1, pp. 18ff., *supra,* and *Or. c. Ar.* 3.10 (Bright, pp. 163–64).

85. Athanasius *Or. c. Ar.* 3.51–52 (Bright, pp. 203–6).

86. Ibid.

87. Ibid.

88. Alexander *Ep. ad Alex.* (Opitz[3], Urk. 14.11, p. 21, lines 15–16).

89. Alexander *Ep. ad Alex.* (Opitz[3], Urk. 14.13, p. 21, lines 19–22).

90. Alexander *Ep. ad Alex.* (Opitz[3], Urk. 14.14, p. 21, lines 22–23). Here, as noted above (p. 53), the Arians quoted in support of their view Ps. 44:7 (LXX).

91. A number of references to Isa. 1:2 indicate that it was a contested text during the controversy. Cf. Athanasius *De Decr.* 10 and *Or. c. Ar.* 1.37, in which the rest of the verse is quoted, with the comment, "And of course, since they were not sons by nature, therefore, when they changed, the Spirit was removed from them and they were disinherited." *Vide* also Eusebius of Nicomedia *Ep. ad Paulin.* (Opitz[3], Urk. 8.7, p. 17, lines 1–2).

92. Alexander *Ep. ad Alex.* (Opitz[3], Urk. 14.11, p. 21).

93. Athanasius *Or. c. Ar.* 3.2 (Bright, p. 156), *NPNF* translation.

94. Athanasius *Or. c. Ar.* 2.19 (Bright, p. 88).

95. Isa. 14:13. Athanasius *Or. c. Ar.* 3.17 (Bright, p. 172).

96. Athanasius *Or. c. Ar.* 1.6, 1.9 (Bright, pp. 6 and 9) and *Ad episc. Aegypti* 12 (Migne PG 25, 564C).

97. Athanasius *Or. c. Ar.* 1.9 (Bright, p. 9). Interestingly, it is only here in the three lengthy orations that Athanasius employs the controversial ὁμοούσιος.

98. Athanasius *Or. c. Ar.* 3.23 (Bright, p. 178).

99. *Vide* Athanasius *Or. c. Ar.* 2.14, 47, 66–70, 74; 3.22–23, 30–33, 38. And *De Inc.* 8, 42–45, 54.

100. Athanasius *Or. c. Ar.* 2.6 (Bright, p. 74).

101. Athanasius *Or. c. Ar.* 1.5 (Bright, p. 6) and *Ad episc. Aegypti* 12 (Migne PG 25, 564C). *Vide* chap. 5 *infra,* pp. 166ff.

102. Athanasius *Or. c. Ar.* 3.10 (Bright, p. 163).

103. Arius *Ep. ad Alex.* (Opitz³, Urk. 6.2, p. 12, line 9): "ἄτρεπτον καὶ ἀναλλοίωτον, κτίσμα τοῦ θεοῦ τέλειον."

104. Irenaeus *Adv. Haer.* 4, Preface. See Ps. 82:6 and John 10:34ff., and Hans von Campenhausen, *The Formation of the Christian Bible* (Philadelphia: Fortress Press, 1972), p. 56 and n. 199.

105. Athanasius *De Decr.* 20 (Opitz², p. 16, line 37).

106. Athanasius *Or. c. Ar.* 1.5–6 (Bright, pp. 5–6).

107. Athanasius *De Decr.* 20 (Opitz², p. 17, line 11).

108. Athanasius *De Decr.* 31 (Opitz², p. 27, lines 27–28).

3

The Obedient Logos

Virtually all modern treatments of Arianism have a common point of departure.[1] Attention falls upon Arian cosmology. Starting from the "top," consideration is given to the exclusive attributes of God the Unbegun, the origination of the Son, and the relationship of that creaturely Son to God and to the rest of the created order. This unanimity is due to the long-operative belief that Arius' own starting point was the protection of the unity of God and his defense against certain tendencies resident in Christologies which spoke of the preexistent Logos of God.

Such a consensus explains why, in their discussions of Arianism and the problems at stake at Nicaea, neither modern surveys of Christian doctrine nor studies in church or late Roman history suggest to readers that the issues and causes of "the Trinitarian controversy" remain in any serious doubt or uncertainty.[2] If there has been broad scholarly agreement about the centrality of the doctrine of God and cosmological concerns in Arian circles, however, sharp disagreements have surfaced as soon as attempts are made to place Arius and his companions in particular philosophical and ecclesiastical traditions. The question of the origins of Arian Christianity was not long ago declared to be "wide open."[3] Similarly, efforts to assemble the known components of Arian teaching into anything approaching a system have proved unsatisfying, recently prompting a specialist in the field to begin an article with the query, "How much do we really know about the theology of Arius?"[4] Though the view has been nearly universally held that the Arians were primarily cosmologians of a philosophical bent, it remains true that no single scholarly account of Arian Christianity—its structure of thought and its sources—has been able to carry the day against competing theories. It can be argued (as some have) that the sources for Arius' thought are too sparse and fragmentary and that reports of his doctrine are unreliable, subject as they are to the polemicists' strategies which frustrate labors of historical reconstruction. Real as those difficulties may be, however, patristic studies have reached more settled conclusions concerning other doctrinal disputes for which fewer primary data survive, and the era is long past when scholars gave unquestioning credence to orthodox descriptions of heretical teachings. And although we possess only those portions of the *Thalia* which Athanasius preserves, either in quotation or paraphrase, the writings of Arius, Eusebius of Nicomedia, and the fragments of Asterius' teaching, when placed alongside the attentive and carefully designed rebuttals of Alexander and Athanasius, comprise a substantial body of material which might have been expected to yield more conclusive results in interpretation.[5]

Our rationale in placing this chapter *after* considerations of Christology and soteriology needs again to be made explicit. In the preceding pages we pointed to the importance of soteriological interests in early Arianism. It is not the Arian plan to demote Christ in order to clear space and secure preeminence for the high God; rather, he is the one upon whom sonship is conferred, his election being signal of the salvation accessible to other creatures. We have no intention of ignoring those carefully framed Arian propositions which can be termed "cosmological," nor do we seek to deny their significance. But the order of our investigation and the place in which cosmology is discussed reflects a fundamental conclusion to which reassessment of the sources has led us: few of the many important Arian cosmological terms and formulas (for example, "God," "Father," "Son," "Word," "Essence," "from the nonexistent," "creature," "work," "by his will and pleasure") are capable of being rightly understood until one has gained a thorough command of this party's soteriological scheme, which pivots on the idea of sonship by adoption/election, both for the Christ and for believers.

The point bears restating. After sketching the portrait of the Arian Christ and the sonship which he models for believers, we are in a position to see the import and the purposes of the cosmological debate. That is, discussion about the things which God *alone* is (μόνον ἀγέννητον, μόνον ἀΐδιον, and so forth), about the Son as "perfect creature," about the status of a "product" and "work," about what a being is by nature and by appointment (φύσει and θέσει), about the question of eternality of the Father and the Son—all these are connected, like spokes to a hub, to the basic question, how is salvation possible? For this was the crux of the battle between orthodox and Arian Christians. When the two views of salvation with their major points of collision have been perceived, the controversy's beginnings no longer have the appearance of an ecclesiastical version of the tussle within the metaphysics of late Platonism, nor of clashing halves of Origen's crumbling theological synthesis, nor even of competing exegetical traditions and methods.[6] Approached as a movement concerned with questions of the "better things that belong to salvation," Arianism is perceived differently and, we think, more comprehensively.[7] Crucial to Arian belief are such matters as the nature and number of God, but only as these issues are linked with the content, shape, and dynamics of salvation. Does the divine drama feature the eternal, consubstantial Son of the Father, whose descent arrests creation from perishability by means of divine power visiting creaturely weakness? Or is the Son a "certain one" among creatures, foreordained and faithful, the servant who brings himself to perfection by discipline and exemplifies the relationship to be had with the Father by "all the rest"? For Arius and Eusebius, no less than for Alexander and Athanasius, there was no significant distance between these questions and the propriety (or impropriety) of claiming that both Father and Son had been in existence "forever." We hope to demonstrate the ways in which Arian insistence that the Son had a beginning, was not "true" Word, and was no "portion" of the paternal essence is of a piece with their commitment to a scheme which calls savior the Christ who is simultaneously a creature and a "strong God."

Another prefatory word is required for this portion of our study. What follows is a *description* of the main and positive lines of argument which define Arian beliefs about God, the Son (or second principle), and creation. As far as possible, attention will be given to the relationship in which Arian tenets stand to each other. Description of the key Arian cosmological and theological assertions cannot, of course, unfold without reference to the ideas of their opponents, but our objective is to bring into sharper relief the dominant features of their thinking and the coherence of Arian propositions on their own terms. For the most part, we shall confine to incidental remarks and notes our observations about the affinity of certain Arian ideas to prevailing or available philosophical and theological traditions, even though it is apparent that Arian leaders attended to their pedigree of right thinkers with zeal equal to that of their foes.[8] A bewildering array of precursors have been postulated for Arian doctrine by modern scholarship: Aristotle, Plato (and Platonists like Atticus and Albinus), Philo, Origen, Lucian, Paul of Samosata, and the exegetes of the "schools" in Alexandria and Antioch.[9] Immunity to the scholarly ailment of finding what one seeks is hard to achieve, but this spate of conflicting theories would seem to dictate the relegation to a secondary and ancillary role the placement of the Arians on the ideological stage of the first Christian centuries. It is our view that the primary task must be an analysis of Arian argumentation which attempts to discern its internal consistency (without too quickly deciding that certain elements are of peripheral or lesser importance than others). Our methodology is controlled by the realization that the immediate *Sitz* of these writings was the strife which erupted in 318; and our examination of the Arian arguments concentrates less on their intellectual lineage than on the purposes for which they were framed.

In the numerous reconstructions of Arian thought, slight notice has been taken of certain themes which are not self-evidently less important than others. Two of these are particularly provocative. Among the opening statements about God which Athanasius quotes from Arius' *Thalia* is the following:

> We call him unbegotten because of (δία) the one by nature begotten;
> We praise this one as without beginning because of (δία) the one having the beginning;
> we worship him as everlasting because of (δία) the one who has come to exist in times.[10]

And in Alexander's encyclical letter composed some five years before Nicaea, the Arians are charged with having said concerning the Son:

> He was made for our sake, in order that God might create us through him, as by an instrument. And he would not have existed, if God had not willed to make us.[11]

We quote these passages because they typify a number of ideas attributed to the Arians which, difficult in themselves, are all the more problematic if the traditional views of Arian intentions are credited. The first, though it sharply delineates differences between the first and second principles (Father and Son), is capable of being read not so much as a statement of contrasts but as a declaration about how God, ineffable in his own nature (as a prior sentence states), can be approached and known. Understood in this way, the repetition of the δία (because of, through) in the sentence indicates a movement in apprehension and worship from the (believer to the) Son to the Father. The idea was by no means new to Christian thought and piety, but it is not what the characterizations of Arius' narrow concern for the doctrine of

God might lead us to expect among his doctrines. What is suggested is the indispensability of the Son for knowledge and reverence of the Father.

The second passage seems at first to make a contrary point about the importance of the Son. The Arians are reported to have argued that the matter of supreme importance to the sovereign Deity was the creation of humankind, for which purpose (and for no other) the Son was made—the Son was created to be a serviceable instrument. As the orthodox writers will restate the proposition, Arians believe the Son came into being for the sake of humankind, not humankind for his. The assertion is not incompatible with what has been considered Arius' compelling motive, the defense of God the absolute; but it does not render direct service to that objective. We venture to ask whether the structure of early Arian teaching can be drawn in a manner sufficiently comprehensive to do justice to these and other themes which heretofore have seemed peripheral or inconsequential to scholars' understanding of this important movement in Christian history.

FATHER AND SON

One of Arius' major objections to the theology voiced by the bishop of Alexandria turned on its uses of such phrases as "always a Father, always a Son." We know this from the earliest correspondence generated by the conflict and from the account of its eruption by the historian Socrates.[12] Arius informs his ally Eusebius that he is driven from the city for his refusal to subscribe to Alexander's view that the Father and Son are together from eternity (ἅμα πατὴρ ἅμα υἱός)—that the Son coexists with God "ingenerately" (ἀγεννήτως) in such a manner that no "idea" or "moment" can be thought to separate the existences of the two.[13] Asserting that their own reading of scripture disallowed this doctrine, Arian spokesmen scored their opponents for teaching two unbegotten first principles (δύο ἀγέννητα), strongly suggesting that they believed Alexander's formulas traceable to emanationist ideas of the Gnostics and the modalist theology of the Sabellians.[14]

The Arian epistles typically cut clear distinctions between propositions which they deem unacceptable and the doctrines which they themselves put forward in the form of positive declarations.[15] The combination of two of these Arian affirmations has long been supposed to comprise the twin planks of a rigidly monotheistic theology. These two tenets, which have dominated

81

the attention of most researchers, are (1) the assertion that God, or the Unbegotten, is *one* (ἕν) and (2) the claim that the Son had a beginning in existence—the idea productive of the slogan thought to epitomize the Arian heresy: "There was when he was not."[16] For Arius these are halves, or mutual implications, of a single idea:

> . . . as monad (μονάς) and beginning (ἀρχή) of all so God is before all. Wherefore he is also before the Son. . . .[17]

According to the traditional view of Arius and his partisans as cosmologians preoccupied with a particular idea of God, the logical sequence of the statement is as follows: the singularity and uniqueness of God as first principle requires that he alone be counted as without beginning and eternal, so that all things, even the Son, are preceded by him. Thus, a doctrine of God is understood to control description of the Son as posterior, secondary to God, and having a beginning (ἀρχή); God's transcendence dictates the Son's subordinate status.

There are compelling reasons for challenging this interpretation of the Arian argument and for asking whether it correctly perceives the purposes which prompted its formulation. Our reexamination begins with the second half of the argument, the assertion that the Son had a beginning in existence. Much attention has been given to Arian efforts to deny that the Son was eternal or eternally begotten (ἀειγεννής)[18] and yet to place his genesis before temporality, or before the rest of creation. The expressions and phrases framed to make the point, which stands over against the orthodox insistence that both Father and Son are ἀεί, are numerous and familiar.

> . . . the Son has subsisted by will and pleasure before times and ages.
>
> And before he was begotten or made or appointed or formed, he was not.
>
> . . . the Son has a beginning, but God is without beginning.
>
> . . . [the Son] did not exist before being begotten . . . being begotten apart from time before all things.
>
> The Unbegun made (ἔθηκε) the Son a beginning (ἀρχήν) of the creatures (τῶν γενητῶν).
>
> . . . the monad was, but the dyad (δυάς) was not before it came to be.
>
> There was when the Son of God was not, and he was begotten later who previously did not exist.

> The Word of God was not forever, but he came to be from the nonexistent (ἐξ οὐκ ὄντων). For God, who is, made (πεποίηκε) him who was not out of the nonexistent.

> The Son was not always; for all things were made from the nonexistent, and all existing creatures and works were made, so also the Word of God himself was made from the nonexistent, and there was when he did not exist, and he was not before he was made, but he also had a beginning of creation.[19]

Taken by themselves, statements of this kind permit the sense which has been attributed to them and can be seen as functioning in support of what has been termed the "limited theological perspective" of the Arian party.[20] This is only possible, however, if the prominent Arian postulate which informs and is inseparable from these passages is either ignored or discounted. This postulate makes clear the fact that for the Arians, paramount importance attaches to the terms "Father" and "Son," not to the term "God." The writings of the Arians themselves and their opponents' reports attest the presence of the assertion in the earliest stages of the controversy. Arius' *Thalia* contains the statement that ". . . when the Son does not exist, the Father is God," and he writes, similarly, to Eusebius that "God precedes in existence the Son."[21] Arius' meaning is unambiguous: prior to the Son's creation, God is God, *not* Father. Thus one must say that God, rather than the Father, precedes the Son in existence. Arians objected to the sempiternity not of God but of God as *Father*. This was clearly recognized by Alexander, whose encyclical epistle preserves the Arian teaching that "God was not always (a) Father, but there was when God was not (a) Father."[22]

In Arian usage, the term "Father" signifies a relationship which God has to the Son, not an attribute which he has in himself. This is attested by the care with which Arius distinguishes between God and Father. God only receives the name Father, he argues, upon the creation of the Son. "Sonship" is, in effect, a determining factor in the concept of divine "fatherhood." This observation, which Athanasius quoted by way of handing down an indictment, represented for Arius and his followers a fundamental and vigorously advocated tenet: "God was not always Father of the Son; but when the Son came into being and was created, then God was called his Father."[23] When the orthodox insisted that if the Son is not eternal we creatures should be called the Son's sons, the Arians retorted, not entirely tongue in cheek, that by the reckoning of their opponents, Christ should be called God's brother, not his Son.[24]

Fatherhood and sonship are neither absolute nor essentialist words in the Arian vocabulary. They pertain to priority of importance, sequence of time, and quality of relationship. The Arian understanding of the terms "Son" and "Father" derive from empirical rather than theoretical notions of sonship. This can be seen in Arius' assertion in the *Thalia* concerning the Son's limited knowledge of the Father, which draws upon the example of human relationship and experience: "What argument allows, then, that he who is begotten from a father knows the one who begot [him] with full comprehension?"[25] Likewise, Athanasius' scorn of the questions which Arians put to the citizenry should not prevent us from thinking that these lines of reasoning were pursued with full seriousness. They ask people on the street, "Did you have a son before you bore him?" and proceed to the answer's implications for doctrine: "Just as you did not, so in the same way, the Son of God was not, before he was begotten."[26] Arian argumentation, proceeding from this empirical way of understanding fatherhood and sonship, moves in a different direction in a literal reading of those passages of scripture which (to the Arians) spoke of the begetting of a second to God. Importantly, in Arian exegesis, "Son" connotes an adoptive relationship to the Father rather than a biological one. We learn from Athanasius that the Arians interpret Christ's sonship by means of passages like Deut. 14:1 ("You are the sons of the Lord your God") and John 1:12 ("But to all who received him, who believed in his name, he gave power to become children of God").[27] As we have noted in the preceding chapters, "Son" is indicative of relationship formed in the conferring of grace which links Son to the Father in a way not radically unlike that which links all believers to God.

There is no sharper contrast to be found between Arian and orthodox thinkers than the manner in which these parties construe language of "begetting." For the Arians, those passages of scripture which speak of the birth of the Son are read along creationist lines, in order to underscore the dependent relationship of the Son to the Father. So Arius denies that the biblical phrases "from him" (Rom. 11:36) and "from the womb" (Ps. 109:3 [LXX]) and "I came forth from the Father and I am come" (John 16:28) support the belief that the Son is "part" of the Father, or "one-in-essence" with him. The Son has received his existence, glories, and life, and "all things have been delivered to him" (Luke 10:22//Matt. 11:27), so that it is fitting to say that God, who rules (ἄρχει) and precedes him, is his origin.[28] (We are told in a brief treatise composed to combat Arian use of this latter

84

text that they employed it in order to stress that the Son "once" did not have the lordship over creation which was thereafter bestowed upon him by his Creator.)²⁹ Reacting in a similar way to essentialist (or "genetic") understandings of the Son as "from" (ἐξ αὐτοῦ) or "out of" (ἀπ' αὐτοῦ) the Father, Eusebius of Nicomedia asserts that the designation of the Son as "created" and "formed" in Prov. 8:22 tells against the theories advanced by Alexander and Athanasius. If, he says, the reference to the Son as "begotten" (in the same text) tempts them to think that the Son alone has an "identical nature" (τὴν ταυτότητα τῆς φύσεως) with the Father, those places in scripture (he cites Isa. 1:2; Deut. 32:18; Job 38:28) should be recalled in which others are called the "begotten" of God. Eusebius presses the point which his texts illuminate: it is not the procession of nature from nature which the passages teach—they describe, rather, the birth of all things created by the will of God.³⁰ Asterius, in remarks which will be treated more extensively below, joins his Arian colleagues in describing Christ's sonship in terms applicable to other creatures, and thus in terms which connote a relationship of thorough dependence upon the Father both for existence and for power. Ranking Christ with the many powers created by God (among whom he is πρωτότοκος and μονογενής), Asterius claims that "all, indeed, are equally (ὁμοίως) dependent upon their possessor (τὸν κεκτημένον)."³¹ Neither the words nor the works of the Son belong, properly speaking, to him, "but to the Father who gave him power."³² The derivative and dependent authority of the Arian Christ which we discussed in the first chapter is by no means confined to the Jesus of history. It is evident in his origination as a creature of God's will, and it will be seen to be a mark of his role as the Son who serves as his Father's creative agent.

The orthodox, by contrast, will only allow that the Son is "from" or "out of" the Father in the sense that he is "offspring of the paternal essence" (τῆς πατρικῆς οὐσίας . . . γέννημα).³³ Biblical passages which suggest the begetting of the Son are understood in a physical sense, so as to emphasize the mutuality and coeternality of the Father and the Son.³⁴ In conceiving the Son's link with the Father in natural terms, Alexander seeks to distinguish his relationship from that in which creatures stand to the Creator. The sonship of the Word, "naturally partaking of the paternal divinity (κατὰ φύσιν τυγχάνουσα τῆς πατρικῆς θεότητος), is unspeakably different from the sonship through him by appointment (δι' αὐτοῦ θέσει)."³⁵ Christ's sonship, he means, belongs to him by virtue of his essence and nature, while creatures come to call God "Father" only by adoption. Accordingly, the Son, being perfect, is unchangeable, while all the rest stand in need of his help.[36]

It is precisely the fear that essential or substantial or eternal linkage between Father and Son will blur or destroy the definition of relationship which stirs Arius' abhorrence of any terms suggestive of communication of the divine substance, priority, or eternality. About the Arian conviction that the Son is "foreign" to the Father in terms of essence we shall have more to say very shortly. The point to be registered at this juncture has to do with the significance which Arians attached to the terms "Father" and "Son." They are descriptive of a relationship in which priority of importance and sequence of time are clear; and they underline, in addition, qualities which define the bond between the one who derives existence and power, submitting (ὑπομένει) himself, and the one who creates, empowers, and rules. It was in order to mark clearly the dependent character of this sonship that the Arians collected texts from the New Testament which emphasized the Son's humiliation and suffering, *but this dependency is proper to the creaturely Son from his beginning before time.* What Alexander and Athanasius unfailingly regard as irreligious efforts to dishonor the Son and demote him to the rank of creature represent an exact rendering of what the Arians consider to be the meaning of sonship both for Christ and for Christians. Athanasius complains, "If . . . the Word is not from (ἐκ) God, as would be a natural and genuine son from a father, but is named as the creatures, because they are framed, he (as all things from God) is neither from the essence (ἐκ τῆς οὐσίας) of the Father nor is himself the Son according to essence, but from virtue (ἐξ ἀρετῆς), as we are called sons according to grace (κατὰ χάριν)."[37] In the Arian view, the Son owes his existence and the powers which enable him to be preeminent among creatures to the Father. This is the doctrine which is served by Arian insistence that "before he was begotten or made or appointed or formed, he was not,"[38] for what is being trumpeted is the gracious purpose of the one who gives life, calling creatures into being as sons. This divine intent and action is revealed in the first creature. In order to make this case, and as an indispensable part of it, the Arians *do* maintain the "transcendence" of God. But it would be more accurate to say that they assert his *unqualified sovereignty.* Their purpose in doing so, however, is to be sought in their sense of what dealings between a Father and a Son (and sons) entail, and the failure to come to terms with this priority in the religious program of the Arians can only result in tying their statements about the Son's beginning to the *idée fixe* of which they have been accused.

How then are we to assess those portions of Arian teaching which enunciate the first tenet, the prior "half" of their supposedly all-consuming defense of God's transcendence—the emphasis, namely, upon the singularity of the Deity (ὁ θεός)? Influenced by his opponents' characterizations, and on the basis of Arius' references to God as "monad" as well as his attention to attributes proper to God "alone," many have inclined to the view expressed in sharpest terms by T. E. Pollard:

> There can be no doubt that the compelling motive of Arianism was the desire to preserve a strict monotheism, but that does not mean that its monotheism was "biblical." The God whom the Arians declare to be "One" is not the Living God of the Bible, but rather the Absolute of the philosophical schools.[39]

It may well be asked whether the kind of polarity assumed in this distinction is serviceable in the interpretation of patristic literature generally, but the question at hand involves the orientation and intentions of Arius and his allies.

Arius' designation of God as μονάς could not be taken as proof of a strictly philosophical viewpoint and interest, even if we lacked abundant evidence (which we do not) of the numerous scriptural texts from which Arian propositions were argued from the beginning. The use of the term for God (in ways that do not at all rule out a "biblical" view of the Deity) is well attested in the intellectual and ecclesiastical tradition of Alexandria which was the possession of both parties in the dispute. Its use by Philo, Clement, and Origen has been noted by G. C. Stead, whose correction of Pollard suggests that "like Philo, Arius is prepared to argue that God is μονάς while giving full recognition to his biblical attributes."[40] It may be added that God is called "monad" by Dionysius of Alexandria in the course of his exchange with his episcopal counterpart in Rome, and we know that one feature of Arian and orthodox warfare involved vying for legitimacy in the genealogy of right thinkers, which agreement with Dionysius was thought to insure.[41] It is interesting to see that Athanasius too speaks of the "monad." This is not his usual and favored designation for God (as it is not, apparently, for Arius), and he employs it primarily in the context of discussion of Arian ideas—but he neither questions the connotations attaching to the word nor displays any reluctance in using it himself.[42] We must conclude that the word, though capable, like others (for example, μοναρχία), of introducing dangerous ideas (particularly Sabellianism, with which Arius himself associates it in his *confessio fidei*), was not itself a signal of erroneous doctrine. It is unwarranted to assume that the presence of the term signifies in his case, more than in that of his predecessors and contemporary combatants in the church, a commitment to settling problems of the definition of God solely, or even primarily, by the canons and specialized terminologies of philosophy.

More vexing to interpreters than his willingness to call God "monad" has been the statement by Arius that though the monad existed eternally, the δυάς "did not exist before it came to be."[43] G. C. Stead may be correct that the translation ("the number two") implies "the second" rather than "the two" (that is, Father and Son), but this is not the only possibility.[44] If his translation is influenced by the supposition that Arius *could not say* "the duality [or "the two"] was not before it came into existence," it is not beyond question; for we have seen that Arius made a claim of precisely this sort. Though he professed the eternality of God, he clearly taught that there was a beginning of the relationship to which the terms "father" and "son" apply. His sense could have been: God the monad was, but the dyad (the pair, Father and Son) was not, before it came to be—that is, before God created the Son, at which point he was called "his Father." It needs also to be said that even if it is maintained that Arius meant by δυάς "the second," or the Son, it is arbitrary to claim that he intended the term to be "almost certainly uncomplimentary."[45] This supposition by Stead assumes a sense of the term which Arius would have entertained because he was primarily a Platonist, though it is *at least* as likely that Arius could have understood "the second" more positively—in a way analogous to Philo's use of it to signify the Word articulated (λόγος κατὰ προφοράν), in contrast to the monad, the unspoken thought.[46] The shape of Arius' "Logos theology," as we shall see, permits such a view of the one who is the second to God.

Rehearsing the faith which he received from his forebears (and which he claims to have learned from his antagonist Alexander, to whom he writes), Arius asserts, "We confess one God, alone unbegotten, alone eternal, alone unbegun, alone true, alone having immortality, alone wise, alone good, alone sovereign, judge, orderer [and] governor of all, unchanging and unalterable, just and good, God of [the] law and prophets and [the] New Testament. . . ."[47] The extended description of ἕνα θεόν, its repetitive μόνον marking the qualities and functions of the Deity, might be considered supportive of a view of Arius' zeal for the monotheistic principle and perhaps a philosopher's strategy for declaring the absolute transcendence of the "One." It is doubtful, however, that the string of phrases is designed for the express purpose of placing in an inferior light the begotten Son who is next described; for there is nothing denigrating (on Arian assumptions) in the designation of this Son as uniquely produced, agent of creation, *also* unchanging and unalterable—even his characterization as perfect creature and (perfect?) offspring. (And of course Arius' *confessio* adheres to the prescribed creedal patterning which dictates the sequence in which the persons are treated.)[48]

What is particularly noteworthy in this Arian description of God is the evidence of its biblical influences, which have been recognized but not sufficiently probed.[49] The words "unbegotten," "eternal," and "unbegun" in the initial phrases fall into the category of theological *topoi* by the fourth century; and though important to the Arian scheme, they are not remarkable. It is instructive to observe that the following five phrases reveal reliance upon or quote exactly (except for endings) language in New Testament writings. When Arius speaks of God as "alone true" (μόνον ἀληθινόν), he echoes the prayer of Jesus in John 17:3 (τὸν μόνον ἀληθινὸν θεόν). The phrase "alone wise" (μόνον σοφόν) corresponds with doxological language of Rom. 16:27 (μόνῳ σοφῷ θεῷ), and reference to the Deity as "alone good" evokes the statement by Jesus in Mark 10:18 (οὐδεὶς ἀγαθὸς εἰ μὴ εἷς ὁ θεός). The remaining two phrases containing μόνον are taken from an eschatological passage in 1 Timothy, which we set here alongside the Arian statement.

Arius' *confessio fidei* (Urk. 6.2)	1 Tim. 6:15–16
. . . ἕνα θεόν	. . . ὁ μακάριος καὶ
μόνον ἀγέννητον, μόνον	μόνος δυνάστης
ἀΐδιον, μόνον ἄναρχον,	ὁ βασιλεὺς τῶν βασιλευόντων
μόνον ἀληθινόν [cf. John 17:3],	καὶ κύριος τῶν κυριευόντων
μόνον ἀθανασίαν ἔχοντα,	ὁ μόνος ἔχων ἀθανασίαν,
μόνον σοφόν [cf. Rom. 16:27],	φῶς οἰκῶν ἀπρόσιτον,
μόνον ἀγαθόν [cf. Mark 10:18],	ὃν εἶδεν οὐδεὶς ἀνθρώπων
μόνον δυνάστην. . . .	οὐδὲ ἰδεῖν δύναται. . . .

The most obvious thing to be observed on the basis of the parallels between Arius' language and these phrases from the New Testament (of which the two from 1 Timothy and the one from John are, for all practical purposes, exact) is that Arius consciously portrays God in language which is, at the very least, consonant with scripture.[50] Further, it is very probable (at the least, arguable) that the very biblical passages to which he alludes are the source of his emphatic reiterations of what God *alone* is—1 Tim. 6:15, 16 and John 17:3 furnishing the construction featuring μόνον.

There are, however, more far-reaching implications in Arius' reliance upon 1 Timothy (an epistle both parties can be seen claiming as support from the dispute's beginning)[51] in his faith declaration about God and the Son. Does a connection exist between the assertion in Timothy (just after the phrase quoted by Arius) that "no man sees or is able to perceive" God and the well-known Arian proposition that God cannot be comprehended by the Son? Two considerations suggest that this is so. First, the doctrine seen in the *Thalia* (and elsewhere) that "God is invisible (ἀόρατος) to all, both to those created by the Son and to the Son himself," points to 1 Tim. 1:17, in which God is termed "the king of the ages, immortal, invisible, only God (. . . τῷ . . . βασιλεῖ τῶν αἰώνιων, ἀφθάρτῳ, ἀοράτῳ, μόνῳ θεῷ)."[52] Secondly, Arius can be expected to have included the Son among the *men* incapable of perceiving the Deity—and to have found this inclusion dictated by the holy and authoritative writing which he is quoting. Both the theme of the oneness *and* distinctness of God, and the clear statement that the Son is, though mediator between God and humanity, a member of the class redeemed through him are present in 1 Tim. 2.5: "For there is one God (εἷς γὰρ θεός), and one mediator between God and men, [the] man (ἄνθρωπος) Christ Jesus." To the number of biblical passages from which we saw the Arians framing christological and soteriological ideas, then, we are justified in adding certain themes in 1 Timothy, which Arius cites in building his doctrine of God and which serves as a likely and natural source and/or support of other concepts important to his religious scheme.[53] But a broader point stands to be made as a result of this examination of an Arian formulation which has been construed as "philosophical" and single-mindedly intent upon the starkest monotheistic definition. Considered on its own terms and in the light of its own evident sources, Arius' statement about God and his attributes does not compel the interpretation frequently given to it. It distinguishes in unambiguous language the sovereign God from the uniquely begotten Son, who subsists by the Father's will, is preeminent among creatures, and as perfect creature shares immutability with his Maker. Of a purposeful depreciation, demotion, or assault upon the honor and status of the Son there is no real evidence—at least no more than can be found in 1 Tim. 2:5.

Arius and his fellow thinkers took with radical seriousness the relationship of the Father and the Son, a relationship in which the former was prior, superior, and dominant. The structure and content of that relationship—what it was and what it was not—were matters of critical importance to Arius, Eusebius, Asterius, and their followers. Both the mode of origination of the Son and the continuing bond between him and the Father were conceived by them in a striking way. Conceived relationally rather than ontologically, and marked by dependence rather than coequality, the "kinship" between the Father and the Son for early Arian thinkers is grounded in the conception of the will of God and the faculty of willing. We have in the preceding chapters treated the importance of this set of ideas to the Arian scheme of salvation.[54] We turn now to those formulas which conceive of the Son's creation and his role in God's "works" in terms of the divine will; for this, according to the Arians, is God's key property and the mode in which he is related to those whom he has made.

FATHER AND SON:
FOREIGN IN ESSENCE, RELATED BY WILL

The cardinal principle of the Arians, as we remarked earlier, applies with equal force to the Jesus of history and to the preexistent Son. It is that all creatures, including the Son and redeemer, are ultimately and radically dependent upon a Creator whose sole means of relating to his creation is by his will (βούλησις) and pleasure (θέλησις).[55] The derivative character of the power and authority manifest in Jesus' ministry was traced by Arian exegetes from a series of biblical texts which spoke of the things bestowed upon him by his Father. These assertions are in complete harmony with what is claimed about the Son created before all ages—both the mode of his origination and his role in God's purposes for the cosmos. Our purpose in what follows is to sketch out the shape of this principle of God's willing as it bears upon the Son's status as creature (κτίσμα) and work (ποίημα)—that is, as a positive vision of God and the drama over which he presides—and to investigate Arian ideas and criticisms concerning the applicability of οὐσία-language to the realities central to the Christian proclamation.

Having placed heavy emphasis upon the relationship denoted by the terms Father and Son, Arian spokesmen were required to explain just how the Father and Son are related to each other since (as they contended) they are not of the same essence. No Arian conviction is more clearly attested than that expressed in their persistent cry that the chief property of the Deity is his θελεῖν, and the unfolding of his οἰκονομία is by his free purpose, his will and pleasure.

The category of "will," whether divine or human, can signify changeability—on this point Arians and orthodox could agree. Their sharp difference, making the question of the will a pivotal one in the controversy, was how or whether willing-language and voluntarist categories could be applied to the data of Christian revelation. One dramatic aspect of this clash we have already investigated: the proclamation by the Arians of a Christ capable of change, improvement, and advance was countered by a Christology which denied mutability to the divine Word. The orthodox strategically invoked the category of "nature" or "essence" in order to rule out the possibility of change and instability in the savior. Athanasius' presentation of the Christ in whom divine nature controls the will is pitted against the carefully articulated view of the Christ who exercised his faith and received a "reward of virtue."

Commitment to the category of will is equally firm in Arian discussion of the origination of the Son. Arius, Eusebius, and Asterius with one voice describe the Son's creation as an act of the Father's will and portray the Son as a product of the Father's intentionality. Their insistence that "the Son has received being from the Father at his will and pleasure (βουλήσει καὶ θελήσει)" insures God's own freedom to act—it is the counterpart to the Christology of promotion.[56] "Unless," the Arians maintain, "he [the Son] has by will come to be, then God had a Son by necessity and against his good pleasure."[57] Just how high the stakes are on this contested point can readily be seen in Athanasius' twofold rebuttal in the third *Oration*. His initial tactic is a form of the *reductio ad haeresim*: Arian belief in a "will" and "pleasure" which precede the Word is, he says, a doctrine closely akin to the "Thought" and "Will" which the Valentinian Ptolemy imagined as the pair first generated by the Unbegotten.[58] This is yet another version of the orthodox accusation that in saying "There was when he was not" the Arians proposed an interval (διάστημα) between God and his Son.[59] By orthodox reckoning, there can be no intervening entity, whether a "moment" or a "precedent will," interrupting the continuity of being or eternity which guarantees the Son's full deity. Such a "break" marks the boundary between Creator and creatures, and Athanasius states accordingly that though it is permissible to speak of God's precedent will with reference to things created (he cites Psalms 115, 111, 135), to say that the Son came into being by God's will is to make him a "work" and one among the other creatures.[60]

Aversion to Gnostic ideas and to substantialist terminology reminiscent of emanationist theologies—so forcefully expressed in Arian correspondence—reveals Athanasius' charge to be transparently false. The antecedents for the contested Arian formula lie not in Gnostic systems but in biblical language and, more particularly, in eminent church writings belonging to the "mainstream." Ignatius had spoken in his letter to the Smyrneans (1.1) of the "Son of God according to the will (θέλημα) and power of God." The Arian idea and its terminology are most closely paralleled in several of Justin Martyr's formulations in the *Dialogue with Trypho*. He speaks of God's lordship over all, including the Christ "who was according to his will (κατὰ βουλήν) his Son, being God"; of the Son as "begotten from the Father at his will (θελήσει)"; and (also in reference to the Son) of the "power . . . begotten from the Father by his power and will (δυνάμει καὶ βουλῇ), but not by abscission, as if the essence of the Father were divided."[61] The concept and its language continued in the writings of Hippolytus (*Contra Noëtum* 16)—". . . whom the Father, willing (βουληθείς), begot as he willed (ὡς ἠθέλησεν)"—and the writing of Clement and Origen.[62] Particular issues stemming from the "Logos theology" enunciated by Justin continue to concern Arius and his followers (as we shall see), but the assertion that the Son is brought into existence by the divine will is meant by them as a statement about the character of God the Father and about the manner in which he acts. Simultaneously, it challenges Athanasius' distinction between modes of generation—one for the Son, a different for creatures. In the midst of his denunciation of Arian teaching about will and willing, Athanasius quotes (with an attempt to distort his opponent's meaning) the remark of Asterius:

> If making at his pleasure (τὸ θέλοντα ποιεῖν) is dishonorable for the Creator, [then] let the being pleased (τὸ θέλειν) [to make] be abolished in the case of all alike, so that the honor may be preserved to him untarnished. Or if the willing

(τὸ βούλεσθαι) is proper to God, let that which is more excellent pertain also to the first offspring. For surely it is not possible that for one and the same God the being pleased [to make] should be fitting, in the case of the things made, and also that the not willing (τὸ μὴ βούλεσθαι) should be appropriate.[63]

Asterius calls for consistency, demanding that God's "willing to make" is proper to him, and thus pertains to creatures *and* to the firstborn among creatures, the Son. God wills and purposes, he makes and creates βουλήσει καὶ θελήσει, and this manner of calling into being things which were not incorporates all, for all depend upon God for their existence. For Asterius, as for the other Arian writers, God's will is not understood as an entity or an existent being, or a divine attribute hypostasized, but as an *action*. It is an action of the kind undertaken by a person, and in this case it is an action of God the Father which initiates transaction between himself and those created.

It is also clear that in asserting the creation of the Son by God's will, the Arians did not think they were in danger of implicating God in a "passion" or "affect" inappropriate to deity. Even though their formulation of the Son's origination was said by Athanasius to suggest human emotions (ἀνθρωποπαθής), the Arians did not believe themselves vulnerable to the charge.[64] The voluntarist cast of their definition of the relationship between Father and Son, compelled by their understanding of sonship in covenant in biblical writings, was legitimized philosophically by means of the Stoic category of εὐπάθειαι (innocent, or worthy, affects). Like Origen, they believed it the same thing to call the redeemer a Son of the Father's love and a Son by the Father's will.[65] On the question of attributing "passion" to God as Father, Arius and his colleagues considered themselves to be securely on the offensive; for the physical sense in which the orthodox spoke of the Son's begetting could be accused of evoking the pornography of Gnostic cosmogonies, with their accounts of the Archons' couplings. This was the exact force of Asterius' attack upon the theory of the generation of the Son advanced by Alexander and Athanasius. In subscribing to the doctrine contained in Eusebius' letter to Paulinus, he understood the Arian view to be the only sound and traditional one:

[For] the gist of the letter is to attribute the generation of the Son to the will (βουλή) of the Father, and to show plainly that the act of generation by God is free of passion (μὴ πάθος), which very thing the wisest of the Fathers

94

proclaimed in their own treatises, defending against the impiety of the heretics, who falsely invented something corporeal and sensuous with respect to the childbearing of God, teaching the emanations.[66]

The point was not made so elaborately by Eusebius himself, but his disapproval of the opponents' description of sonship from paternal essence was thorough—he thought it an inexcusably somatic idea of God's operations, suggesting "some corporeal thing which has been subject to change."[67]

For the Arians, the use of the category of will and willing excluded any idea of substantial commonality between the Father and Son, making it possible to describe both the chief property of God and his way of relating himself to all his creatures. Athanasius suffered under no illusions about their objective, as the second part of his attack in the third *Oration* reveals. To the Arian insistence that the Son came to be by will, not by necessity or contrary to God's intention, Athanasius retorts:

> Who is it then who imposes necessity on him? . . . for what is contrary to will they see; but what is greater and transcends it has escaped their perception. For as what is beside purpose is contrary to will, so what is according to nature transcends and precedes counseling. . . . As far then as the Son transcends the creature, by so much does what is by nature transcend the will.[68]

For Athanasius, as for Alexander, categories of nature or essence have to take precedence over and secure the will in unchangeability. Just as the way the orthodox read the Gospels led them to divinize the will of Christ, locating the willing faculty in the immutable Logos (but weakness and fear in his flesh),[69] so they argue the origin of the Son from the Father's οὐσία, for "essence" and "nature" surpass the category of willing. The Arian view is, of course, just the opposite: as the ministry of Christ recorded in the New Testament, by their reading, revealed a morally changeable servant of the Father's purpose, so they understand the Son's creation in terms of what Asterius calls "that which is more excellent"—that is, in terms of the paternal will and pleasure.

Further definition and amplification of the importance of the idea of the Son's subsistence by the Father's will and pleasure can be gained from the Arian documents. First, we know that this allowed them to say that the Son was "begotten"(γεννηθῇ), and to add as parallel verbs (under the guidance of Prov. 8:22ff.) "made" (κτισθῇ), "appointed" (ὁρισθῇ), and "formed" (or "established"—θεμελιωθῇ).[70] The same, or very similar, claims about the character of the Son could be made by these verbs—the first was not, as it was for the orthodox, an antonym of the latter three. More is being indicated here than the basic Arian proposition that the Son was a begotten creature. The idea that he was appointed or ordained (ὁρισθῇ) leads to a second point which, we are told, the Arians made emphatically. The Son's creation is in the interest of the larger divine purpose; the firstborn has his *raison d'être* and his definition in relation to the works God intends to accomplish. So God, "wishing to form us (θελήσας ἡμᾶς δημιουργῆσαι), there-upon . . . made a certain one, and called him Word and Wisdom and Son, in order that we might be formed by him."[71] Alexander also reports the doctrine "he was made for our sake (δι' ἡμᾶς), in order that God might create (κτίσῃ) us through him, as by an instrument."[72] The will of God is worked for creation through the agency, the service, of the one begotten and made. The third, and for the Arians the all-important, point is already intimated in the reference to God's creation of "a certain one." It is stated in provocative language in the *Thalia*:

> The Unbegun made (or instituted—ἔθηκε) the Son as a beginning (or office of power/sovereignty—ἀρχήν) of the other things made (τῶν γενητῶν) and raised (ἤνεγκεν) him for a Son to himself, adopting him (τεκνοποιήσας).[73]

The phrase yields to a double interpretation with philosophical and political connotations. It affirms (1) that the Son is made a beginning of the products of God and (2) that the Son is elevated to a magistracy (after the model of imperial adoptions in Roman antiquity). But the primary point about what has been effected by the divine will is this: creation is election, and the generation of the Son is at the same time adoption. Arians speak of the Son by the will and pleasure of God not only to give an account of the beginnings of the cosmos but with a view to rehearsing God's dispensations on behalf of the created order.[74] Arian attention to chronology and to the broader drama of the biblical record is evident in their account of the Son's origination:

> God, foreknowing that he would be good, proleptically gave to him that glory which afterward he had also as man by means of [his] virtue; thus, on the basis of his works, which God foreknew, he made such a one as him now to be begotten.[75]

Divine volition and creaturely freedom to choose and act are prerequisites of a view of relationship which features sovereignty and obedience—that is to say, a view which has the structure of covenant. These are fundamental elements of the Arian religious scheme. Without pursuing at this point how the two kinds of statements interacted with each other, we may be certain that Arian Christians appreciated the coherence and connection between two remarks which strike modern analysts as belonging to quite different doctrinal categories. Asterius' remark ("If the willing of God has pervaded all works in succession, certainly the Son also, being a work, has come into being and been made according to his will") and the doctrine attributed to Arius ("And by nature, as all others, so also the Word himself is changeable, but by his own choice, when he wills, he remains good") were, to the Arians, more intelligible together than either could be singly.[76] The Son created before the ages, like all creatures, depends upon the will of God for his existence; and his works as preexistent Son and Christ of history consist in learning and doing what God's economy demands.

The traditional view of the Arian controversy as a clash between contrary Trinitarian schemes—one stressing equality of Persons, the other maintaining a graded hierarchy—is not a complete misperception. It is, however, oversimple and basically off target in that it does not bring us close enough to the truly incendiary issues in the conflict. In their endeavor to express and defend the cardinal beliefs of Christianity, Arians embraced a conceptual and linguistic framework which centered in will and willing, thus depicting the relationship between Father and Son, Creator and creatures in voluntarist terms. Convinced as they were that the gospel of God's promises in his Son needed to be proclaimed in this way, they were deeply suspicious of a presentation of the divine drama which invoked the problematic language of οὐσία and φύσις. Assertions by Bishops Alexander and Athanasius that the Father and Son were one-in-essence and related through identity of nature seemed to Arian churchmen destructive of core meanings in the record of God's actions in the Testaments.

With a variety of sharp propositions Arius assaulted the formulas which argued for commonality of essence between Father and Son. He denied any notion of that relationship which suggested that the Son was "from" the one who begot him as a portion or an emanation.[77] The Son could not be thought of as coeternal (συναΐδιος) or co-unbegotten (συναγέννητος) or consubstantial (ὁμοούσιος) with the Father.[78] Certain metaphors intended to describe the relationship were disallowed: light from light, or a lamp made into two.[79] Neither could the philosophical category of relations (πρός τι) be employed to speak of the Son being with the Father in such a way as to maintain that there were two unbegotten principles.[80] Arius' argument that God is beyond comprehension since he is "to himself" has its counterpart in the statements that the Son is distinct καθ' ἑαυτόν and possesses nothing which is God's own "in proper subsistence."[81] The preserved utterances of Arius about the Trinity are vivid—their purpose is to prohibit belief in any substantialist connection between the Persons:

> . . . there is a Triad not in equal glories; their subsistences (ὑποστάσεις) are unmixed with each other, one infinitely more estimable in glories than the other.
>
> The essences (οὐσίαι) of the Father and the Son and the Holy Spirit are separate in nature (μεμερισμέναι τῇ φύσει), and are estranged, unconnected, alien (ἀπεξωμέναι, ἀπεσχοινισμέναι, ἀλλότριοι), and without participation in each other (ἀμέτεχοί εἰσιν ἀλλήλων) . . . . They are utterly dissimilar from each other with respect to both essences and glories to infinity.[82]

The question at issue, though the Triad is referred to, is how the Son and Father may and may not be thought to be related. In his letter to Alexander, Arius contrasts God, who is cause (αἴτιος) of all, without beginning and most solitary (μονώτατος), with the Son begotten, created, and established by the Father, and alone made to exist by the Father alone.[83] The denial, in its several forms, that the Son is an offspring of the Father's essence may be seen as the negative form of what, in unison with his allies, Arius states positively and insistently in the *Thalia*: ". . . being Son, he truly existed by the will of the Father," and "by God's will the Son is as strong and as great as he is."[84]

There is between the Father and Son (or between the members of the Triad) no *analogia entis*—there is only the will of the Creator upon which the creature is radically dependent for both being and knowledge. A close examination of the difficult letter of Eusebius highlights the importance of this assertion to the Arians. From the things created by God—for example, rebellious sons, inconstant creatures, or drops of dew (Isa. 1:2; Deut. 32:18; Job 38:28)—one can deduce nothing whatever about God's own nature, for as he tells Paulinus:

> There is nothing which is from his essence, but all things having been created by his will, each exists just as, indeed, it was created. For on the one hand there is God, but on the other there are the things which are going to be like his Word in relation to his likeness, [and there are] the things created by free will.[85]

It is not certain whether, in the final phrase, Eusebius seeks to differentiate between rational beings and other creatures called into existence by God's superabundant beneficence.[86] The primary distinction he wishes to make, however, is not in any doubt. There is God the Creator, and there are his creatures, who are (as the next line indicates) "from God" in one sense only—they are (ἐκ τοῦ θεοῦ) "by his will," not "out of his substance."

One among these creatures is the Son. Arius is reported to have advanced much the same argument, teaching that "since all beings are foreign and different from God in essence, so also the Word is alien and different from the essence and individuality of the Father in all respects, but he belongs to those things originated and made (γενητῶν καὶ κτισμάτων) and is one of these."[87] On the subject of how the Son is related to the Father, although they possess different essences or natures, Eusebius has more to say. His exposition of the question is tied to the interpretation of the three verbs appearing in the controverted passage Prov. 8:22ff. Denouncing a theology which intimates two Unbegottens or imagines God's begetting in a corporeal manner, he asserts:

Rather [we have learned and believed] the unbegotten is one, and one is that which was created truly (ἀληθῶς . . . γεγονός) by him—and was not from his essence, not participating at all in the unbegotten nature (καθόλου τῆς φύσεως τῆς ἀγεννήτου μὴ μετέχον) nor existing from his essence, but being entirely different with reference to the nature and might [that is, of the unbegotten], made according to perfect likeness of disposition and power of the one who had created him (πρὸς τελείαν ὁμοιότητα διαθέσεώς τε καὶ δυνάμεως); whose beginning is inexpressible by word and also by thought, not only of man, but we have believed it is also incomprehensible to the thought of all creatures above man. We utter these things, not by way of proposing our own thoughts, but because we have learned that he is "created" and "formed" and "begotten" with respect to the essence and to the immutable and inexpressible nature, and to a likeness relative to his Maker (ὁμοιότητι τῇ πρὸς τὸν πεποιηκότα), as the Lord himself says: "God created me in the beginning of his ways, and he formed me before the age; and before all hills he begets me."[88]

Researchers have paid little attention to Eusebius' argument, even though it is one of the lengthier pieces of sustained Arian reasoning preserved from the controversy. The reason for its frequent mistranslation *and* misinterpretation resides in the failure to recognize the pivotal significance of the category of will in earliest Arian teaching.[89] But there is nothing obscure in Eusebius' claims. The Son is not from the Father's οὐσία and does not in any way partake of the unbegotten φύσις. His own nature and power are of a different order than that of God himself. Toward the end of the passage, the

Son is described as one created, formed, and begotten (for Eusebius the verbs are virtually synonymous) with respect to his Creator's ineffable, immutable nature, and with respect to a likeness (ὁμοιότητα) to his Maker. A *similarity* exists, he says, between the originate Son and the Creator-Father. This similarity is not, he emphatically states a few lines later, an "identity of nature." The preference which some had for "likeness" over "identity" was to have a colorful history in the controversy, but this distinction is not in itself the objective Eusebius is pursuing. The important issue is, in what does this "likeness relative to his maker" consist? The clue to Eusebius' meaning resides in the parallel language he has employed in the preceding (lengthy) sentence. It is a τελείαν ὁμοιότητα διαθέσεώς τε καὶ δυνάμεως, "a perfect likeness of disposition and power."[90] We have translated δυνάμεως as "power" in order to convey *both* the writer's differentiation between the "might" (δυνάμει) of the Creator and of the one truly created (is it an "infinite" difference, as in the case of the respective "glories" of the members of the Triad?) *and* his insistence that the Son too has power relative to the God who empowers. Father *and* Son possess δύναμις; that belonging to the Son is "lesser," or rather it is *derived*, since he is recipient, not source. This line of reasoning, if it represents what Eusebius intended, would accord fully with what is known to us from the *Thalia*—namely that the Son, a strong God, praises the Superior in his degree, and that by the power with which God sees, the Son undertakes to see his Father in his own measure.[91]

One sense of the word διάθεσις, "disposition," has to do with ordering and arranging and refers, typically, to stones in a wall or elements comprising a rhetorical piece.[92] By the Aristotelian definition, which speaks of "arrangement of that which has parts, either in space or in potentiality or in form," "disposition" could be descriptive of the organization of things in the world.[93] On this reading, Eusebius might be understood to be speaking of the Son's likeness to the Father as the Creator's instrument—that is, as one who works the ordering and power which stem from God. Consonant with this kind of interpretation is a remark Eusebius makes late in the letter: "And all things were created by God through him, but all things are from God."[94] The word "disposition" can also refer, of course, to one's attitude or condition. In a complimentary address to Eusebius, Arius speaks of the former's "innate love and disposition (διάθεσιν) . . . toward his brothers on account of God and his Christ."[95] Athanasius has the monk Antony

100

employ the term in contrasting the skill which produces dialectic with the attitude of the soul (διαθέσεως ψυχῆς) which produces faith.[96] Similarly, Philo speaks of the wise man who puts on "that surest and most stable quality (τὴν ὀχυρωτάτην καὶ βεβαιοτάτην διάθεσιν), faith," and elsewhere teaches that God takes delight more in the "blameless intention (ἀνυπαι-τίῳ . . . διαθέσει) of the votary" than in the flesh of the animals sacrificed.[97]

In fact the two qualifying words which accompany the idea of perfect likeness remove any uncertainty as to Eusebius' meaning, for they are technical terms from the ethics of the Stoa. Plutarch records that the great Stoics defined virtue as "a certain disposition of the governing portion of the soul and a power produced by reason (διάθεσιν τινα καὶ δύναμιν)."[98] As J. N. Rist has noted, Stoics chose διάθεσις rather than ἕξις in their search for a word suggestive of "stability of character"; they meant by it a "fixity of purpose."[99] Likewise, in calling virtue a "power," the Stoics did not intend to endorse a potentiality which might go either way but thought rather of a person who, as Rist has written, "has the power and will always use the power to act virtuously."[100] In embracing these terms and setting this phrase over against all essentialist language, Eusebius proclaimed the Son's perfect likeness to his Father to be one of virtue! In his steadfast purpose and effective discipline, the Son is related to the one who created, formed, and begot him by his will and pleasure.

One consequence of the Arian bishop's conception of the Son's likeness to the Father was not to be missed. The fact that he is called "begotten" does not locate the Son in an order of being alien from other creatures, "as if he had been created from the paternal essence, and so had the identical nature because of this."[101] Eusebius reminds Paulinus of others called "begotten" in scripture; they too were called into relationship with God by his will, and they no less than the Son, their fellow creature, may demonstrate obedience to him by their "disposition" and "power."

We have taken note of Arian emphasis upon the relationship denoted by "father" and "son" and have proceeded to examine the ground and dynamic of that relationship in will and willing—both the free action of the Sovereign and the Son's purposive response in virtue. Two tasks remain. It must be asked how the Arians supposed they were advancing their cause in proclaiming that the Son was not God's "true" Word. And finally, attention must be given to the character and role which Arian doctrine ascribes to the preincarnate Son, who is the Father's student and apprentice.

101

THE ONE CALLED "WORD"
BY GRACE AND PARTICIPATION

Could the Arian teaching about the Logos have been as confused and confusing as the polemic of their critics makes it seem? Athanasius is our primary source for the reports that the Arians taught multiple Words and Powers and Wisdoms of God, that they refused to call the Son "true" God, and that they believed he merely held by a trick of language the appellations "Son," "Word," and "Wisdom." The bishop is at his rhetorical best in these joustings with Arian pronouncements, which he quotes selectively, connects together as his agenda of ridicule dictates, and (not infrequently) pushes to conclusions which we may be sure the Arians themselves would have disowned. It is argument by misrepresentation, but it is misrepresentation through distortion rather than bald fabrication. The Arian views are actually given; they are presented partially, however, and without their own emphases, rationale, and objectives in view. Athanasius' account, consequently, preserves valuable information about Arian opinions concerning God's Word and "Word," but his rhetorical art holds traps for the historian, and his description of the doctrine of the Arians on this subject (like others) requires the control available from their own remarks.

According to Athanasius, the Arians held that God was "once" without Word (Reason) and Wisdom (an inevitable consequence, he intimates, of their claim that the Son has a beginning).[102] He reports their belief in "two Wisdoms" and in "another Word in God besides the Son," as well as their conviction that Christ's power is not "true power of God," since he is only one of the many powers over whom (as the Psalter teaches) the Lord God presides.[103] Arians dare to say that the Word is not "true God" but is merely called such by grace, like others.[104] The characterization is not so inaccurate as it is misleading.

The basic shape of what we might call the "*logoi* theology" of the early Arians can be recovered by working from Arius' own words (in the letters and excerpts from the *Thalia*) and by using carefully and judiciously the information supplied by Athanasius and Alexander. The scheme is not complex, and though we are not able to sketch out all the details, Arius and his allies seem to have been intent upon clarification and defense of a number of familiar Christian beliefs which seemed to them to be in jeopardy.

We have seen that the Son in whom Arian Christians believed was a

102

product of God's will and pleasure, who neither shared his Father's essence nor participated in his unbegotten nature. Eusebius insists that he was "truly (ἀληθῶς) created" and Arius that he "truly (ἀληθῶς) existed by the will of the Father."[105] The reality and authenticity of the Son's being and of his relationship with the Father are caught up in his character as one freely created and bound to the Father by will. On the assumptions which govern the thinking of the orthodox, the adjectival and adverbial terms marking reality can only have reference to essence and nature. So the Son is "true" (ἀληθινός) Son, "true" (ἀληθῆ) offspring, and "truly" (ἀληθῶς) God because he is one-in-essence with his divine Begetter.[106] As Alexander and Athanasius use the term "true," therefore, the Arians could not and would not say that the preexistent Son (or the incarnate Christ) was true Son or Word or Wisdom. To have done so would have meant equating the word "true" with the word "essential" (in its strict sense), and it would have signaled capitulation to the entire substantialist frame of reference upon which the theology of the Alexandrian bishops depended.

As the structures of reality are differently drawn by the early Arians, they argue that God's "true" Reason and Wisdom—that is, the Λόγος and Σοφία which belong to his nature alone—are his intrinsic attributes. Contrary to the charges leveled at them, the Arians do not teach that God was ever without *his own* Word and Wisdom. Athanasius knows this, for he preserves their doctrine of the one Wisdom which is God's own and exists in him (τὴν ἰδίαν καὶ συνϋπάρχουσαν τῷ θεῷ), distinguishable from the Son, and their parallel doctrine of the Word, other than the Son, which is in God.[107] The accusation contained in Alexander's encyclical is correct: the Arians say that the Son "is neither similar to the Father in essence, nor is he truly and by nature (ἀληθινὸς καὶ φύσει) the Word of God, nor is he true (ἀληθινή) Wisdom. . . ."[108] On the basis of language in 1 Cor. 1:24, Asterius extends the Arian argument, stated more positively, to include God's power.

> For the blessed Paul did not say that he preached Christ, his [that is, God's] "own power" or "wisdom," but without the article, "God's Power and God's Wisdom" (1 Cor. 1:24), preaching that the power of God himself was distinct (ἄλλην), which was innate and existent with him unoriginately (τὴν ἔμφυτον αὐτῷ καὶ συνϋπάρχουσαν αὐτῷ ἀγενήτως), generative indeed of Christ, creative of the whole world, concerning which he teaches in his Epistle to the Romans, thus, "Ever since the creation of the world his invisible nature, namely

103

his eternal power and deity, has been clearly perceived in the things which were made" (Rom. 1:20). For as no one would say that the Deity mentioned there was Christ, but the Father himself, so, as I believe, his eternal power is also not the only-begotten God (John 1:18) but the Father who begot him. And he teaches us of another (ἄλλην) Power and Wisdom of God, namely, that which is revealed through Christ, and made known through the works themselves of his ministry (τῆς διακονίας).[109]

Important for our purposes here is Asterius' delineation of the Power and Wisdom which are intrinsic or innate (ἔμφυτος) to God.[110] He strives to underline the properties, the eternal attributes of the sovereign God, and to distinguish these from the derivative power and wisdom manifested in the savior. Asterius shares with Arius the suspicion that essentialist definitions of sonship threaten, among other things, to diminish or subtract from the Father. This is the precise force of Arius' remark to Alexander:

> The Father did not, when giving [the Son] the inheritance (κληρονομίαν) of all things, deprive (ἐστέρησεν) himself of those things which he has ingenerately in himself. For he is the source of all things.[111]

Drawn from Heb. 1:2b (which refers to God's appointed heir and creative agent), the image belongs to that set of Arian depictions of God which visualize personal interactions involving choice and performance. It is an image, like Arius' declaration about God's elevation and adoption of a certain one to the role and status of Son, which is transactional rather than genetic. The reminder that God retains his own reason, wisdom, and power may be viewed as a defensive measure by the Arians—a protection of God's enduring attributes and a warning against views of the Son's begetting which qualify the divine majesty or intimate its displacement to the Second Person of the Trinity. Theories of God's Word "articulated" (προφορικός), when framed aggressively in terms of shared essence or nature, could only suggest (despite all reassurances that divine paternity bore no resemblance to human) partition and depletion. More sharply than Justin, whose concepts and language stand behind his remarks, Arius combats views of the Son as God's Word which might result in confusion as to the "source of all things." The apologist had been willing to utilize the metaphor of fire kindled from fire when he spoke of the "beginning" God begot before all creatures by his will. Before quoting Prov. 8:21ff. in support of his argument, Justin tells us that this one called by several names (for example, "Glory of the Lord," "Son," "Wisdom," "Angel," "Word") was begotten in a way analogous to a word spoken by us, "but not by abscission, so as to lessen the reason in us, when we put it forth."[112] It is because of the invocation of essence language by the opposition that the Arians put the argument more stringently. God is diminished in no way by his bestowal of all things upon his designated creature, who is unlike him in essence and dependent upon his will for his existence and for such power and wisdom as he possesses. No theory of the Word issuing from God which obscures God's full sovereignty or the utter dependency of the Son is allowable. But the Arians' caution and critique is, in actuality, the obverse of what they advance as a positive and definite way of understanding how it is that the Son has gained his names and what these names signify about him.

Arius and his allies were fond of thinking and speaking of God's eternal Word, Wisdom, and Power (his inseparable properties) and of God's Son, who held the titles "Word," "Wisdom," and "Power." The distinction underlies Arius' statements that the Son sees God by the power (τῇ δυνάμει) with which God is able (δύναται) to see and that "Wisdom existed as Wisdom by the will of the wise God." This potentially confusing scheme has been characterized by G. C. Stead as a "two-level" theory of the Logos in which "terms such as 'wisdom' and 'logos' have two meanings, whereas 'Son' is presumably distinctive; the generated Logos is the Son, the ingenerate Logos is the inalienable possession of the Father."[113]

What the Arians intend to convey in their references to multiple Words, Wisdoms, and so forth, can be more fully elucidated in the reports of Alexander and Athanasius. Alexander tells us that Arian refusal to call the Son "truly and by nature" God's Word and Wisdom continues with the claim that

> . . . he is one of the things made (ποιημάτων) and produced (γενητῶν), but he is called Word and Wisdom inexactly (κατακρηστικῶς), since he himself came into being by God's own Word and by the Wisdom in God, in which God made not only all things, but him also.[114]

From the Athanasian account we learn the basis upon which, according to Arius' viewpoint, the Son has these designations. He says that Arius teaches that

> there is another Word in God besides the Son, and partaking (μετέχοντα) of this, the Son himself . . . is named by grace Word and Son.[115]

And the Arians dare to claim:

105

> The Word is not true God. But if he is called God, nevertheless he is not true [God]; but by participation of grace (μετοχῇ χάριτος), just as even all others, so he also is only called God by a title.[116]

It is not immediately apparent how these ideas could have helped to advance the cause of Arian Christianity. What purpose did they serve? In the Arian soteriology, as we saw above, the phrases "by grace" and "by participation" denoted a sonship by adoption, as opposed to "natural" sonship.[117] It is intriguing that these phrases also made possible the definition of the chief actors in the Arian account of the creation of the cosmos. The one possessing the names "Word," "Wisdom," and "Power" κατὰ χάριν or μετοχῇ or μετοχῇ χάριτος (the phrases are, in the debate, interchangeable) is identified as a creature, like others, of God's intrinsic Word, Wisdom, and Power. He is, by Arian categories of thought, a true creature of the paternal will; it is as a "partaker" of the Father's reason, skill, and might that he is capable of performing the works for which he has been called into being. Athanasius, of course, sees the matter differently. On his terms, Christians may choose to believe *either* in a son who is "true" (that is, from the Father's essence) *or* in a creature who is a son "by adoption (θέσει) and by participation (μετοχῇ) and in idea (κατ' ἐπίνοιαν)."[118]

Many of the sharpest edges of the debate between orthodoxy and Arianism are visible in the wrangle which surrounded the latter's desire to describe the Son's relationship to the Father as one of "participation." There can be no real doubt that Arians used and attached special significance to the terms μετέχειν, μετοχή, and μέτοχος. Beyond his report of this concept and its language in his summary of the *Thalia*, Athanasius attacks the idea with a vengeance at numerous other points in the *Orations* and takes pains to correct interpretations of biblical passages on the basis of which the Arians have developed their model of sonship μετοχῇ.[119]

A series of arguments registers Athanasius' protest. If the Son partakes of the Father, he says, it must be of the Father's essence, for in partaking of anything external to the Father, "this entity, whatever it is, [would be] found between the Father and the essence of the Son."[120] His argument, dictated by the concretizing tendencies of his substantialist viewpoint, contrives to make the thing partaken (like the "interval" and "precedent will" he extrapolated as consequences of other Arian tenets) an interruption of the coessential unity of Father and Son. In a deft but problematic counterproposal, Athanasius equates God's being "wholly participated" with his begetting and proceeds to argue that the Son *is* the essence of God of which all things partake "according to the grace of the Spirit coming from him."[121] Another ploy involves Athanasius' feigned confusion over how the Son, who through improvement and advance came *later*, as a man, to his divine status, could have been available as the Word to be partaken of by Moses and the illustrious saints of the earlier dispensation. Adoption and deification, as well as knowledge of God as Father, depend, he insists, upon one who is eternally "true" Son and, like the Father, unchangeable—he is the one through whom creatures receive sonship "by participation." Elsewhere the Arians are accused of distorting the "religious" meaning of Ps. 44:7 (LXX), with its declaration about the Son: "You have loved righteousness and hated lawlessness, therefore God, your God, has anointed you with the oil of gladness above your fellows (παρὰ τοὺς μετόχους)." The true Word, Radiance, and Wisdom of the Father is not to be grouped among the "fellows" or "partakers" mentioned by the psalmist; if he were one of the originate beings, then he too would be one of those who partake (εἷς . . . τῶν μετεχόντων).[122] Athanasius is obliged, in two other instances, to correct Arian exegesis. When Heb. 3:2 refers to the Son as "faithful," it indicates that he is the fitting recipient of our faith, not that he himself partakes of faith (οὐ πίστεως μετέχων) like believers who stand in need.[123] Likewise the Father is not "in the Son" (John 14:10) in the way that he visits saints to empower them, for the Son is God's own offspring, while creatures "are sanctified by participation of him in the Spirit (μετοχῇ τούτου ἐν Πνεύματι ἁγιάζεται)."[124] And to these attacks on the Arian understanding of sonship μετοχή we may add a provocative passage from the third *Oration*. In it Athanasius treats as a hypothetical Arian belief, as a deduction from their premises, what he knew they taught quite explicitly—namely that the Son "is called 'God' according to participation (κατὰ μετοχήν) just as also all the others."[125]

Committed to the proposition that it is not possible for the one who participates to give what he receives, orthodoxy must maintain that "the Son himself partakes of nothing, but what is partaken from the Father is the Son."[126] Against the Arian claim that the Son, like other creatures of God, partakes of the Creator's Word, Wisdom, and Power, they propose a divine Triad in which there is no partaking, but community and equality of essence—it is creatures who need to partake of God. The promise of Ps. 82:6 ("You are Gods") has no bearing on the consubstantial Son but was directed to believers, who "had this grace from the Father, only by participation of the Word, through the Spirit."[127] We meet in this formula yet another strategic defense of Alexander's inviolable principle that there is no real commonality between the sonship of the savior and the sonship of these who in saying "Abba" become the elect of God.

It is evident that Arian Christians relied upon an idea of the Son's partaking of God which was definite and forceful—at least sufficiently so to call forth a battery of rebuttals from the opposition. It would be good to know with more precision what they sought to convey in speaking of the one named "Word" and "Wisdom" μετοχῇ. The word and its derivatives were encountered with some frequency in the Septuagint and in the New Testament writings. Beyond the psalm passage in which Arians discerned a notice of the Son as one anointed from among other "partakers," there could be seen other references to "partaking"—of the law, of holy things and sacred meals, of actions good (education, fear of the Lord) and evil (idolatry, intermarriage, ritual pollution, attendance at games and exercise at the palaestra) and their consequences.[128] In the Epistle to the Hebrews, a favored resource for Arian exegetes, the idea appears in the quotation of Ps. 44:7 (LXX) in ethical contexts, in the claim that the steady confidence of believers makes them partakers of Christ, and in the proclamation that Christ partook (μετέσχεν) of the same flesh and blood as the children and brothers "he had to make like . . . in every respect."[129] None of these passages, however, suggests the precise point under consideration.

It has been tempting to search the philosophical and exegetical traditions for more exact correspondence to the Arian concept of participation in God. Special attention has centered in (1) the Platonic notion of the immanence of the "idea" in the "particulars," along with later Platonists' use of terms connoting participation "to express the connection and dependence between successive levels of reality,"[130] and in (2) the subordinationist theology of Origen, and his doctrine of the ἐπίνοιαι or θεωρήματα through which the Logos, though himself one, shares in the multiplicity of creatures.[131] Of the kinds of passages which suggest themselves, we may quote characteristic excerpts from Philo and from Origen. In the treatise *Allegorical Interpretation*, Philo writes of the "idea" of a particular and individual mind which exists before it as an archetype and paradigm. He continues,

Just so, before the individual objects of intellectual perception came into being, there was existing as a genus the "intellectually perceptible" itself, by participation in which the name has been given to the members of the genus (κατὰ μετοχὴν καὶ τὰ ἄλλα ὠνόμασται).[132]

He states in another work,

Of the power of reasoning God is not, indeed, partaker (οὐ μετέχει μεν . . . ὁ θεός) but originator, being the fountain (πηγή) of archetypal reason.[133]

Both in the connection made between participation and naming, and in the insistence that, as source, God himself does not partake, a resemblance to Arian thinking is visible. More closely parallel to their doctrine in content and language is a celebrated passage from Origen's *Commentary on John* in which the distinction is made between ὁ θεός and θεός:

It must be said that the God (ὁ θεός) is God-himself (αὐτόθεος), even as the savior said in the prayer to the Father, "that they may know you, the only true God" (John 17:3), and that everything which is outside of God-himself, being made God by participation of his divinity (μετοχῇ τῆς ἐκείνου θεότητος), could not be called *the* God (ὁ θεός), but God (θεός), which name belongs especially to "the firstborn of all creation" (Col. 1:15); being first by virtue of being next to God, drawing the divinity to himself, he is superior to other Gods of whom God is *the* God, as it is written, "The God of Gods, the Lord, has spoken and called the earth" (Ps. 49:1 [LXX]), assisting them to become Gods, and drawing from God abundantly the means by which they may be made divine and communicating it to them according to his own goodness. The God, then, is true (ἀληθινός) God; the others are Gods formed according to him as images of the prototype. But again, of the many images, the archetypal image is he who is with God, the Word, who was in the beginning because he was God always dwelling (ἀεὶ μένων) with God.[134]

The similarities are at once more extensive and more provocative. Even if Arius would have rejected the idea that the Son was "always dwelling" with God, he shared Origen's desire to mark clearly the sovereign position and status of the Father. We have noted already that John 17:3 is reflected in the definition of God in Arius' "confession of faith." Of particular interest to us is Origen's assertion that the firstborn is made God μετοχῇ in the Father's divinity—a concept apparently very much like the Arian belief that the Son is called God, though not "true," "by participation."

Not surprisingly, the writings of these two Alexandrian theologian-exegetes, both thoroughly at home in the Platonism of their era, have been thought likely influences upon the cosmological scheme of the Arians.

Enthusiasm for seeing kinship of ideas and terminology cannot be allowed, however, to obscure important differences and dissimilarities. And in fact, Arian resistance to one of the axiomatic assumptions of the philosophical tradition upon which Philo and Origen depend does more than merely qualify the parallels which are frequently drawn from these alleged precursors.

What is at issue here may best be stated in reference to Origen, though the same holds true for Philo and other Platonizing theologians or philosophers who might have been cited. The position of the Son in the cosmos as a mediator (through his multiple "aspects"), the designation of the Word as God's "image" (with its indebtedness to the doctrine of ideas), the notion of eternal begetting and the entire redemptive drama which Origen sketches—all of these depend upon a view of the universe which perceives living entities and their relationships in terms of communicated being, in terms of essence, which flows from God himself as if from a fountain. A specific result of this view, as Henri Crouzel has shown convincingly, is that for Origen the term μετοχή is indicative not of "participation" but of "communication"; to claim that the firstborn was made God μετοχῇ τῆς [τοῦ ἀληθινοῦ θεοῦ] θεότητος was to claim that "the Father and the Son possess a common nature, of which the Father is the origin and which he communicates to the Son."[135]

Nothing could have been farther from the thinking of Arius and Eusebius of Nicomedia. Whatever correspondences exist between Arian description of the Son's relationship to the Father and various "Middle" and "Neo-" Platonist accounts of the articulation of the universe by first and second Gods, or by the Existent and the demiurge, Arian churchmen departed in the most radical way from the prevalent view that the actions of God and the experience of humans could be recounted and understood in terms of shared οὐσία and communicated φύσις.[136] For this reason they used the word ἀμέτοχος to rule out any participation in *essence* between persons in the Trinity and to deny that the Son had a share in the unbegotten *nature*. It is worth noting in this connection that the Arians themselves did not, so far as we can tell, employ the word μετουσία when speaking of the Son's bond with the Father. It simply could not be for them, as it was for other writers of the period, including Athanasius, a synonym for μετοχή. "Things according to nature" and "things according to participation" were contrasted by the Stoics.[137] In the Arian controversy the categories have

110

become polar opposites. Consequently, Athanasius challenges the Arian portrait of the Son by pitting "true" (he means consubstantial) against θέσει and μετοχῇ, adoption and participation—both of which are understood as antitheses of sonship "by nature." We are safe in assuming that Arian Christians welcomed the inference that one who partakes is not the equal of the one partaken; the Son's participation in the Father marks him as a dependent being whose power, reason, and wisdom can only be derivative and relative. In speaking of sonship μετοχῇ, therefore, the Arians rejected any notion of ontic identity and relation.

But their primary purpose was to invoke another meaning which attaches to μετοχή in philosophical writings of the period—one which belongs to the realm of ethics. The Stoics gave particular sharpness to the idea by frequent references to "participation" in virtue or in vice and by making "virtue, or partaking of virtue (τὸ μετέχον ἀρετῆς)," equivalent with traditional descriptions of "the good life."[138] Stoic definitions of the good man as one who partakes of virtue and of goodness as actions which do the same are seen to be part of the working ethical vocabulary of late antique authors, non-Christian and Christian.[139] Themes in Philo can be taken as illustrative; God has no need for improvement (βελτίωσιν) and does not partake of anything outside himself, but instead imparts to others; aware of his own excellence and of creaturely weakness, God "wills not to dispense benefit or punishment according to his own power, but according to the measure of capacity which he sees in those who are to participate in either of those dispensations."[140] Dominant in this strain of Philonic thought is the vision of a God who deals with morally accountable creatures, each possessed of the capacity to partake of virtue.[141] In his analysis of Num. 28:2, Philo makes use of a distinction and terminology which bring us quite close to familiar Arian themes. He argues that "gifts" (δῶρα) which God bestows upon the perfect excel "grants" (δόματα) partaken by ascetics who are advancing (οἱ . . . ἀσκηταὶ οἱ προκόπτοντες).[142] The Christ of the Arians qualifies for both of Philo's categories: he is the creature whose perfection was achieved by discipline and moral advance.

The Arian doctrine of God's intrinsic Word and the Son named "Word" has a double purpose. It seeks to maintain the plenary and undiminished sovereignty of the Father, by whose Word, Wisdom, and Power the firstborn was brought into being and is enabled to do his Lord's bidding. Secondly, in their insistence that the Son holds his titles κατὰ χάριν and μετοχῇ, the

111

Arians underline their conviction that all relationship with the Father is adoptive, built upon the favor which he bestows upon those who, in pursuing virtue, cry "Abba" and come to know him. No different from other sons and daughters in this regard is the uniquely begotten Son; his creation is also election, and his status as the Father's beloved is, as in the case of the rest, an adoption which is "the reward of virtue." As in the minds of Arius and his allies no onus attached to the word "creature," neither did they count it a denigration of the Son to speak of his partaking of the Father, by which means he is empowered both to understand and accomplish the divine command. Sonship μετοχῇ is no inferior relationship. As far as Arian thinkers are concerned it is simply *the* mode of relationship which the Father has established between himself and those to whom he has given life. The firstborn of the creatures exercises his capacity to choose what is good. His unwavering obedience wins him preeminence among originate beings; as one who proves to be unchangeably and unalterably obedient, he is "a perfect creature of God, but not as one of the creatures."[143] He is nevertheless related to the Father in exactly the same manner as others and, as Asterius wrote, one among those dependent upon their master.[144] For Christians of Arian persuasion, the Son who was "faithful to him who appointed him" was both exemplar to, and one among, those holy brothers mentioned in Hebrews who are "partakers of the heavenly calling (κλησέως ἐπουρανίου μέτοχοι)."[145]

It needs to be asked whether the Arians took the commonality of the sonship of the "Word" and other creatures with such seriousness that they understood these created beings to possess, like the firstborn, their titles and favored status by grace and by participation. Such is the testimony of Athanasius, who reports their belief that

> . . . there are many powers; for the one [power] of God is his own by nature and eternal, but that of Christ, on the other hand, is not true power of God, but even he is one of those called "powers," of whom one also is pronounced not only "power" but "great power"—namely the locust and the caterpillar (cf. Joel 2:25). The others are many and like the Son, and about them also David speaks in the Psalms when he says, "Lord of the powers" (Ps. 24:10).[146]

Of scholarly reluctance to credit this Arian teaching G. C. Stead's recent work is typical. It is Athanasius, he argues, who makes Arius place "the heavenly Son within the homogeneous mass" of originate beings, while Arius thought instead of "a hierarchial Trinity . . . perfectly intelligible to anyone familiar with the Origenistic tradition."[147] In order to sustain this interpretation, however, it becomes necessary to read Arius' claim that "one equal to the Son the Superior is able to beget" in a wholly arbitrary way—namely, that though God could have created other sons, "he has not exercised this privilege."[148] No conclusion of this kind is compelled (or, we think, plausible) when the determinative Arian convictions about fatherhood and sonship are accorded their full weight. Because others share the creaturehood of the Son, they may be presumed also to partake of the Word, Wisdom, and Power which exists inalienably in the God who is source of all. And they too may be considered to be similar in disposition and power to the one who made them. Arians are arguing not for the stratification of the universe but for the dynamics of redemption whereby creatures, in emulation of the creature of perfect discipline, may be themselves begotten as equals to the Son. Athanasius preserves from the *Thalia* Arius' proposition that God is able to have sons like, though not more excellent than, the firstborn. There is no reason to assume that Arius thought this a divine option which had not been and would not be exercised; the real force of the statement resides in its assumption that morally free and changeable creatures might be responsive to the paternal will and be recipients of his saving favor. So at any rate Asterius seems to have thought, judging from his repeated declarations about the multiplicity of creatures who share title and service with the firstborn. The Reason of God is one, as is the Wisdom of God, but there are many things rational, wise, and beautiful; the Son is first of the originate beings, and one among the intellectual natures—like the sun among the phenomena, which illuminates at the command of the Maker, the Son enlightens other inhabitants of the intellectual world.[149] With more precision than Athanasius of Anazarba, who argued simply that Arius and his companions did nothing illegitimate in understanding the Son as one among the hundred sheep of the parable, Asterius teaches that many powers are created by God, of which Christ is πρωτότοκος and μονογενής. These powers, including the locust who worked God's punishment in Egypt, are invited to praise God by David, "who does not flinch from calling them servants of God, and instructs them to do [God's] will."[150] The burden of the evidence indicates that the assertion of the Son's fundamental identity with other creatures was from the beginning of the dispute axiomatic for Arian Christians, and that they "dated" this creaturehood of the Son not merely from his human ministry but from his beginning before the ages. We are also

113

justified in thinking that the concept of sonship by grace and participation, which defined the relationship of all creatures to God, impelled Arian spokesmen to speak of other beings who might lay claim, along with Christ, to such titles as "Word," "Wisdom," "Power," "Image," and "Glory."[151] Indeed, they thought the names applicable even to themselves, for they too expected to be in the company of those God willed to exalt and adopt as sons.

GOD'S SUBORDINATE:
THE PERFECT CREATURE

We sought in the first chapter to demonstrate how Arian exegetes were led to portray the redeemer Jesus as "the good person who partakes of virtue."[152] We turn now to their description of the Son as God's creative agent, "the beginning of his works," which does not depart from that characterization. Even in the exalted role of framer of the cosmos, the Son is perfect *creature*, and he acts under the limitations of his status as a being possessing derivative and dependent authority. As such, he stands in need of training and direction, and his glory consists in a subservience which ennobles rather than demeans.

Asterius tells us that the Son was created and made by the Father in his "beneficent liberality" and "superabundance of power."[153] Like a physician who possesses the skill of curing prior to his exercise of it, the Father had "anticipatory knowledge of the begetting (προϋπάρχουσαν . . . τὴν τοῦ γεννᾶν ἐπιστήμην)" which he brought to effect by his will and pleasure. So God acted, "willing to create originate nature," or to say the same thing, "willing to fashion us."[154] Of creatures only the Son was created by the Father acting alone, for the Father, foreknowing the glory he would acquire by his virtue, made this "certain one" and raised him to a position of favor. To say that the Son was μονογενής, then, carried dual but inseparable meanings: he was created by the Father directly, and as firstborn he was the beloved creature, honored "above his fellows."[155]

Arian accounts of God's initial work of creation emphasize both his freedom to act and the eternality of his attributes of knowledge and power. Beyond that, the effort is made to illustrate the ways in which the Father's relationship to the Son manifests the covenant of intention which has been struck between the Creator and all over whom he exercises his saving

114

sovereignty. There is no evidence that these thinkers, in describing the firstborn as the creative ὄργανον through whom the ages and the universe came into existence, sought by this way of speaking to degrade or dishonor the Son of God. It is said emphatically that the Father rules (ἄρχει) his elect Son, who submits (ὑπομένει) to him—no other view of the Father's and the Son's standing with each other was feasible, given the Arian understanding of the divine *modus operandi* and the voluntarist cast of their vision of dealings between characters in the divine drama.[156]

We noted earlier that Arians qualified the Son's power of perception and knowledge, which he had "in his measure." Reminders of his ignorance of the "hour" and his questioning of the Father from the cross were connected with the assertion that he was likewise incapable of comprehending either his Creator's essence or his own. Though Athanasius was sufficiently appalled by the suggestion that the Word, as Jesus, was one who "had to learn by inquiry," the Arian designation of the Son as learner was by no means restricted to his earthly ministry.[157] In the *Thalia* Arius taught that "God is wise, in that he is teacher of the Wisdom." The sense of the saying is not certain, since we are left in doubt whether it is the content or the recipient of the divine pedagogy which is being described. No ambiguity whatever surrounds Asterius' conception of the Son's identity as student:

> He is a creature and belongs to the things made. But he has learned (μεμαθήκε) to frame (δημιουργεῖν) as if at the side of a teacher and artisan (παρὰ διδασκάλου καὶ τεχνίτου), and thus he rendered service (ὑπηρέτησε) to the God who taught (διδάξαντι) him.[158]

The Son depends upon the Father for training whereby he will fashion the cosmos. It is learning which is acquired rather than natural, and the Arians presumably had no difficulty in thinking of increase in the Son's expertise. Describing the Son's training by the Father as a process, Asterius appears to be applying the Arian interpretation of Luke 2:52 to the Son's activity "before the ages": as God's creative assistant before the creation of the world, he "advanced in wisdom," becoming competent to discharge the command to create. This is precisely the conclusion reached by Athanasius, who quickly, on the basis of this Asterian doctrine, groups him among those who depict a Wisdom who makes progress toward wisdom.[159]

When Asterius speaks of the one called Son and Word as the necessary "medium" (μέσου) between "the untempered hand of the Father" and originate nature, he does not thereby intend to separate him from the many "powers" who are ministers of God and are taught to do his will.[160] Prominent in his teaching are the terms which express the unmistakably subordinate role of the πρωτότοκος and μονογενής. Arius reportedly took over from him the idea that the Son, calling other creatures into being, served in the capacity of "underworker and assistant (ὑπουργοῦ καὶ βοηθοῦ)." [161] The orthodox response to this line of reasoning is seen in Athanasius' second *Oration*. The first argument is in defense of God, and takes two forms: the Almighty is neither so wearied by ordering (προστάττων) that after the creation of the Son alone he needs assistance; nor is there such vanity (τῦφος) in God that rather than condescending himself, he sends an aide.[162] Secondly, Athanasius questions how, if the Word is himself creature, he withstood the "untempered hand of the Father," for by his presuppositions the Son's φύσις is determinative, not the excellence on account of which he was appointed to be God's instrument of creation. The basis of the attack is Athanasius' conviction that a creature is incapable of creating another creature since none of the things brought to be is an efficient cause.[163] The retort of the Arians is most provocative. They say,

> Behold, through Moses [God] led the people out of Egypt, and through him he gave the law, and yet he was man—so that it is possible for the like (τὰ ὅμοια) to be brought into being (γίνεσθαι) through the like (διὰ τοῦ ὁμοίου).[164]

Arians liken the creative activity of the Son to the work of Moses, the one under divine orders. "Bringing into being" or "creating" has less to do with genetic laws or ontological categories than with the willed actions of the sovereign God; and existence, by implication, is defined not by the "stable state" dictated by one's nature but by the events—each having its own "when" or ὅτε—which signal the creature's election into a relationship of promise.

What most troubled the orthodox spokesmen, in the end, was the portrait of the Son of God as an underworker and assistant, with its clear message that this creaturely Son was one "under orders" and thus obliged to bend his will to the purposes of his Master. Over against their claim that the Son was God's βουλή and that between Son and Father there were no negotiations, no "questioning and answer," stood the radically different Arian estimate of the Son:[165]

> By nature, as all others, . . . the Word himself is alterable, and remains good by his own free will, while he chooses.[166]

116

The servant's response to command, for early Arianism, is the chief element in the narrative of God's dealings with his anointed—it is just as centrally present in the account of the Son's activity as instrument of creation as in the drama of Jesus' ministry and passion. So the designations of him as slave (δοῦλος), servant (διάκονος), minister (ὑπηρέτης), and the like are pointed declarations of their vision of the way in which the two persons are related:[167]

> . . . what the Father wills, the Son wills also, and does not oppose either the purposes or judgments of the Father. Rather, he is in all respects in accord (ἐν πᾶσίν ἐστι σύμφωνος) with him, declaring the very same doctrines and a word consistent and united with the Father's teaching (διδασκαλία). It is in this way that he and the Father are one (cf. John 10:30).[168]

As framer of the cosmos, the agent of God's creation, the Son acts in the capacity of assistant (βοηθός) to his Father.[169] These works too are among those which belong ultimately not to him but to the one upon whom he depends—the Father who empowers him to participate in his purposes and judgments. A product of the paternal will, he abides in the Father, as John 14:10 teaches, by virtue, conforming his will to that of the Sovereign.[170]

The Son believed in by the Arians could only be a particular kind of mediator. It is incorrect to hold them responsible for a doctrine of Christ as a demi-God—the alleged *tertium quid*—who is neither fully God nor fully a creature. It is in fact Alexander whose language comes closest to this idea. He professes faith in the Son's only-begotten nature which stands in a middle position in the vast distance separating the unbegotten Father from those beings produced out of the nonexistent.[171]

Consistent with the assertion in 1 Tim. 2:5 that the mediator between God and man was the *man* Christ Jesus, the Arians proclaimed the μέσον of God's κτίσις to be a perfected κτίσμα. As one elect and anointed, he was recipient of the knowledge and power by which he undertook τὸ δημιουργεῖν; and as one who attained sonship by obedience to the commandments of his Father, he was the champion and exemplar of that adoption which awaited other creaturely partakers of the heavenly calling. Arius and his allies believed in a created Creator as well as a saved savior!

We have seen that central to the Arian understanding of salvation was the view that Christ attained his favor with God through the machinery of ethical advance and thus established a like goal for all true believers. This soteriology made Arian propaganda potentially appealing to the largest and

117

most influential group of strivers for perfection in the fourth century: the monks. The holy men of the desert were to tip the balance of power and dominate the Christian imagination for hundreds of years. The monk represents the earthly image of perfection for clergy and laity in both East and West. Would the perfect monk be painted in Arian or in orthodox brushstrokes?

With the Arian soteriology and cosmology exposed to view, Athanasius' *Life of Antony* becomes the locus of conflicting claims about the way of virtue and the nature of Christian redemption. It is to these conflicting claims that we must now turn.

NOTES

1. A notable exception, as indicated earlier, is C. W. Mönnich, "De Achtergrond van de arianse Christologie," *Nederlande Theologisch Tijdschrift* 4 (1950): 378–412. *Vide* also Maurice F. Wiles, *The Making of Christian Doctrine* (Cambridge: Cambridge University Press, 1967), pp. 95ff.; idem, "In Defense of Arius," *JThS* 13 (1962): 343ff.

2. See, for example, the doctrinal studies by A. C. McGiffert, *A History of Christian Thought* (New York and London: Charles Scribner's Sons, 1932–33); J. N. D. Kelly, *Early Christian Doctrines*⁴ (London: Adam & Charles Black, 1968); Bernhard Lohse, *A Short History of Christian Doctrine* (Philadelphia: Fortress Press, 1966); Bernard Lonergan, *The Way to Nicea,* trans. Conn O'Donovan (Philadelphia: Westminster Press, 1976). *Vide* also the historical treatments of Christianity and late antiquity by Henry Chadwick, *The Early Church* (Harmondsworth, England: Penguin Publishing Co., 1967); A. H. M. Jones, *The Decline of the Ancient World* (London: Longman, 1966); Robert M. Grant, *Augustus to Constantine* (New York: Harper & Row, Publishers, 1970); F. E. Peters, *The Harvest of Hellenism* (New York: Simon & Schuster, 1970); and Peter Brown, *The Word of Late Antiquity* (London: Thames & Hudson, 1971).

3. T. E. Pollard, "The Origins of Arianism," *JThS* 9 (1958): 103.

4. G. C. Stead, "The *Thalia* of Arius and the Testimony of Athanasius," *JThS* 29 (1978): 20.

5. Ibid., and see n. 19 *infra*.

6. Cf. Pollard, "Origins"; Wiles, "Defense"; H. A. Wolfson, "Philosophical Implications of Arianism and Apollinarianism," *Dumbarton Oaks Papers* 12 (1958); G. C. Stead, "The Platonism of Arius," *JThS* 15 (1964): 16–31; idem, "The Concept of Divine Substance," *VC* 29 (1975); idem, *"Thalia* of Arius"; F. Ricken, "Nikaia als Krisis des altchristlichen Platonismus," *Theologie und Philosophie* 44 (1969): 321–41; E. P. Meijering, "ΗΝ ΠΟΤΕ ΟΤΕ ΟΥΚ ΗΝ Ο ΥΙΟΣ; A Discussion on Time and Eternity," *VC* 28 (1974): 161–68; and É. Boularand, *L' Hérésie d'Arius et la*

"foi" de Nicée (Paris: Latouzey & Ané, 1972). Free of oversimple assumptions about exegetical "traditions" and "schools," Rowan Greer greatly advances our understanding of how orthodox and Arian thinkers made use of the Epistle to the Hebrews. *Vide* R. Greer, *The Captain of Our Salvation* (Tübingen: J. C. B. Mohr, 1973).

7. Heb. 6:9.

8. Beyond Arius' generalized references to his forebears in the faith, whom he calls "orthodox," "God-taught," and "elect" (Arius *Ep. ad Eus.* [Opitz³, Urk. 6, p. 12, lines 3–4] and Athanasius *Or. c. Ar.* 1.5 [Bright, p. 5]), there is the much-discussed reference to Lucian of Antioch which figures in G. Bardy's *Recherches sur Saint Lucien d'Antioche et son école* (Paris: Gabriel Beauchesne et ses fils, 1936) and the evidence that the Arians argued for the continuity of their teaching with that of Dionysius of Alexandria in Athanasius *De sententia Dionysii*.

9. See n. 6 *supra*. Since the early nineteenth century, the origins of Arius' ideas have been located in the writings of Plato, Aristotle, Philo, various "Middle Platonists," and the Christian "schools" of Alexandria and Antioch. In a recent survey of possible sources of Arian doctrine, É. Boularand attempts to straddle the latter two options. He suggests that Arius drew the *"formules-clés"* of his heresy from Alexandrian theology of the era of Bishop Dionysius while also inheriting from Antioch Lucian's exegetical method and Paul of Samosata's *monothéisme judaïsant*. *Vide* Boularand, *L'Hérésie d'Arius,* pp. 101–74.

10. Athanasius *De Syn.* 15 (Opitz², p. 242, lines 11–13).

11. Alexander *Ep. Encycl.* (Opitz³, Urk. 4b.9, p. 8, lines 6–7).

12. Arius *Ep. ad Eus.* (Opitz³, Urk. 1.2); Alexander *Ep. Encycl.* (Opitz³, Urk. 4b.7, p. 7, line 19), *Ep. ad Alex.* (Opitz³, Urk. 14.26, p. 23, lines 29–31); Athanasius *De Decr.* 3.6 (Opitz², p. 5, lines 23–26). Cf. Socrates *H.E.* 1.5.

13. Arius *Ep. ad Eus.* (Opitz³, Urk. 1.2, p. 2, line 2).

14. Both Arius and Eusebius of Nicomedia make the charge that their opponents teach two unbegotten beings, and Alexander of Alexandria registers that he has been so accused: Arius, *Ep. ad Alex.* (Opitz³, Urk. 6.4, p. 13, line 12 (δύο ἀγεννήτος ἄρχας); Eusebius of Nicomedia *Ep. ad Paulin.* 3 (Opitz³, Urk. 8, p. 16, line 1); and Alexander *Ep. ad Alex.* (Opitz³, Urk. 14.44, p. 26, lines 23–24). For the charges that orthodox propositions about the Father and the Son smack of Gnostic notions of "emanation" and "portion," see Arius *Ep. ad Alex.* (Opitz³, Urk. 6.3, p. 12, lines 10–11) and Eusebius *Ep. ad Paulin.* (Opitz³, Urk. 8.5, p. 16, lines 12–13).

15. *Vide* Arius *Ep. ad Eus.* (Opitz³, Urk. 1.2–4, pp. 1–2), *Ep. ad Alex.* (Opitz³, Urk. 6.2–4, pp. 12–13). There is attention to counterposing ideas of the two parties in the orthodox writings as well. The structure of Alexander's *Ep. ad Alex.* is (*a*) presentation of Arian belief, (*b*) rebuttal, then (*c*) defense against charges (with creedal statement). Athanasius in *Or. c. Ar.* 1.9 (Bright, pp. 9–10) juxtaposes a synopsis of the two theologies and concludes with a tightly drawn set of antitheses.

16. . . . ἦν ποτε ὅτε οὐκ ἦν ὁ Υἱὸς τοῦ θεοῦ: Alexander *Ep. ad Alex.* (Opitz³, Urk. 14.10, p. 21, line 8). *Vide* Socrates *H.E.* 1.5; Athanasius *Or. c. Ar.* 1.10, 11, 22; *De Decr.* 18; *Ep. ad Afros* 6.

17. Arius *Ep. ad Alex.* (Opitz³, Urk. 6.4, p. 13, lines 12–13). *Vide* also Athanasius *De Syn.* 15: "σύνες ὅτι ἡ μονὰς ἦν ἡ δυὰς δὲ οὐκ ἦν πρὶν ὑπάρξη." G. C. Stead, "Platonism of Arius," p. 19, qualifies his own suggestion that δυάς "is almost certainly uncomplimentary" by references to other possibilities—notably, that it is a synonym for δεύτερος θεός. His chief point, however, is that the use of the term μονάς does not necessarily indicate (as Pollard thinks) Arian preference for conceiving of God as an Absolute—that is, in philosophical rather than biblical terms.

18. Arius *Ep. ad Eus. (Opitz³, Urk. 1.2, p. 2, line 2).*

19. Arius *Ep. ad Eus.* (Opitz³, Urk. 1.4, 1.5, p. 3, lines 1, 3, 4); *Ep. ad Alex.* (Opitz³, Urk. 6.4, p. 13, lines 9–10); Athanasius *De Syn.* 15 (Opitz², p. 242, line 14 and p. 243, line 1); Alexander *Ep. ad Alex.* (Opitz³, Urk. 14.10, p. 21, lines 8–9); Alexander *Ep. Encycl.* (Opitz³, Urk. 4b.7, p. 7, lines 19–20); Athanasius *Or. c. Ar.* 1.5 (Bright, p. 5). G. C. Stead, *"Thalia* of Arius," using *De Syn.* 15 (with its elusive and problematic metrics) as a control for examining the testimony of Athanasius concerning Arius' teaching, is wary of the reported doctrines in *Or. c. Ar.* 1.5, though he acknowledges 1.6 contains a portion which, though not metrical, conforms closely in content and language to other known Arian utterances. The effort to gain criteria for assessing Athanasian reports is welcome, even if Stead's isolation of *De Syn.* 15 as the "centerpiece of this argument" is, as we think, not without difficulties. Some of these are important: first, because we do not have all of the *Thalia,* its excerpts cannot be assumed to set the limits on what this Arian piece taught—and other elements might well be thought to be contained in the reports of people like Alexander and Athanasius; secondly, it is clear that there was more to early Arian argumentation than the propositional assertions associated with the *Thalia*—specifically, the biblical texts advanced and fought for from an early point in the dispute. More serious still is Stead's desire to tighten Arius' identity as a subordinationist and theologian in the tradition of Origen and Middle Platonism. It must be asked whether narrowing the focus to *De Syn.* 15, and to particular emphases within it (Stead does not probe the importance of "changeability" there), does not make that identification easier to establish than it actually is. Is it because of his estimate of "the philosophical tradition presupposed by Arius" (Stead, "Platonism of Arius," p. 17) that Stead resists, for example, crediting Athanasius' persistent claim that Arius ranged the Son among the creatures ("within this homogeneous mass," p. 31)? Beyond the particular points of disagreement with Stead about the content of Arius' teaching within what he counts as reliable source material (to be treated in the notes following), there is a larger consideration which has to do with the historical phenomenon which we are calling "early Arianism." As an ecclesiastical and political reality, "early Arianism" cannot be reduced to or even defined by the verse of Arius and those ideas from other sources which concur with the portions of the *Thalia* which Athanasius chose to report in *De Synodis* 15. Arius wrote more than poetry, and there were more Arians than Arius—the ideas of Eusebius and Asterius were influential in the movement. Furthermore, signs of exegetical conflict mark the

earliest reports of the controversy, and the combated texts are numerous. And surely it is not insignificant that Alexander is aware of soteriological arguments advanced before Nicaea which do not appear in the same explicit form in *De Syn.* 15 (see chap. 2, pp. 63ff.).

20. Stead, *"Thalia* of Arius," p. 39.

21. Athanasius *De Syn.* 15 (Opitz², p. 243, line 2) and Arius *Ep. ad Eus.* (Opitz³, Urk. 1.3, p. 2, line 6) respectively. Cf. Athanasius *De Decr.* 3.6. See Stead's difficulty with the text in *De Syn.* 15, which can only mean that God's paternity is not eternal but "dates" from the generation of the Son (Stead, *"Thalia* of Arius," p. 29).

22. Alexander *Ep. Encycl.* (Opitz³, Urk. 4b. 7, p. 7, line 19). *Vide* also Athanasius *Or. c. Ar.* 1.9, where among the things he says his enemies advance from the *Thalia,* he recapitulates: "οὐκ ἀεὶ ὁ θεὸς Πατὴρ ἦν, ἀλλ᾽ ὕστερον γέγενον· οὐκ ἀεὶ ἦν ὁ Υἱὸς, οὐ γὰρ ἦν πρὶν γεννηθῇ."

23. Athanasius *De Decr.* 3.6 (Opitz², p. 6, lines 25-26). Alexander's line of reasoning is seen in *Ep. ad Alex.* (Opitz³, Urk. 14.26, p. 23, lines 28–29): it is necessary to hold that the Father is forever Father (τὸν πατέρα ἀεὶ εἶναι πατέρα). Since the Son is eternally with the Father, on which account he has the name of Father, the Father is ever perfect (ἀεὶ . . . τέλειος), lacking nothing good (which Fatherhood is).

24. Athanasius *Or. c. Ar.* 1.14 (Bright, p. 15).

25. Athanasius *De Syn.* 15 (Opitz², p. 243, lines 20–21). Note the mistranslation in NPNF version.

26. Athanasius *Or. c. Ar.* 1.22 (Bright, p. 24). *Vide* also Asterius frg. XXV (Bardy, *Lucien,* p. 351).

27. *Vide* chap. 1, p. 9 and n. 43. The pertinent text is Athanasius *De. Decr.* 3.6 (Opitz², p. 6, lines 15–20). Cf. Athanasius *Or. c. Ar.* 2.4 (Bright, pp. 71–72).

28. Arius *Ep. ad Alex.* (Opitz³, Urk. 6.5, p. 13, lines 15–16).

29. Athanasius *Hom. in Mt. 11:27* 1 (Migne PG 25, 209). Athanasius' argument is that the text refers not to dominion over creation but to the incarnation.

30. Eusebius *Ep. ad Paulin.* 6 (Opitz³, Urk. 8.6, p. 16, lines 15–18).

31. Asterius frg. IIa (Bardy, *Lucien,* p. 342).

32. Asterius frg. XIII (Bardy, *Lucien,* p. 346).

33. Athanasius *Or. c. Ar.* 3.6 (Bright, p. 159). *Vide* also *De Syn.* 48.3 (Opitz², p. 272, lines 29–30): "ἡ δὲ οὐσία αὕτη τῆς οὐσίας τῆς πατρικῆς ἐστι γέννημα καὶ ὁμοιότης αὐτῆς ὥσπερ καὶ τὸ ἀπαύγασμα τοῦ φωτός." See also Athanasius *Or. c. Ar.* 1.17.

34. Athanasius *De Decr.* 3.6 (Opitz², p. 6, lines 3ff.).

35. Alexander *Ep. ad Alex.* (Opitz³, Urk. 14.29, p. 24, lines 8–12).

36. Ibid.

37. Athanasius *De Decr.* 5.22 (Opitz², p. 19, lines 4–8).

38. Arius *Ep. ad Eus.* (Opitz³, Urk. 1.5, p. 3, line 3).

39. Pollard, "Origins," p. 104.

40. Stead, "Platonism of Arius," p. 19.

41. Athanasius *De Sent. Dionys.* 17 (Opitz², p. 59, lines 24–25). In *De Decr.* 26 (Opitz², p. 22, lines 6ff.) Dionysius of Rome is reported to have complained of those who divide τὴν ἁγίαν μονάδα into three hypostases foreign to each other, and to have warned against partitioning τὴν θαυμαστὴν καὶ θείαν μονάδα into three Godheads.

42. Athanasius *Hom. in Mt. 11:27*6 (NPNF translation): "For the Triad, praised, reverenced and adored, is one and indivisible without degrees. It is united without confusion, just as the Monad also is distinguished without separation." And *Or. c. Ar.* 1.17 (*NPNF* translation): ". . . for if the Word is not with the Father from everlasting, the Triad is not from everlasting; but a Monad was first, and afterward by addition it became a Triad . . . ; if the Son is not proper offspring of the Father's essence, but of nothing has come to be, then of nothing the Triad consists, and once there was not a Triad, but a Monad."

43. Athanasius *De Syn.* 15 (Opitz², p. 243, line 1).

44. Stead, "Platonism of Arius," p. 19.

45. Ibid.

46. Ibid. Stead himself notes this possibility, and says Arius may have "simply used δυάς as a synonym for the more familiar δεύτερος (θεός), *metri gratia.*"

47. Arius *Ep. ad Alex.* (Opitz³, Urk. 6.2, p. 12, lines 4–7).

48. Arius' letter to Eusebius of Nicomedia, like Alexander's encyclical and his epistle to his namesake in Constantinople, develops their claims, charges, and defenses within this creedal sequence, which first treats God the Father and then the Son.

49. G. C. Stead pointed to the presence of five scriptural phrases but did not pursue their significance. See Stead, "Platonism of Arius," p. 17.

50. As of course Arius makes explicit in the words "God of the law and prophets and the New Testament."

51. *Vide* Alexander *Ep. ad Alex.* (Opitz³, Urk. 14.56, p. 27, line 27, through p. 29, line 2).

52. Athanasius *De Syn.* 15 (Opitz², p. 242, lines 19–20). See also Alexander *Ep. Encycl.* (Opitz³, Urk. 4b.8) and Athanasius *Or. c. Ar.* 1.6 (Bright, p. 6).

53. Designation of God as "judge of all" (πάντων κριτήν) may well draw upon Heb. 12:23, which speaks of the believers' approach to "the assembly of the first-born (πρωτοτόκων) who are enrolled in heaven," and "to a judge who is God of all (κριτῇ θεῷ πάντων) and to the spirits of just men made perfect, and to Jesus the mediator of a new covenant (διαθήκης νέας)."

54. See pp. 5–6, 13–30, 53–57 *supra.*

55. Arius *Ep. ad Eus.* (Opitz³, Urk. 1.4, p. 2, line 9, through p. 3, line 3); *Ep. ad Alex.* (Opitz³, Urk. 6, p. 12, lines 8–9); Eusebius *Ep. ad Paulin.* (Opitz³, Urk. 8, pp. 16–17); Athanasius *De Syn* 15 (Opitz², p. 243, lines 3, 11).

56. Athanasius *Or. c. Ar.* 3.59 (Bright, p. 212).

57. Athanasius *Or. c. Ar.* 3.62 (Bright, p. 215).

58. Athanasius *Or. c. Ar.* 3.60 (Bright, p. 213).

59. Athanasius *Or. c. Ar.* 1.12, 14 (Bright, pp. 13, 16). In Alexander *Ep. ad Alex.* (Opitz³, Urk. 14.23–24, p. 23, lines 15–22), the bishop argues that the "interval" (διάστημα) during which the Arians say the Son "still unbegotten of the Father was prior to the Wisdom of God, by whom all things were created" (*NPNF* translation). The charge misunderstands (intentionally or not) the Arian view according to which the Wisdom intrinsic to God is eternal, while the one "called 'wisdom' by participation (μετοχῇ)" has a beginning. "Wisdom," or the Son, precedes the beings for whose creation he was made. It seems likely that the argument concerning a διάστημα was less the reason for Arian development of a "Logos theology" than a complaint resulting from its advocacy. But here, as elsewhere, it is not an easy matter to uncover the sequence of elements in the debate.

60. Athanasius *Or. c. Ar.* 3.60 (Bright, p. 213).

61. Justin *Dial.* 127;61; 128 (*ANF* translation). The passages hold interest for us on several counts. The first mentions that the Son "ministered to his [that is, God's] will," employing a form of ὑπηρετέω (see note 167 *infra*). *Dial.* 61 is taken up with an interpretation of Prov. 8:22, which Justin (like Arius, and unlike Athanasius) understands to refer to the origination of the Son before all creatures. In the final text we see Justin's insistence that the one called "God" and "Angel" (that is, the Word) is indeed "numerically distinct" from the Father who begot him "by his power and will."

62. Hippolytus *Noët.* 16; Clement *Prot.* 10, *Strom.* 5.1; Origen *De Prin.* 4.4.1.

63. Asterius, frg. XV (Bardy, *Lucien*, pp. 346–47). Athanasius (in *Or. c. Ar.* 3.60, in which the Asterian remark is found) argues that the Arians seek to establish a precedent (προηγουμένην) will, like Ptolemy. This important section of the third *Oration* includes the insistence that "the Son is by nature and not by will" (*Or. c. Ar.* 3.66), and that as a category "nature" transcends "willing." We note, however, that Asterius has called "willing" τὸ κρεῖττον.

64. Athanasius *De Decr.* 10.5 (Opitz², p. 9, lines 23–24). *Vide* also Athanasius' reference (in *Or. c. Ar.* 3.65) to God's possession of ἕξις (*habitus*).

65. See above, pp. 15–18.

66. Asterius, frg. XVIII (Bardy, *Lucien*, p. 348).

67. Eusebius *Ep. ad Paulin.* (Opitz³, Urk. 8.3, p. 16, lines 1–2). In Arius *Ep. ad. Alex.* (Opitz³, Urk. 6.5, p. 13, lines 15–20) we read: "So far then as he has existence and [the] glories and [the] life from God, and all things have been delivered to him (Matt. 11:27//Luke 10:22), in this sense God is his origin. For he rules him as being his God, and as being before him. But if the terms 'from him' and 'from the womb' and 'I came forth from the Father, and I am come' (Rom. 11:36; Ps. 109:3 [LXX]; John 16:28) are understood by some to mean as a part of him, one-in-essence, or as an emanation, then the Father is synthetic and divisible and changeable and body, the incorporeal God suffering the somatic consequences, as far as their belief goes."

68. Athanasius *Or. c. Ar.* 3.62 (Bright, p. 215), *NPNF* translation.

69. Athanasius *Or. c. Ar.* 3.57 (Bright, p. 209).

70. Arius *Ep. ad Eus.* (Opitz³, Urk. 1.4, p. 3, line 3). The repeated ἤτοι between the verbs suggests that for Arius the terms are virtually interchangeable.

71. Athanasius *Or. c. Ar.* 1.5 (Bright, p. 5).

72. Alexander *Ep. Encycl.* (Opitz³, Urk. 4b.9, p. 8, lines 5–6).

73. Athanasius *De Syn.* 15 (Opitz², p. 242, lines 14–15).

74. We find ourselves in total disagreement with Pollard ("Origins," p. 104), who remarks that Arianism "had no conception of a God who acts in history in creation, election, self-revelation, redemption, and sanctification." Even if the documents of the controversy did not contain evidence to controvert his statement, historians would be taxed to explain how the movement—assuming his description to be accurate—could have presented the slightest appeal to Christians who can be assumed to have continued in worship, exposure to scripture, and the like.

75. Athanasius *Or. c. Ar.* 1.5 (Bright, p. 5).

76. Asterius, frg. VI (Bardy, *Lucien,* p. 344), and Athanasius *Or. c. Ar.* 1.5 (Bright, p. 5).

77. Arius *Ep. ad Alex.* (Opitz³, Urk. 6.3, p. 12, line 10, through p. 13, line 6).

78. Arius *Ep. ad Alex.* (Opitz³, Urk. 6.4, p. 13, lines 10–12), and Athanasius *De Syn.* 15 (Opitz², p. 242, line 17).

79. Arius *Ep. ad Alex.* (Opitz³, Urk. 6.3, p. 13, line 1).

80. Arius *Ep. ad Alex.* (Opitz³, Urk. 6.4, p. 13, line 12).

81. Athanasius *Or. c. Ar.* 1.6 (Bright, p. 6) and *De Syn.* 15. (Opitz², p. 242, line 16). The translation "proper subsistence" is from *NPNF.*

82. Athanasius *De Syn.* 15 (p. 242, lines 24–26) and *Or. c. Ar.* 1.6 (Bright, p. 6).

83. Arius *Ep. ad Alex.* (Opitz³, Urk. 6.4, p. 13, line 10). *Vide* Athanasius *Or. c. Ar.* 1.7 (Bright, p. 7).

84. Athanasius *De Syn.* 15 (Opitz², p. 243, lines 11, 19).

85. Eusebius *Ep. ad Paulin.* (Opitz³, Urk. 8.7–8, p. 17, lines 4–6).

86. Some such distinction seems to be indicated by the unexpected term ἐκουσιασμόν, with its connotations of a freewill offering.

87. Athanasius *Or. c. Ar.* 1.6 (Bright, p. 6). Stead's desire to fit Arius' doctrine into a Platonic scheme leads him to downplay Arius' own insistence that the Son was one of the creatures. But it is Alexander, as we see (Opitz³, Urk. 14.44–45, p. 26, lines 20 26), who tries to position the Son as mediator between Deity and humanity. Furthermore, though Stead argues that "Athanasius wants to represent Arius as teaching that the Son is merely part of the created order," we note that Alexander reports the idea on more than one occasion (Opitz³, Urk. 14.4, p. 20, lines 5–10, and Urk. 14.17, p. 22, lines 13–15). Arius himself states that the Son is κτίσμα and belongs to that order of being. The qualification that, though a creature, he is not as one of the creatures is a statement about the Son's preeminence on account of his virtue (as we have argued) and cannot be made to suggest an ontic "middle ground" of the sort Stead is inclined to hypothesize. See Stead, "*Thalia* of Arius," pp. 24ff.

88. Eusebius *Ep. ad Paulin.* (Opitz³, Urk. 8.3–4, p. 16, lines 2–12).

89. *Vide* Theodoret *E.H.* 1.5 (translation in *NPNF,* Second Series, vol. 3, p. 42).

90. Eusebius' idea of "perfect likeness" is meant to counter such formulas as Alexander's concept, grounded in substantialist thinking, of the Son's "exact likeness (ἐμφέρειαν) in all things to the form and impress of the Father" (Opitz³, Urk. 14.53, p. 28, lines 5–7). Alexander's description of the Son as εἰκών . . . ἀπαράλλακτος of the Father (Opitz³, Urk. 14.47, p. 27, line 15) is not at all similar in meaning, despite verbal correspondence, to the remark attributed to Asterius (in Eusebius of Caesarea C. Marc. 1.4.33). For Asterius the emphasis falls on the image as distinct from the archetype, and his thinking is analogous to that which led later Arians to agree to certain formulas involving the terms ὅμοιος and ὁμοιούσιος. His teaching is reported as follows: "For the Father who begot out of himself the only-begotten Word and firstborn of all creation is of another sort; one only begot one only; perfect begot perfect; king begot king, lord begot lord, God begot God; he begot an identical image of the substance and will and glory and power (οὐσίας τε καὶ βουλῆς καὶ δόξης καὶ δυνάμεως ἀπαράλλακτον εἰκόνα)"—in Asterius frg. XXI (Bardy, Lucien, p. 349). Despite Asterius' conviction that the phrase involved no compromise of the distinction between the Father and Son, the Arian historian Philostorgius (H.E. 2.15) complained that this amounted to a betrayal of the party's cause.

91. Athanasius De Syn. 15 (Optiz², p. 242, line 22).

92. Philo De cher. 30; Athanasius Or. c. Ar. 2.4 (Bright, p. 72).

93. Aristotle Metaphysics 5.19 (translation from Loeb Classical Library).

94. Eusebius Ep. ad Paulin. (Opitz³, Urk. 8.8, p. 17, line 7).

95. Ep. ad Eus. (Opitz³, Urk. 1.2, p. 1, line 6).

96. Athanasius V. Anton. 77.

97. Philo De conf. ling. 9; De spec. leg. 2.9 (translation from Loeb Classical Library).

98. Plutarch De virt. mor. c. 3 p. 441c (SVF 1, p. 49, no. 202).

99. J. M. Rist, Stoic Philosophy (Cambridge: Cambridge University Press, 1969), p. 3.

100. Ibid., pp. 3–4.

101. Eusebius Ep. ad Paulin. (Opitz³, Urk. 8.6, p. 16, line 15, through p. 17, line 1).

102. Athanasius Or. c. Ar. 1.19–20 (Bright, pp. 20–22).

103. Athanasius Or. c. Ar. 1.5 (Bright, p. 5).

104. Athanasius Or. c. Ar. 1.5–6 (Bright, pp. 5–6).

105. Eusebius Ep. ad Paulin. (Opitz³, Urk. 8.3, p. 16, line 3) and Athanasius De Syn. 15 (Opitz², p. 243, line 19).

106. E.g. Athanasius Or. c. Ar. 1.9, 1.28, and 3.9 (Bright, pp. 9, 27–28, and 163). See Alexander Ep. ad Alex. (Opitz³, Urk. 14.32, p. 24, line 25), which refers to "τὴν . . . γνησίαν αὐτοῖ καὶ ἰδιότροπον καὶ φυσικὴν καὶ κατ' ἐξαίρετον υἱότητα."

107. Athanasius Or. c. Ar. 1.5 (Bright, p. 5).

108. Alexander Ep. Encycl. (Opitz³, Urk. 4b.7, p. 7, lines 21–24).

109. Asterius, frg. I (Bardy, Lucien, pp. 341–42).

110. On the meanings of ἔμφυτος see G. W. H. Lampe, *A Patristic Greek Lexicon* (Oxford: Clarendon Press, 1961), p. 459. Here Asterius refers to the "inborn" or "innate" properties peculiar to God. Cf. Arius *Ep. ad Eus.* (Opitz³, Urk. 1.2, p. 1, line 5).

111. Arius *Ep. ad Alex.* (Opitz³, Urk. 6.4, p. 13, lines 5–6).

112. Justin *Dial.* 61; 128.

113. Stead, "Platonism of Arius," p. 20. Stead is certainly right in speaking of the double application of "Word" and "Wisdom" to the Unbegotten and to the firstborn, but the Arian use of the term "Son" is more complex than he suggests. Though clearly "Son" is not an inalienable attribute of the Father and cannot be referred to him, it too (according to Athanasius) is one of the names (along with "Word," "Wisdom," "Power," "God") given to the first creature (see n. 115 *infra*). Athanasius may be extending the series of titles beyond those specified by the Arians themselves, but even if that is the case, we know that the term "Son" was not reserved for a single being. In Arian thinking it was a term equally appropriate for the firstborn and for other adopted creatures related to the Father in the same way.

114. Alexander *Ep. Encycl.* (Opitz³, Urk. 4b.7, p. 7, line 24, through p. 8, line 2).

115. Athanasius *Or. c. Ar.* 1.5 (Bright, p. 5).

116. Athanasius *Or. c. Ar.* 1.6 (Bright, p. 6).

117. *Vide supra,* chap. 2, pp. 55–58.

118. Athanasius *Or. c. Ar.* 1.9 (Bright, p. 10).

119. Athanasius *Or. c. Ar.* 1.9, 15, 16, 28, 39, 46, 56; 2.9, 37–38. For μετουσία see *Or. c. Ar.* 3.1, 6, 15, 51. Athanasius employs μετουσία, κοινωνία, and forms of μεταλαμβάνω as synonyms for μετέχω and its derivatives. The Arians, we may assume, were more cautious. See *infra,* pp. 110–11ff.

120. Athanasius *Or. c. Ar.* 1.15 (Bright, p. 17).

121. Athanasius *Or. c. Ar.* 1.16 (Bright, p. 17).

122. Athanasius *Or. c. Ar.* 1.46 (Bright, pp. 47–48). Athanasius insists (*Or. c. Ar.* 1.56), in his treatment of Heb. 1:4, that "things originate cannot be called generate, God's handiwork as they are, except so far as after their making they partake of the generate Son, and are therefore said to have been generated also, not at all in their own nature, but because of their participation of the Son in the Spirit" (*NPNF* translation). Stead appears to misconstrue the importance to Athanasius of the formula μετοχῇ τοῦ Λόγου διὰ τοῦ Πνεύματος in the treatment of Ps. 82:6, for in *Or. c. Ar.* 1.9 Athanasius gives *his,* not the Arians', interpretation. See Stead, "*Thalia* of Arius," p. 37.

123. Athanasius *Or. c. Ar.* 2.9 (Bright, p. 77).

124. Athanasius *Or. c. Ar.* 3.1 (Bright, p. 155).

125. Athanasius *Or. c. Ar.* 3.15 (Bright, p. 169). *Vide* Athanasius *Or. c. Ar.* 1.9; Alexander *Ep. ad Alex.* (Opitz³, Urk. 14.11ff., pp. 21ff.). *Vide supra,* chap. 2, pp. 56–57, 67.

126. Athanasius *Or. c. Ar.* 1.16 (Bright, p. 17). *Vide* Athanasius *De Syn.* 51 (NPNF translation, altered): ". . . if . . . the Son is not such by participation, but

while all things originated have by participation the grace of God, he is the Father's Wisdom and Word of which all things partake, it follows that he, being the deifying and enlightening power of the Father . . . is not alien in essence from the Father, but coessential. For by partaking of him, we partake of the Father; because the Word is the Father's own. Whence, if he was himself also from participation, and not from the Father his essential Godhead and Image, he would not deify, being himself deified. For it is not possible that he who merely possesses from participation should impart of that partaking to others, since what he has is not his own, but the giver's; and what he has received is barely the grace sufficient for himself." See also Athanasius *Or. c. Ar.* 1.9 (Bright, p. 10).

127. Athanasius *Or. c. Ar.* 1.9 (Bright, p. 9).

128. *Vide* Wisd. of Sol. 19:16; 1 Esd. 5:40; 1 Cor. 10:17; Ecclus. 51:28 and Heb. 12:7–8; Ps. 118:63 (LXX); Hos. 4:17; 1 Esd. 8:70; 2 Macc. 4:14 and 5:27; Prov. 1:18; 29:10; Esther 8:13.

129. Heb. 5:13; 12:7–8; 3:14; 2:14.

130. David L. Balas, ΜΕΤΟΥΣΙΑ ΘΕΟΥ, *Studia Anselmia* fasc. LV (Rome: Libreria Herder, 1966), p. 5.

131. Stead, "*Thalia* of Arius," pp. 34ff.

132. Philo *Leg. Alleg.* 1.22 (9) (Loeb Classical Library translation).

133. Philo *Quod det. potiori* 82(27) (Loeb Classical Library translation).

134. Origen *Jo.* 2.17–18 (SC, pp. 216–18).

135. H. Crouzel, *Théologie de l'image de Dieu* (Paris: Aubier, 1956), p. 110, quoted in T. E. Pollard, *Johannine Christology and the Early Church,* Society for New Testament Studies, Monograph Series 13 (Cambridge: Cambridge University Press, 1970), p. 94.

136. Though he was clearly a subordinationist of Origenist sympathies, Eusebius of Caesarea seems to be in close proximity to the essentialist thinking of Athanasius. For example, he writes in *H.E.* 1.3.13 that Jesus Christ, unlike other anointed prophets and kings, "has received the oil, not that prepared of material substances, but the oil of the Divine Spirit as befits his divinity, by his participation in that divine nature which is unbegotten and of the Father (ἀλλ' αὐτὸ δὴ πνεύματι θείῳ τὸ θεοπρεπές, μετοχῇ τῆς ἀγεννήτου καὶ πατρικῆς θεότητος ἀπείληφει)." He, nearly as much as Alexander and Athanasius, was at odds with the position expressed by Eusebius of Nicomedia in his letter to Paulinus.

137. Stobaeus *ecl.* 2.82 (*SVF* 3, p. 34, no. 141). *Vide* H. Hanse, "Metechō," *Theologisches Wörterbuch zum Neuen Testament* (Stuttgart: W. Kolhammer, 1935), 2:830–32. Philo, in *De opif. mund.* 73 (24), describes plants and animals as existences which "partake neither of virtue nor of vice" and proceeds to speak of other beings which "have partnership (κεκοινώηκεν) with virtue only and have no part or lot (ἀμέτοχα) in vice" (Loeb Classical Library translation).

138. *SVF* 3, p. 6, no. 16; p. 17, no. 70; p. 19, no. 76.

139. Diogenes Laertius VII.94; Clement *Strom.* IV.6 (concerning things which

partake of the goods—that is, τὰς καλὰς πράξεις). Also, *SVF* 3, p. 27, no. 114; p. 19, no. 76.

140. Philo *De cherub.* 86 (25); *Quod Deus sit immut.* 80 (17) (translation from Loeb Classical Library).

141. *Vide* Philo *Leg. Alleg.* 3.1.

142. Philo *Leg. Alleg.* 3.70.

143. Arius *Ep. ad Alex.* (Opitz³, Urk. 6.2, p. 12, lines 9–10). On Stead's treatment of this idea in "*Thalia* of Arius," pp. 30–31, see *supra*, n. 19.

144. *Vide* n. 31 *supra*.

145. Heb. 3:1.

146. Athanasius *Or. c. Ar.* 1.5 (Bright, p. 5). See also Athanasius *De Decr.* 16 (Opitz², p. 13, lines 18ff.).

147. Stead, "*Thalia* of Arius," pp. 31, 30.

148. Ibid., p. 30.

149. Asterius, frgs. XI, III (Bardy, *Lucien*, pp. 345, 343).

150. Asterius, frg. IIa (Bardy, *Lucien*, pp. 342–43).

151. *Vide* Athanasius *Ep. ad Afros* 5, which is a parallel account of the events described in *De Decr.* 20 (Opitz², pp. 16–17).

152. Asterius, frg. V (Bardy, *Lucien*, p. 344). Cf. Philo *De Opif. mund.* 21–23 and *Leg. Alleg.* 3.78.

153. Asterius, frg. IV (Bardy, *Lucien*, p. 343). Though Arius argued that before the Son's existence God was not [a] Father, Asterius' remark seems to provide for a "science" of paternity or generation prior to the generation itself. The ἐπιστήμη or intellective power of the God is safeguarded by distinguishing it from the Son (whom some identify as "Logos" in a way which seems to deny the "true" Reason which is God's own attribute). Here the prominent theme has to do with divine forethought and foreknowledge directed to the genesis of the Son. Methodius speaks of the divine ἐπιστήμη which led God to create (in *Arbit.* 22 and also in *Creat.* 6).

154. Asterius, frg. VIII (Bardy, *Lucien*, p. 344): θέλων ὁ θεὸς τὴν γενητικὴν κτίσαι φύσιν, and Athanasius *Or. c. Ar.* 1.5 (Bright, p. 5): θελήσας ἡμᾶς δημιουργῆσαι.

155. Arius *Ep. ad Alex.* (Opitz³, Urk. 6.4, p. 13, line 10), Asterius, frg. VIII(b) (Bardy, *Lucien*, p. 344), and Gregg and Groh, pp. 276–78.

156. Arius *Ep. ad. Alex.* (Opitz³, Urk. 6.5, p. 13, lines 15–16), and Athanasius *De Syn.* 15 (Opitz², p. 242, line 23).

157. Athanasius *Or. c. Ar.* 3.27 (Bright, p. 182).

158. Asterius, frg. IX (Bardy, *Lucien*, p. 345).

159. Athanasius *Or. c. Ar.* 2.28 (Bright, p. 97).

160. Asterius, frg. VIII (Bardy, *Lucien*, p. 344).

161. Asterius, frg. VIII(b) (Bardy, *Lucien*, p. 344).

162. Athanasius *Or. c. Ar.* 2.24 (Bright, p. 93).

163. Athanasius *Or. c. Ar.* 2.26 (Bright, p. 95).

164. Athanasius *Or. c. Ar.* 2.27 (Bright, pp. 95–96).

165. Athanasius *Or. c. Ar.* 2.31 (Bright, p. 100).

166. Athanasius *Or. c. Ar.* 1.5 (Bright, p. 6).

167. See the use of ὑπηρετέω and ὑπηρέτης in Justin *Dial.* 57.3, 61.1; Origen *Hom. 20.1 in Jerem.* (Migne PG 13 500D); Philostorgius *H.E.* 9.14 and 6.2. For the sharp statement of the Son's role as one who does as commanded, *vide* Hippolytus *c. Noët* 14.

168. Asterius, frg. XIV (Bardy, *Lucien,* p. 346). *Vide* Origen *c. Cels.* 8.12; Theodore Mopsuestia *fr. in Jo.* 5.19 (Migne PG 66 744B). The symbol of Antioch in 341 spoke of "three in *hypostasis,* but one in concord," and the idea of συμφωνία figured at the Council of Sardica, as we learn from Theodoret (*H.E.* 2.8.45). Athanasius comments on John 10:30 and 14:9 in *De Syn.* 48: "Now as to its [i.e., the union] consisting in agreement of doctrines, and in the Son's not disagreeing with the Father, as the Arians say, such an interpretation is a sorry one, for both the saints, and still more angels and archangels have such an agreement with God, and there is no disagreement among them" (*NPNF* translation). Asterius' endorsement of this kind of moral union between Father and Son is attested also in frg. XXXII (Bardy, *Lucien,* p. 352), and in fragments 73 and 74 of Marcellus (GCS 4, pp. 198–200).

169. Asterius, frg. VIII(b) (Bardy, *Lucien,* p. 344).

170. Asterius, frg. XIII (Bardy, *Lucien,* p. 346).

171. Alexander *Ep. ad Alex.* (Opitz[3], Urk. 14.44–45, p. 26, lines 20–29).

4

Claims on the
Life of St. Antony

PERCEPTIONS OF ANTONY

There are differences, as H. Dörries pointed out nearly thirty years ago, between the Antony who speaks and is spoken of in *Verba Seniorum* and the Antony who is featured in the *Vita Antonii,* that work of profound and enduring influence which, if not Athanasian, was written by someone never out of the Alexandrian bishop's earshot.[1] If it were possible to be confident in the former work about the connection of these pieces of desert wisdom and lore to particular personages, and if their collection could be more precisely dated, Dörries' contrast of the "historical" Antony of the *Sayings* with the "idealized" Antony of the *Life* might still be compelling. However, whether the *Sayings* source provides a glimpse of a more "primitive" Antony or not, the man portrayed there *is* distinguishable from the demon-tested thaumaturge who battles pagans and heretics (Satan's dupes and allies) in Athanasius' hagiography. The Antony of the *Sayings* bears clearer marks of humanity, specifically of human vulnerability. He is not merely subject to physical abuse, his spirit remaining unconquered—this would be the Athanasian athlete who returns to the tombs for more combat, bloody but unbowed by demonic assaults. More typical of the Antony met in the collection of sayings is a certain tentativeness or susceptibility to discouragement, which is one of the characteristics which led Dörries to call him a "penitent."[2] "Troubled by boredom and irritation" in his cell, Antony prayed to be delivered from distraction, to be made whole. Going outside, he saw someone "like himself" doing the monk's toil—alternately standing for prayer and weaving palm fronds—and was instructed by this stand-in, a correcting angel, to do the same. Regaining his confidence, Antony renewed his labor, and (in the words which conclude the story) "found the salvation which he was seeking."[3]

Though Athanasius' desert hero has his perplexities *de rerum natura et futura* resolved in prayer by divine providence, this Antony is shown agonizing about various questions of theodicy—about unequal life spans and unrighteous wealthy who oppress the righteous poor. A voice commands: "Antony, look to yourself: these are the judgments of God, and it is not good for you to know them."[4] Antony, like others called "Abba" in the *Sayings,* confronts and examines others who pursue virtue. He visits a monk of great reputation and heaps abuse upon him as a test.[5] A monk who did not surrender all his wealth is made an object lesson: ordered to purchase meat with his withheld funds and hang it around his neck, he is attacked by dogs and birds—a pale imitation, Antony warns, of the damage done by demons to those whose cords to the world are not completely severed.[6]

This Antonian sharpness is balanced by several anecdotes which sound a note of moderation. He teaches that immoderate fasting can put a monk farther from God.[7] A hunter who is displeased when he happens upon Antony and others enjoying conversation is instructed by the example of a bow which is stretched too taut and snaps.[8] A penitent monk is rebuffed by the community which expelled him and finds a forceful advocate in Antony, who convinces the monks with Abba Elias that it is unwise "to run a rescued ship aground and sink it."[9] This nonrigorist stance is paralleled in a letter (reproduced by Ammon as Antony's) in which a revelation provides a warrant for forgiveness of postbaptismal sins.[10]

Like other wise men who appear in the *Sayings,* Antony's utterances are philosophical in a restricted sense—they address practical and ethical questions at the popular level. So there is simple advice on how to please God, analysis of harmless and harmful movements which occur in the body, and advice on the control of tongue and belly.[11] This brand of wisdom makes the transition from declaratory to hortatory with ease. From the observation that God prized equally the hospitality of Abraham, the quietness of Elijah, and the humility of David, Antony proceeds to urge that "whatever you find your soul wills in following God's will, do it, and keep your heart."[12] The importance of the aspirant's intention is similarly stressed in the response made to a monk who asks Antony to pray for him: "Neither I nor God will have mercy on you unless you take trouble about yourself and ask God's help."[13] Antony does not indulge in speculation about the divine nature or about the generation of the Son of God. The issues which occupied Christian thinkers in metropolitan areas in the third and fourth centuries are nowhere in view. Pondering of the ways of God takes a very different form, as seen in Antony's reflection that God does not visit inner wars on the current generation because he knows they are not durable enough![14]

In the *Life of Antony,* an altogether different person and mind is encountered. Though Athanasius' model monk is locked in battle with Satan throughout his ordeal of nearly ninety years, he suffers no setbacks. A clear victor from the outset, the aura of invincibility surrounds both the accounts of wrestling and the periodic reminders that Antony intensified his discipline. The suggestion has been made that the temptation narrative of the New Testament provides the broad framework of the narrative, but Antony accomplishes feats which go far beyond the endurance of testing. He prophesies, exorcises, predicts calamities which will befall heretics, corrects bad doctrine, silences and astounds Greek sophists, corresponds with emperors, and manages during the twenty years of self-confinement in a deserted fortress to retard change in his physique. Athanasius' designation of the hermit from the "inner mountain" as "man of God" seems inadequate. He is theologian, humble (and powerful) ally of orthodox bishops, wonder-worker—he is a holy hero, larger than life, who is nevertheless to be emulated by the people. Antony, as Dörries wrote, "represents the type of the Christian, the ideal portrait of the human being, as he should be."[15]

Because of the variety of themes and elements which comprise the *Vita Antonii,* scholars have succeeded in discovering in it nearly everything they looked for—the evolution and elaboration of ascetic tendencies already evident among the apostles, the pattern of staged eremitic withdrawal from society, borrowings from stories of Hellenic greats like Pythagoras, a θεῖος ἀνήρ designed to surpass Apollonius of Tyana, and (in reaction to these last interpretations) a holy man modeled exclusively after the biblical presentations of the prophets, disciples, martyrs, and angels.[16] A double message about its purposes and intended audience is conveyed by the treatise itself. The author introduces his work as a guide for those who desire to undertake the new discipline, but concludes with the suggestion that Antony's story be used as an apology among nonbelievers.

ANTONY IN THE ARIAN CONTROVERSY

The portrayal of Antony as a monk who is not hostile toward clergy and who eagerly joins the cause of bishops against heterodoxy and schism has been noted by most commentators, who variously assess the correspondence between Antony's loyalties and his biographer's known commitments. Between the view that Antony actually was the ecclesiastically connected figure he appears in the *Life* to be and the supposition that Athanasius has made the monk over in the image of his own concerns and programs, a number of positions can be taken. E. R. Hardy argued in his *Christian Egypt* that while Athanasius made certain that the hero about whom he wrote emerged as a "loyal orthodox monk," the work "doubtless served as a relief from the struggle" with the Arians.[17]

However, a perception of the Arian controversy as a clash of two soteriologies, each with its own understanding of the spiritual progress or sanctification of believers, makes this estimate of Antony's attraction for Athanasius less likely. To a degree unrecognized heretofore, the *Life of Antony* must be regarded as a major offensive in that battle which occupied the Alexandrian bishop's entire career. Its anti-Arian agenda is *not* limited to the several passages in which Antony delivers patented Athanasian denunciations and warnings about the "Christ-fighters." Feats of the desert wrestler of demons, and the interpretive framework in which they are set, reveal consciousness of the soteriological issues which sharply divide orthodox and Arian spokesmen for the Christian faith.

The dramatic profile of the monk (Antony, or any celebrated ascetic) and the way in which he pursues the "way of virtue" were destined to be contestable by two parties within the church which promoted distinctive and opposing schemes of salvation. As the exemplar of holy living, the monk personifies the process by which redemption is secured. As the hero who symbolizes the religious aspirations of the people, he is a political force emperors soon learn they cannot ignore and contending ecclesiastical groups know from the start they must enlist as ally. When the battle for the monk (or for the continued or the increased support of the monk) is joined, it might be expected to proceed on two fronts: the practical work of contact, correspondence, and negotiation, and the related but more theoretical task of propaganda—specifically, the development of the view that the monastic ideal is the product, the legitimate offspring, of only one set of christological and soteriological ideas. To anticipate the results of our investigation, the *Vita Antonii* preserves one side of the bid for monastic support in the Arian controversy, fastening upon the career of a celebrated monk whose recent death made him a propitious subject and a fine polemical agent just at a point in the history of the strife when its outcome was far from predictable. Theory about the monk takes the form of editorial control and presentation of the lore. It is articulated along lines familiar in other polemical writings evoked by the dispute. The Arian could be relied upon to assert that the holiness of the desert dweller is none other than that progress in moral excellence which imitates Christ, the first among creatures who proved himself through obedience. While capable also of speaking about Jesus' imitability, the orthodox wished to interpret the wilderness discipline by means of concepts harmonious with their teaching of the Logos who descends to dispense power, who lends the divine assistance without which there is no catharsis of passions or redemption of the flesh. Advocates of both soteriological schemes, it must be supposed, faced the tricky task of transplanting the doctrinal and political concerns which beset church and empire in a setting to which they were foreign, or at most intrusive, echoes from the world. At least as they appear to us in the collected apothegms, the desert fathers manifest slight interest in those problems which occupied urban Christian intellectuals or caused bishops to convene synods. Despite the fact that both Athanasius and Arius were honored as "ascetic" by their devotees, it is probable that they had more in common with each other as Alexandrian Christian professionals (certainly in terms of biblical understanding and doctrinal vocabulary) than either had in common with those who embraced the stark instincts and practices flourishing among anchorites in middle Egypt.[18]

Evidence of Athanasius' dealings with monks is extensive. A number of epistles are addressed to the monastics and to particular monks, discussing questions of doctrine, ascetical theory, and in one case, the necessity of a monk's acceptance of election to the episcopate. Athanasius apparently had ascetics in his company when his exile from Alexandria resulted in a visit to Rome in 340.[19] It is more difficult to know with any accuracy how large or representative a group of monastics were known to Athanasius and whether they counted themselves his supporters. It is safe to assume that there were clusters of monks (like those in the Meletian monastery which existed in the 330s at Hathor in the Upper Cynopolite nome) who viewed the orthodox leadership in Alexandria with suspicion or enmity.[20] Athanasius and other historians of the period complain of the alliance of Arians and Meletians, and it is reported that a search for Arsenius, with whose murder Athanasius was charged, was conducted in Meletian communities.[21] In the surviving fourth- and fifth-century sources upon which we depend for our knowledge of early monasticism, however, the name of Athanasius surfaces regularly, and never in an unfavorable light. He is mentioned in the *Verba Seniorum* only as one who on occasion summoned monks to Alexandria (hence Abba Pambo's famous musings about the actress he saw in the city), but the sources which show familiarity with the *Vita Antonii* accord him a more prominent role. The bishop's journeys on the Nile bring monks to its banks for a glimpse and, sometimes, consultation. A working alliance between the monastic leaders and Athanasius is assumed. Didymus' trance-inspired prescience of the Emperor Julian's death contains the directive to inform the bishop.[22] Traditions are preserved in the *Life of Pachomius* suggesting that Athanasius, Antony, and Pachomius (and his successors) enjoyed a cooperative relationship which included a number of mutually beneficial transactions. A lector from the Alexandrian church gains admission to the Pachomian community, his orthodoxy insured by his close association with the bishop, who is described as "a spring gushing up to eternal life."[23] A search party commissioned by Constantius to locate and capture Athanasius is frustrated by the monks at Pabau, one of whom, it is interesting to note, admits to the presiding officer, Artemius, that although the bishop is their father, he has never seen his face.[24] The closing pages of the work recount Athanasius' visit to the monasteries (then under the direction of Theodore) and note that the bishop was cheered to discover "that the disposition of the brothers towards him was most genuine."[25] In response to a compliment from Athanasius about the good order found in the monasteries, Theodore remarks, "Through our father the grace of God is among us, but when we see you it is as if we see Christ."[26] These and other passages preserve and continue a tradition which links Athanasius and orthodoxy unambiguously to the desert's most celebrated heroes.

How well, and in what context, did Athanasius and Antony know each other? The question of Athanasius' relationship to "the great one" (as Palladius calls Antony) presents some difficulties. As a result of the rapid popularity of the *Vita Antonii,* by the end of the fourth century the two names are often mentioned in the same breath.[27] But the nature of the bishop's familiarity with his subject is problematic. Some commentators have stressed remarks in the proem of the *Life of Antony* in which the writer claims to have seen the monk on numerous occasions, followed him "more than a few times," and served him by pouring water over his hands.[28] This assertion of firsthand knowledge justifies the rushed completion of the treatise, however, in order that it could be sent before the end of good sailing weather. Athanasius says he had hoped to consult certain monks who had been with Antony more frequently. In addition, the suspicion that contact between the famous hermit and his hagiographer was limited is heightened by the appearance, late in the work, of a "we passage"—the reference to what appears to have been an official episcopal escort of the monk at the end of one of his dramatic visitations to Alexandria.[29] The "we passage" is most striking for the fact that it stands alone—it is implausible that Athanasius would have refrained from placing himself at other events and sites described in the *Life,* had he been able, credibly, to do so. At any rate, nothing in the *Vita Antonii* itself indicates that encounters between the two men were regular or substantial—only that they took place in the context of affairs in Alexandria. In short, the diversity of the materials which the reader meets in this story of Antony and the distance which seems to stand between the narrator and his hero lend credence to the evidence available from the *Life of Pachomius* which, in reference to the *Vita Antonii,* makes no mention of Athanasius' personal contact with the monk but reports his use of "informed monastic sources."[30]

Whatever historical actuality may stand behind the association of these two figures before Antony's death in 355, Athanasius' interest in the career of the monk (and his own connection with it) was inspired by more than a friend's desire to honor the monk's memory with a combination panegyric and biography. There are good reasons to believe that the Antony "project" was undertaken for the express purpose of combating attempts by the Arians to enlist the monks in support of their cause. No evidence of Arian success in this venture survives. But Athanasius himself reveals by his correspondence that the Arian strategy was sufficiently threatening to require episcopal advice and admonition. He is aware of Arians who visit monasteries and use their familiarity with the monks as a selling point among the Christian populace. He is also cognizant of monastics who, though they give assurances that they do not share the views of the Arians, are nevertheless willing to worship with them.[31] Athanasius warns the ascetics to whom he writes to avoid scandalizing simple believers; they compromise their own piety by associating with the heretics, or with those who tolerate their company. The monks are urged "to shun those who hold the Arian impiety, and . . . to avoid those who, while they pretend not to hold with Arius, yet worship with the impious."[32] Another epistle, also thought to be written to monks, corrects in a few sentences heretical willingness to link originate nature with deity, then moves to the most telling condemnation of the Arians—the sign of God's punishment in the inglamorous demise of Arius while perched upon a Constantinopolitan toilet, *before* he could be restored to communion with the orthodox.[33] If the letter was written around 358, as generally supposed, it indicates concern for the doctrinal alignment of the monks just at the time when the composition of the *Vita Antonii* is usually dated—in 356 or 357, just after the monk's death.[34]

Is there further evidence of a contest for the loyalty of the ascetics in the 350s—one in which the stakes are visibly high for both orthodox and Arian spokesmen? An incidental remark in the *Life* is especially provocative in this regard. Setting the scene for Antony's appearance in the capital city as a representative of orthodoxy, Athanasius reports the Arian claim "that he [Antony] held the same view as they."[35] It is hard to imagine why this information would be revealed if entirely fictitious, since Athanasius' treatise labors to create the impression that no such view could possibly be held. Athanasius does add quickly that Antony's fury at the misuse of his name by the opposition was one of the things which brought him down from his mountain retreat. We know that both Arians and the orthodox worked to obtain the monks as important allies. In this single remark Athanasius provides a reason for wondering whether Antony himself was the (or a) symbolic figure in whom this battle centered, each party claiming the monk's allegiance, or each attempting to win the followers by co-opting the life and teaching of the prestigious hero. The timing of Antony's death may well have made him a prime candidate for such a competition, even if he was not, before Athanasius' treatment of him, the most noteworthy of the monks or "on record" concerning the doctrinal issues dividing the church. The apparently immediate impact of this Athanasian portrait of Antony as an orthodox ally is probably indicative of an important win in this phase of the extended polemical struggle. For some (perhaps most) in the Christian community, a desert saint's endorsement of orthodoxy and the orthodox bishop might prove more compelling than the exegetical and philosophical joustings which filled episcopal correspondence, reports on synods, and dogmatic treatises like Athanasius' three books against the Arians. It needs to be said also that Athanasius' task in showing Antony to be on his side may have been made easier by its basis in fact, by the monk's actual opposition to the Arians (as K. Heussi thinks)—if not as one thoroughly capable of arguing the intricacies of the debate, at least as one with certain ties to the orthodox episcopate in Alexandria.[36] However, the claims which orthodoxy wanted to make about the celebrated anchorite were not so ironclad as to disallow Arians from making similar ones. This was one of the primary reasons for the writing of the *Life*. Arian designs upon or inroads among the monks, a politically potent group, necessitated the particular kind of portrait which Athanasius produced. And whether or not the Arians could carry their case about the concurrence of Antony's views with theirs, it is not to be doubted that they claimed a congruency between Arian ideas and the ascetic ideal. Athanasius' consciousness of the shape of this Arian contention is manifest at numerous places in the *Life*—blatantly in those instances in which the heresy is under direct attack, and more subtly (but just as surely) at other points in the narrative. The *Vita Antonii* is constructed with a view to counteracting the Arian concept of adopted sonship as a progress in virtue. Antony's story, and through it the pattern of the monastic life, are presented as the natural and legitimate expression of orthodox soteriology, *and of that soteriology alone.*

The more explicit presentation of Antony as a champion of orthodoxy occurs toward the end of the *Vita*. His withdrawal from the world, his warfare with demons in the tomb and twenty-year confinement in the fortress set the stage for a lengthy address to the monks. A description of Antony's bold but unsuccessful actions (he desired martyrdom) during the persecution of Maximin resumes the narrative, which continues in a series of episodes highlighting his intensified discipline, advice to visitors, and his prodigious accomplishments as a healer. Attention then shifts (in chap. 67) to Antony's character as churchman. In describing him as a strict observer of the rule of the church, and as one whose deference to clergy extended even to "giving place in prayer" to deacons, Athanasius is touching upon an issue important to the ecclesiastical hierarchy—the anticlerical bias found among monastics, whose retreat from the world expressed also a judgment upon a worldly church. Athanasius' epistle imploring the ascetic Dracontius to accept his election as bishop of Hermupolis Parva addresses the suspicion harbored by the monks that close association with church officialdom threatens corruption of those who pursue virtue.[37] In his respect for church order and orders, Athanasius' Antony is indeed "model"—his example is meant to correct attitudes inimical to the welfare of the orthodox community.

In his correctness of belief Antony is similarly rigorous, refusing to have dealings with Meletians, Manichees, or any other enemies of piety. The confrontation with the demonic has simply moved into the arena of doctrine, for these groups threaten the same "destruction of the soul." Singled out for special attention in this display of the monk's ecclesiastical fidelity are the "Ariomaniacs," as Athanasius is fond of calling his opponents.[38] Arians, we are told, once visited Antony in his mountain hermitage but were chased away after his interrogation uncovered their irreligion. The image employed to denounce them is commonplace in the polemical writings of the bishop: the doctrine of the Arians is "worse than the venom of serpents."[39] Responding to an appeal from "the bishops and all the brothers," Antony descends the mountain and enters Alexandria for the purpose of renouncing Arianism as "the last heresy and the forerunner of the Antichrist."[40] To those familiar with the writings of Bishops Alexander and Athanasius, the monk's brief disputation holds no surprises of either content or vocabulary. It capsulizes Arian tenets in denying them: the Son of God is no creature, is not from nonbeing but always coexisted with the Father, the eternal Word and Wisdom from his essence.[41] The warning which follows, to avoid fellowship with the Arians because "light has no fellowship with darkness" (2 Cor. 6:14), and the comparison of the heretics with the pagans, who also worship the creature rather than the Creator (Rom. 1:25), are met elsewhere in Athanasius' works.[42] Dörries called this Antony the product of a "law of transmutation"—the father of the monks is made into an exemplary figure who must battle on fronts on which he himself had to fight less than his biographer.[43] Though Antony's time in the city is taken up with his dealings with an aggressive throng trying to lay eyes and hands on this powerful thaumaturge, Athanasius' own primary interests are made theirs. He says the people rejoiced to hear the heresy which contends against Christ (τὴν Χριστομάχον αἵρεσιν) "condemned by such a man."[44]

Antony's concern over the heretics does not abate after his departure from the capital. Back in his hermitage, Antony the seer continues his activity as heresy fighter. In the first of two anti-Arian visions, mules are seen kicking within the church and a voice predicts the profanation of its altar. The narrator confirms the vision's fulfillment in "the current assault of the Arians," which resulted in plunder of the churches and the removal of sacred vessels.[45] The monk's prophecy includes notes of consolation and exhortation: those being persecuted for their orthodoxy will be restored, enjoying the freedom to speak boldly wherever they please. In the meantime, Antony advises (as Athanasius' letter also counsels the monks), "do not defile yourselves with the Arians."[46] A second piece of foretelling concerns General Balacius, a harsh enforcer for the Arian party. Antony sends a letter warning Balacius that he is soon to be visited by divine wrath. The general's scorn and his vow to pursue Antony himself are rewarded five days later with a horse-bite which proves to be fatal.[47]

After it is revealed to Antony that his death is imminent (he is, Athanasius reports, nearly 105), the revered monk delivers two farewell discourses. The speeches can be understood to function in the treatise as reiterations of the main lessons to be learned from the desert hero's career. To the monks gathered in the outer mountain he encourages endurance in *askēsis*, reminding them "to live as though dying daily." Finally, they are to have nothing to do with the Meletian schismatics, nor are they to have communion with the Arians, whose current favor with judges and whose fantasizing posture (φαντασία) will soon come to an end.[48] Identical advice is communicated to the two monks (Palladius gives their names as Macarius and Amatas) who attended the aged Antony in the inner mountain: the discipline is to be kept as if they were making a new beginning in the pursuit of virtue. Antony's parting words again sound the alarm: "Let there be no fellowship between you and the schismatics, and have nothing at all to do with the heretical Arians. You know how I avoided them because of their Christ-battling and heterodox teaching."[49] To Athanasius and Serapion, orthodox bishops, and to the two monks he bequeaths his few possessions and dies (it is related) with his feet in the air, as if in preparation for a journey from the earth.[50] The conclusion of the *Life* serves to underscore the point that Antony was the dedicated and persistent ally of those locked in conflict with the Arians. And if the alliance has some basis in fact, it is presented here not merely as report but in the undisguised form of propaganda. Apparently the political climate at the time of the work's composition demanded it. The monks, for whom the work is primarily written, and the pagans who may read it are to be left in no doubt that Antony, "the man of God," was under divine direction when his opposition to demonic forces compelled him to join the battle against the Arian blasphemy. The commonplace which punctuates Athanasius' *Orations against the Arians*—that the father of the Arian assault upon Christ is Satan himself—is vividly played out in the saga of the great monk. The orthodox stand, the champion Antony in their ranks, defending (to use the phrase placed on the monk's lips by his biographer) "the traditions of the fathers, and especially the holy faith in our Lord Jesus Christ."[51]

The *Vita Antonii* does not, however, confine its effort in claiming the great monk (and thereby the monks) for orthodoxy to those open denunciations of the Arians just reviewed. Antony's entire career, with all the *agonismata* which reveal his excellence and power, could be turned to polemical purposes not to be mistaken by those alert to the dispute's implications for the definition of Christian living. The clash between early Arians and the Alexandrian episcopate centered on the character of the savior and the character of the salvation available to the believer. For the articulation of a soteriological scheme, no more ready (and potentially effective) vehicle could be found than the *Vita* of a monk. As the ideal Christian, the athlete whose discipline promises redemption, the monk's story could be designed and related in a manner which made plain the particular Christology and soteriology which supports and makes possible his saintly attainments. At the same time, the structure and rationale provided for this life of virtue could be made to militate against competing schemes. Are there indications that the teaching and feats associated with Antony's name were perceived by his biographer as explicable by more than one scheme of salvation? And did Athanasius purposely construct this paradigm of the Christian's journey in "the way of virtue" in such a way as to frustrate the soteriology advocated by the Arians who claimed Antony as "their" man? Both questions anticipate affirmative answers, but several procedural problems keep them from being rhetorical. The first difficulty has to do with the distinction between Antony-traditions and the Antony of Athanasius. Athanasian motifs are of course expected to exercise their influence in the *Vita Antonii*. What else is there in the account? Can tensions be detected between particular actions attributed to Antony and the interpretive remarks which frame them and are recognizable as Athanasian themes? If no such tensions were discernible within the narrative, one could assume either that Athanasius and the monk actually "spoke the same language," sharing a common religious and theological idiom (which the *Life* preserves accurately), or that Antony has been so successfully cast in the role designed by Athanasius that no disparities, no redactional "seams" are visible. In asking whether Antony's career spent in pursuit of virtue could have lent itself to an Arian soteriological understanding as readily as to an Athanasian, our task becomes the subtle one of spying out in the *Life* attempts to rule out possible connections between the monk's life of discipline and the Arian conception of discipleship. At this point another issue presents itself and needs to be stated with as much precision as our sources allow. How did Arian and orthodox understandings of the Christian life, the believer's progress toward God, differ? Although the *Life* contains statements about the nature of the savior in the monk's corrections of Arian and pagan doctrines, the work's subject is Antony, a creature and a holy man who presses on toward perfection. He is the type of the pious Christian, even if his piety is, as we read repeatedly, "wondrous." Both parties in the dispute have theories of the advance of the believer, and both orthodox and Arian Christians are capable of speaking of their lives as imitative of Christ. Their theories of moral advancement and *imitatio* are grounded, however, in radically different Christologies.

For the orthodox spokesmen Alexander and Athanasius, "progress in virtue" and "diligence of conduct" are marks of the adoptive sonship by which creatures are saved. Different from the savior, who is divine by nature, those who would be redeemed depend upon his grace, which enables and empowers the life of obedience. In denying any commonality between the sonship of Christ and the sonship of the rest of men, Alexander writes:

> His sonship, which is endowed with the paternal divinity by nature (κατὰ φύσιν), surpasses by an inexpressible preeminence the sonship of those who have been adopted as sons through his appointment (δι' αὐτοῦ θέσει). He is, on the one hand, unchangeable, being perfect and sufficient in all respects, while they, on the other hand, liable to [the] turning in both directions, stand in need of his assistance (βοηθεία).[52]

Against the same opponents Athanasius extends his assertion that "the Word is unlike us and like the Father" by insisting that Christ does not urge believers to follow and learn from him as if they might achieve equality with him—a clear impossibility. Rather, humans receive from him the pattern (παράδειγμα) enabling them to live with *each other* in meekness and humility. The safe course for creatures, subject as they are to changeable conduct, is to model themselves, as far as they are able, after unchangeable nature.[53] Creaturely perfection, while parallel or analogous to the natural perfection of the savior, is not and cannot be the same thing. But, Arian exegetes point out, Christ, like other creatures, said that power was given to him. Athanasius answers: The redeemer received power as a man which was his eternal possession as God. As incarnate Lord, he did this in order to secure grace for humankind, which in Adam revealed its creaturely susceptibility to loss of what it had once received.[54] The orthodox formula for sanctification of believers turns upon the full divinity of the Son of God, whose incarnation effected redemption and whose continuing help makes possible that progress in holiness to be consummated in paradise. Adoption as sons and daughters of God depends entirely upon the eternal deity of the one who descended in order to save, the Christ in whom, as Athanasius says, "was stored the grace which has reached us."[55]

The Arian scheme of *askēsis* proceeds from the axiomatic identification of Christ with creatures. Possible of attainment by other originate beings is his progress in wisdom, stature, and divine favor. As Christ was chosen and named "Son" because of the works he performed (works foreknown by God), so believers are adopted and perfected by following in the way of his obedience and moral excellence, his works done as a creature. The exemplar is not categorically other, "unlike us and like the Father"; hence the imitation envisioned is straightforward and strictly possible. The reason Arian Christians can assert, "we too are able to become sons of God, just as (ὥσπερ) [Christ]," is unambiguous: Christ's election as a reward for his discipline, for his perseverance in the good by choice, is within the reach of fellow creatures.[56] Athanasius protests his opponents' insolent claim to be Christ's equal, and in the process describes their position exactly:

> There will be no difference between him and those who receive the name [that is, of "son"] after their actions (πράξεις), as this is the ground upon which he also has been declared to be Son.[57]

Within this soteriological plan the word χάρις carries a distinctive meaning. In contrast to orthodoxy's substantialist concept of grace as something "stored" in and dispensed from divine nature, Arianism attaches connotations of volition and transaction to the term. For Arius both Christ and creatures possess sonship "by grace," and both can be said to have grace only derivatively—by attribution rather than by nature. It is the same thing to say that the savior is Son "by adoption," "by participation," and "by grace."[58] Although the election of the Son is a gracious act of God in the sense that divine initiative is involved, this "certain one" is named "Son" because his virtuous conduct merits the appellation. His grace, like his glory, though bestowed by God, is won by his own consistent choice of the good.

144

Likewise, as Arian believers aspired to fulfill their adopted sonship in emulation of "the pioneer and perfecter of their faith," they attained grace through moral diligence and discipline. When in *De Decretis* 9 Athanasius describes the sonship of the Arian Christ by saying that the "name was by grace united to him . . . for his virtue's sake," he also describes the dynamic which Arians see at work in the believers' progress toward God, and the foundation for their idea of *askēsis*.[59] Perfected sonship consists in doing the works and enduring the testings accomplished first by the one Arius called "the perfect creature of God."[60]

Important purposes in Athanasius' portrait of Antony are illuminated by an awareness of these opposing soteriologies. And the converse is also true, since the monk's exploits become the platform for an orthodox exposition-by-narrative of doctrines which in the dogmatic treatises can only be stated as propositions.

Of particular interest is Athanasius' depiction of Antony's deeds, his trials and his healing miracles, both of which represent contests with demons. One of the most detailed accounts of the hermit's temptations occurs early in the *Life*. Attacked by manifestations of the tempter as seductress and as a black youth who introduces himself as "the spirit of lust," Antony proves his adversaries weak by his πόνοις, his labors. The narrator concludes the episode with this sentence: "This was Antony's first contest (πρῶτον ἆθλον) against the devil, or rather (μᾶλλον δε) this was the success (κατόρθωμα) of the savior in Antony."[61] The correction is no casual afterthought. The reader has been informed a few lines earlier that during his encounter with Satan Antony had been inspired to nobility by thinking about Christ.[62] The remark that working with (συνήργει) Antony was the Lord, "who bore flesh for us, and gave to the body victory over the devil," sounds one of Athanasius' dominant soteriological themes.[63] Countering the Arian claim that the savior advanced in God's favor "like the rest," in the *Orations* Athanasius describes Christ as "God bearing flesh" and challenges his opponents by asking, "How did he who gives grace to others . . . advance in grace?"[64] The Athanasian point with reference to Antony, however, concerns the source of his heroics. The monk labors to resist temptation, but the triumph is his only because he is a recipient of grace. So alongside notices of the monk's own pursuit of more severe discipline and of his sharpened purpose in his obedience to God's will stands Antony's recitation of the Pauline confession: "Not I, but the grace of God which is with me."[65]

145

From this initial contest Antony moves to the burial grounds and there in the haunt of evil spirits engages in a strenuous battle. Rescued by a friend after having been beaten senseless by his demon adversaries, Antony chooses to return to the tomb, this time to be assaulted by a menagerie of malevolent beasts. At the end of the story a curious exchange takes place between Antony and the Lord. Antony asks where the Lord was when he needed him—apparently the monk had struggled alone. An answering voice informs him that his ἀγώνισμα had been carefully observed and that now, *since he has prevailed,* divine aid will henceforth be his. Immediately Antony becomes conscious of new power.[66]

If, as the presence of this conversation suggests, the story of Antony's trial in the tomb once described the perseverance of a hero who fought without benefit of heavenly assistance, who strived to maintain tranquillity of soul in the midst of physical distress, and *thus* won the favor of the divine spectator, its emphasis has been altered in the Athanasian retelling. Prior to the exchange, we are told that Antony was not bereft of the Lord's help while fighting the beasts. At a critical point in the contest, when no longer able to stand, he looked to the tomb's ceiling, which seemed to open, and saw a ray of light (ἀκτῖνα φωτός) descending, a beam which dispersed the demons and healed his body.[67] Athanasius is capable in other contexts of speaking of such divine intervention from above, and indeed of a saving ἀκτῖνα. Again criticizing the Arian view that Christ shared with other creatures that progress which depends upon steadfast choice of the good, he argues that there can be no advance in the savior, since he is God's own Word, Wisdom, Son, and Power. If anyone is able to partake from his divine brilliance "one ray, so to speak (ὡς ἀκτῖνα), such a person becomes all-perfect among men, and equal to angels."[68] Delivered from the hands of the enemy by an act which replicates the eternal Word's saving condescension, Athanasius' Antony *is* such a person, an example of how, according to orthodox teaching, the Christian is saved and sanctified. Without this motif the episode's emphasis might have fallen upon the monk's purposefulness and upon God's disposition to bestow favor as a reward for ascetic performance. The ideas were not impossible for Athanasius to hold (he too, like Alexandrian ascetical theorists before him, embraces the Pauline injunction to "press on toward the goal for the prize" [Phil. 3:14]), but unless qualified—that is, connected with the concept of descending grace—these ideas were too permissive of an Arian understanding of the monk's progress in virtue after the model of the "advancing" Christ.[69]

146

Antony's twenty-year self-imprisonment in the abandoned fortress stands in the narrative as a demonstration of his newly empowered *askēsis*.[70] Several features in this unusual story invite speculation about the particular interest Athanasius might have had in recounting it. Though visitors to the place hear battle sounds within, they discover that the monk, neutralizing evil spirits by the sign of the cross, dwells inside unperturbed and unharmed—the wailings belong to the frustrated demons.[71] Antony is not this time wearied by struggle, since he is aided by visions from above. There is no suggestion of wrestling or intense effort on his part, and when he emerges from the battlement, which is twice described as his "shrine" (ἄδυτος), his body shows no signs of wear or aging—it is in "the same state" as when he entered. The elimination of any evidence of the monk's striving, coupled with the phenomenon of the arrest of physical decay, is intended to intimate one of Athanasius' favorite themes. Antony appears to be receiving a foretaste, a first installment, of his eventual deification, which in Athanasian theory entailed the arrest of fleshly corruption and the transformation of the perishable by the imperishable nature of Godhead.[72] Antony, departing the fort, is called a mystagogue and θεοφορούμενος, "God-bearer." In the dogmatic vocabulary of Athanasius the term has a specific meaning—one which militates against the Arian claim that believers, by perfection in willing, may enjoy union with the Father just as the Son does. Athanasius insists that no such equality is possible between creatures and the uncreated redeemer. In the mode of the Johannine "farewell discourse," he imagines the savior saying to the Father,

> Their [that is, the believers'] perfecting shows that your Word has dwelled among them; and the world seeing them perfect and bearing God (τελείους καὶ θεοφορουμένους) will believe that you have sent me.[73]

Antony's sojourn in the fortress provides his episcopal biographer with an opportunity to place a particular construction upon his celebrated spiritual power. Supported by visions and the apotropaic sign of the cross, his advance in perfection comes not through striving for equality with Christ but by protection and intervention from above. Antony's holiness is not achieved, it is received. Only the true Son can perform works of power by his own endowment, which is the divine essence shared with the Father; all other sons of God require his saving βοηθεία.[74]

Evidence that this formula controls Athanasius' presentation of Antony's accomplishments appears in numerous other places in the treatise. An insistent counterpoint sounds throughout the song of Antony's feats and his injunctions to renew daily the zeal for discipline: the monk's deeds are not, strictly speaking, his own. The gruesome maladies of a woman from Busiris Tripolitana are cured even while her parents negotiate her admittance into Antony's presence. "This success (again, κατόρθωμα)," he explains, "is not mine . . . rather, her healing is from the savior who works his mercy everywhere for those who call upon him."[75] As a correction of the inclination to attribute the power and the deed to the monk himself, the explanation repeats the interpretation given to Antony's "first struggle" and is representative of a great many such reminders found in the treatise. Antony says he "gave glory to the Lord" for his resistance to the demons who attempted by flattery, by singing hymns and reciting scripture to beguile him.[76] Wonders are done and demons expelled, he instructs his fellow ascetics, because these are works of the savior, products of the grace he gives.[77] Repeatedly disavowing his own role in the conquest of evil spirits, Antony's use of Luke 10:18, 19 conforms with Athanasian employment of the same texts in *De Incarnatione* and in several of the festal letters.[78] It is because of the grace given to the faithful that demonic beings cower, and when Satan himself appears at the monk's cell to admit his defeat in the face of the proliferation of holy men in his territory, Antony marvels at the Lord's χάριν, which has vanquished the evil one.[79]

Empowered by the grace which issues from the savior (who, according to Athanasian doctrine, possesses it eternally as God), Antony advances in virtue and becomes the scourge of demons. The theme is bolstered by notices that the Lord was "with Antony" and "with the holy ones" in their endeavors, and that as the Lord "worked with" (συνήργει) him, so he is "co-worker" (συνεργός) with other desert athletes in their victories over the devil.[80] Apparently the use of this last term by the Arian Asterius to describe Christ's apprenticeship to God did not deter Athanasius, who in the *Life* makes it connote (as he believed it connoted in Rom. 8:28) the dependency of the creature upon the saving power of God.[81] So we are told that the great monk did not heal by commanding but by prayer and by invocation of the name of Christ. "It was clear to all," his biographer records, "that it was not he himself who worked, but the Lord, who through Antony acted mercifully and healed the sufferers."[82]

148

The point needs to be reiterated that these reminders about the enabling grace and assistance from the Lord *interpret* the monk's success in ascetic rigor and his performance of wonders. It is not too much to say that they control, as editorial refrains, the manner in which the reader is to construe the monk's virtue and power, which are Christ-derived. But these motifs do not displace testimony from or in reference to Antony about the value and necessity of striving after holiness. Antony urges recollection of the deeds of the saints and an adherence to commandments which emulates their zeal.[83] He admonishes the monks to stand firm in discipline, "ever striving" (ἀγωνιῶντες ἀεὶ) and mindful of the judgment.[84] In a striking passage in chapter 20, Antony asserts that virtue is "easy" (εὔκολος) for those who will it; virtue "is not far from us, nor does it exist outside of us, but is within us," as Luke 17:21 teaches. Steady inclination toward the good, or advance in virtue, it is explained, comes through keeping the intellectual part of the soul in its natural state.[85] The monk's theory of the soul has become more complex and recognizably philosophical, and the simpler idea that the ascetic's routine is its own reward ("There is much virtue in those plaits," Antony tells Macarius about his weaving of palm leaves) seems distant, but Athanasius' Antony speaks of the need for dedication and effort in ways not discontinuous with the traditions from the *Sayings of the Fathers*.[86] The *Vita Antonii* is laced with remarks about the importance of the aspirant's willingness (τοῦ θέλειν), desire (πόθος), and fixed purpose (προαίρε-σις).[87] At one level, Antony's earnest striving which allows the Lord to work through him is simply the monastic elaboration of a motif familiar in biblical (particularly Pauline) writings and the martyrologies.[88] But the Arian Christology and its correlate idea of the believer's imitative advance in virtue made the correct interpretation of the monk's success the vital business of orthodoxy. Sayings like that of Arsenius to Evagrius—"These Egyptian peasants have acquired virtues by hard work"[89]—needed clarification. Did one pursue the good, obtain virtue, earn favor through diligence, as Christ the creature had, or did the aspirations of the one seeking holiness depend upon the power dispensed by the savior who, fully God and morally unchangeable, is more the rescuer of the helpless faithful than their companion in *agones*? Thirty years before Athanasius claimed Antony for the orthodox party, the grounds for distinguishing between Christ's virtue and that of Christians had been set down by his predecessor in office. Against the Arian doctrine that believers were God's sons in the same way as

Christ, Alexander argued that the Word's sonship is incapable of falling (ἀμετάπτωτον), invulnerable to "slippage." By contrast, he insisted, the sonship of adoption available to creatures is not sonship "by nature," but "by fitness of character and grace" (τρόπων ἐπιτηδειότητι καὶ δωρεᾷ)—it leaves creatures capable of falling away.[90] Improvability cannot be entertained for God's own Word, but men and angels have received blessings in order that they might advance toward sinlessness through discipline and the keeping of commandments.[91] The *Vita Antonii* features an adopted son par excellence, for Antony is orthodoxy's model of earnest endeavor inspired and empowered by the grace of the eternal Logos. His discipline and works are to be admired and imitated; they provide a "sufficient pattern" for others to follow. But Antony's greatness is to be made transparent to the savior he serves, the Christ worshiped by Athanasius, who is decidedly *not* the Christ of the Arians and who does not encourage creatures to attain the very same sonship he has won through his labors.

It is of course possible that Athanasius had other reasons for qualifying the deeds of Antony as he did, for bringing his heroics under the control of this scheme of grace. Obviously he did not desire to "play down" the accomplishments of the celebrated personage he was making a champion of Alexandrian orthodoxy. But Antony's reputation as thaumaturge and the reports which circulated about his prodigious powers were capable of being misunderstood by the populace. A representative of ecclesiastical order and of its supportive theology might be expected to have an interest in making plain the source *and the limits* of the δύναμις of this and other desert holy men. The *Life* shows no interest in suppressing notices of the popular excitement caused by Antony's mighty acts. The people's response to Antony's power as healer and doer of signs is described in the idiom of the New Testament, and the problems posed for the wonder-worker (and for his biographer) are familiar: crowd management, the logic and necessity of retreat, and most importantly, proper understanding of the signs. In chapter 49, Antony is shown withdrawing to the Thebaid, seeking relief from those who camped outside his cell hoping for cure. His departure is prompted, according to Athanasius, by a double danger stemming from "the signs which the Lord accomplished by him"—his own pridefulness and erroneous overestimation of him by others. During a visit to Alexandria, his dealings with the crowd receive different treatment. It is reported that the whole city ran to see him, Greeks and their priests entering the church to see the "man of God," and many seeking to be healed by touching him. A year's crop of converts to Christianity is garnered in a few days. When attempts are made to protect Antony from the enthusiastic masses, he remarks tranquilly that he contends with a greater number of demons in his mountain cell. The episode bears all the traits of a story about a divine man and his thaumaturgy, but Athanasius has framed it in such a way as to make it both more and less than that. No mere healer, Antony is a champion of orthodoxy. He came to the city to denounce the Arians, and the public furor was touched off by his theological address, the people stirred by hearing heresy anathematized "by such a man."[92] And Antony's ability to work wonders is explained in familiar terms: in his actions "the Lord cleansed many of the demons and cured those who were mad."[93] As Luke had been obliged to interpret the marvelous powers of Peter and Paul, whose shadows and handkerchiefs restored people to health, so Athanasius makes clear who is at work in the πράξεις of his hero.[94] The danger of public exaggeration of the holy man's might and authority is checked even while the effects of his deeds are celebrated: he is the agent through whom the power of deity is manifested, not himself the Deity. Antony and other ascetics tap a source the channels of which are defined by the church and presided over, proximately, if not ultimately, by the bishop.

Even if Athanasius thought it beneficial for readers to understand Antony as a humble servant of the church and no competitor to the authority resident in the episcopate, the Arian crisis made the monk's role as fellow combatant a great deal more important. Athanasius does take pains to show that Antony is a "servant of God" rather than a divine man, but the more pressing concern is to portray him, in his words and works, as a monk whose holiness and virtue can only issue from his reliance upon the savior so carefully delineated in orthodox teaching.[95] Should the efforts and accomplishments of Antony suggest a glory in him which approaches or rivals that of Christ, the issues confronting Athanasius have to do less with putting a θεῖος ἀνήρ under orders than with contesting the Arian soteriology, which couches the hope of believers in language promising a sonship equal in glory to that of their creaturely savior, their fellow pilgrim in askēsis.

It is tempting to ask how the Arians might have characterized the Antony expressive of their soteriological understanding and objectives. Do the sharpest features of the Athanasian portrait suggest the profile of an Arian counterpart? If so, we might suppose that the monk (thus the true Christian) of Arian design would not have been energized by grace of the kind which is visited upon the hero of the *Vita Antonii*. That intervening substantial χάρις, the efficacy of which turns upon its bestowal by one who is "unlike us and like the Father," was thoroughly inappropriate to a scheme in which redeemer and redeemed share creaturehood and are by their common nature equipped with similar potencies. The Arian Christ's status as son is held μετοχῇ—that is, by his voluntary participation in the purposes, not the οὐσία, of God. For other sons and daughters of God the same must be said. The monk as representative Christian is the imitator of Christ's unswerving obedience to the paternal will, an ascetic whose excellence God rewards with favor and power. As told by the Arians, Antony's story would be one in which his holiness, his perfected sonship, is the result of perseverance in virtue. The power and glory which attach to his name are prizes for his works. He is one who followed the forerunner in the way of virtue. To such an understanding of the dynamic and purposes of the life of discipline the Egyptian desert athletes of the fourth century cannot have been entirely hostile. Undertaking the ascetic regimen in order to attain purity and salvation, the monks who sought humility and *apatheia* considered even these to be achievements bearing upon their future rewards. So they were capable of speaking of *deserved* grace,[96] and three monks reassessed the significance of effort after observing the προκοπή of Pachomius, who was born of pagan parents. Jettisoning their former belief that "all the holy ones were made saintly by God in their mothers' wombs, and that they were also made unchangeable and without free will," the three join his community, convinced that they "and all others" can be led to God by him.[97]

The ideal Arian Christian is a close copy of the Christ whom he considers first among many brothers. His progress toward becoming, like the redeemer, an "unalterable . . . unchangeable, perfect creature of God" consists in striving to remain obedient to the Father's will. An Antony who shared the views of the Arians, then, would have been a rigorous seeker of virtue's reward. Believing himself armed for the contest with exactly the same powers with which his redeemer stood the test, this Antony is the product of the hero or leader Christology visible in Hebrews' proclamation of Jesus as the "pioneer of salvation" (ἀρχηγὸν τῆς σωτερίας).[98] The glory to which he aspires is none other than that which belongs to God's sons. What is predicated of the redeemer must be predicated of the redeemed.

Athanasius had the program of his opponents firmly in mind when he became Antony's hagiographer and provided the paradigm for those who wished to imitate him. The monk's refutation of Arian precepts and warnings against communion with heretics constitute only a part of the assault on their attempt to align their ideas with the ascetic ideal. Antony's *acta* have been fashioned and narrated in such a way as to preclude the Arian understanding of Christ and the vision of Christian *askēsis* which it supports. In his *Orations* Athanasius argued that the Arians were reckless and blasphemous in claiming that each of them was able to say along with Christ, "I in the Father and the Father in me." He pointed out that none of the prophets took credit for the signs and wonders they performed but professed them to be the works of God "who gave the power." In the same way the apostles testified that it was "not in their own power that they did miracles, but in the Lord's grace."[99] From this formula, with all that it signifies in the dispute with Arian ideas of salvation, Athanasius makes no significant departure as he recounts the virtuous deeds of Antony, making him both a spokesman for orthodoxy and the model for sanctification according to the dynamic of orthodox soteriology. The great monk defends the eternity and full deity of the Logos whose descending grace works both his miracles and his own perfection.

A carefully fashioned polemical weapon, the Antony presented by Athanasius stands as a sharp alternative to the Arian scheme of salvation and its attendant idea of discipleship. As symbol of ascetic greatness, the desert hero becomes also the vehicle for orthodoxy's campaign to undo threatening (perhaps successful) Arian bids for monastic support.

NOTES

1. Hermann Dörries, *Die Vita Antonii als Geschichtsquelle*, Nachrichten der Akademie der Wissenschaften in Göttingen I, Philologische-Historische Klasse 14 (Göttingen: Vandenhoeck und Ruprecht, 1949), p. 376.

2. Ibid.

3. *Verba Seniorum* 7.1, LCC[12], p. 83. *Vide* Athanasius *V. Anton.* 66.

4. *Verba Seniorum* 15.1, LCC[12], p. 156. The lesson in the apothegm from *Verba Seniorum* is echoed, however, in *V. Anton.* 34.

5. *Verba Seniorum* 8.2.

6. Ibid., 6.1.

7. Ibid., 10.1.

8. Ibid., 10.2.

9. Ibid., 9.1.

10. Migne PG 40, 1065. The epistle is attributed to Antony and reproduced by Ammon. A tradition concerning Antony's compassion is indicated also in *Verba Seniorum* 16.20, which involves the forgiveness of a prostitute named Thais. The story is, according to Owen Chadwick, a later addition to the *Verba Seniorum; vide* LCC[12], p. 180.

11. *Verba Seniorum* 1.1; 5.1.

12. Ibid., 1.11, LCC[12], p. 39.

13. Ibid., 10.3, LCC[12], p. 106.

14. Ibid., 10.4, LCC[12], p. 106.

15. Dörries, *Geschichtsquelle*, p. 389.

16. Basilii Steidle, "Homo Dei Antonius," *Antonius Magnus Eremita 356–1956,* Studia Anselmiana XXXVIII (Rome: Pontificum Institutem S. Anselmi, 1956). *Vide* particularly pp. 182–83.

17. Edward Rochie Hardy, *Christian Egypt: Church and People* (New York: Oxford University Press, 1952), p. 52. Hardy notes, however, that during his third exile Athanasius was very much occupied with the continuation of the polemical struggle, composing his *Apology to Constantius, History of the Arians, Defense of His Flight,* and the *Orations against the Arians.* Can an Athanasius seeking a respite from the contest with the followers of Arius be imagined? It should be noted that Hardy accepted a much later date for Athanasius' *Orations* than we do. We prefer A. Gaudel's dating of the *Orations* to A.D. 339–45 (and preferably the earlier date) for the reasons Gaudel gives: "La Théologie du Logos chez Saint Athanase," *Revue des sciences religieuses* 9 (1929): 538–39.

18. Athanasius is referred to as "one of the ascetics" in *Apol. c. Ar.* 6, which reports an encyclical composed by Egyptian bishops in his defense. Epiphanius *Haer.* 69.1.2–3 records the admiration which many felt for Arius' ascetic life.

19. Palladius *H. Laus.* 1.4, W. K. Lowther Clarke, ed. and trans., *The Lausiac History of Palladius,* Translations of Christian Literatures, Series I (New York: The Macmillan Company, 1918), p. 48. *Vide* also Hardy, *Christian Egypt,* p. 73.

20. *Vide* Hardy, *Christian Egypt,* p. 72, and H. Idris Bell, *Jews and Christians in Egypt: The Jewish Troubles in Alexandria and the Athanasian Controversy* (London: British Museum, 1924), pp. 45–97.

21. Athanasius *Apol. c. Ar.* 4ff.; *Fest. Ep.* 10.9; Socrates *H.E.* 1.29; Sozomen *H.E.* 2.23.

22. Palladius *H. Laus.* 4.3, Clark, p. 52.

23. *V. Pach.* 94, Apostolos N. Athanassakis, trans., *The Life of Pachomius (Vita Prima Graeca),* Society of Biblical Literature Texts and Translations 7, Early Christian Literature Series 2 (Missoula, Mont.: Scholars Press, 1975), p. 135.

24. *V. Pach.* 137–38.

25. Ibid., 144, Athanassakis, p. 189.

26. Ibid. Note the role of Antony in the intriguing passage in *V. Pach.* 120, in which he is made to give his approval to the cenobitism of the Pachomians. If communal monasteries had been in existence when he undertook the discipline, Antony hints, his lot and theirs would have been the same. Antony endorses Orisius as successor to Abbot Petronius and asks that his concern for the community be conveyed to "Athanasius, who is so worthy of the office of bishop" (Athanassakis, p. 165).

27. Jerome *De vir. ill.* 87, 88, 125; Gregory of Nazianzus *Or.* 21; Palladius *H. Laus.* 8.

28. Athanasius *V. Anton.* Proem. On the problems surrounding the text dealing with hand washing, *vide* Robert T. Meyer, *St. Athanasius: The Life of Saint Antony,* Ancient Christian Writers 10 (Westminster, Md.: The Newman Press, 1950), p. 106, n. 4.

29. Athanasius *V. Anton.* 71.

30. *V. Pach.* 99, Athanassakis, p. 141.

31. Migne PG 25, 691: *Ep.* 52, *Ad Monachos* I, *NPNF,* vol. 4, p. 563.

32. Ibid. (*NPNF* translation).

33. Migne PG 26, 1185: *Ep.* 53, *Ad Monachos* II, *NPNF,* vol. 4, p. 564.

34. The *V. Anton.* is generally dated in or about the year 357, and the disturbances referred to in chap. 82 are associated with the events Athanasius recounts in *Apol. de fuga* 24ff. *Vide* L. V. Hertling, *Antonius der Einsiedler* (Innsbruck, 1929) for a later dating—between 365 and 373. *Vide* also L. W. Barnard, "The Date of S. Athanasius' *Vita Antonii,*" *VC* 28 (1974): 169–75, and the response by B. R. Brennan, "Dating Athanasius' *Vita Antonii,*" *VC* 30 (1976): 52–54. *Epistle* 52 is ordinarily dated in relation to the letter to Serapion (*Ep.* 54, *NPNF,* vol. 4, pp. 564ff.), which it preceded, and is fixed in the year 358. *Vide NPNF,* vol. 4, p. 563, n. 1.

35. Athanasius *V. Anton.* 69.

36. Karl Heussi, *Der Ursprung des Mönchtums* (Tübingen: J. C. B. Mohr, 1936), p. 101: "Geschichtlich ist auch die Stellungnahme des Antonius gegen die Arianer. Beweis: der Briefwechsel des Antonius mit Konstantin d. Gr. nach der Synode von Tyrus, sowie der Brief des Antonius, der in der Balakiusgeschichte eine Rolle spielt. . . . Allerdings wird Antonius von den dogmatischen Streitfragen nicht allzuviel verstanden haben [Heussi adds the remark of Amélineau: "Il est plus que probable que toute la théologie d'Antoine se borna à une confiance aveugle en l'archevêque d'Alexandrie, Athanase"]. Aber bei dem Ansehen, das er genoss, war er für den Bischof im kirchenpolitischen Kampf eine wertvolle Hilfe."

37. Athanasius *Ep. Drac.* 9 (*vide NPNF,* vol. 4, pp. 557ff.). The tale of Pachomius' attempt to elude ordination by Athanasius may preserve a notice of this ascetic suspicion of ecclesiastical involvement.

38. Athanasius *V. Anton.* 68. *Vide,* e.g., *Or. c. Ar.* 1.4; 2.70.

39. Ibid. *Vide* Athanasius *Or. c. Ar.* 1.1, 26, 30; 2.19, 43; 3.1; *Ep. Aeg.* 9; *H. Ar.* 66.

40. Athanasius *V. Anton.* 69. On the basis of information given in the Festal Index, the visit has been dated to late July of 337 or 338, at which time Antony reportedly "shewed himself wonderful in many things, and healed many" (translation from *NPNF,* vol. 4, p. 503). The problem caused by the chronology given in Socrates *H.E.* 4.25 is discussed in Meyer, *Antony,* pp. 128ff. Designation of Arianism as "the last heresy," etc., occurs also in *Or. c. Ar.* 1.1; 1.17.

41. Athanasius *V. Anton.* 69. For similar statements of the Arian teaching (and orthodox refutation of it) see *Or. c. Ar.* 1.9, *Ep.* 52, *Fest. Ep.* 9.10, *Ep. Aeg.* 13. Dörries, *Geschichtsquelle,* p. 387, writes: "Die Gegenargumente der *Vita Antonii* gegen die Arianer sind die in der antiarianische Polemik des Athanasius so geläufigen, dass ein Einzelnachweis nicht erforderlich ist."

42. Athanasius *Ap. c. Ar.* 43; *Fest. Ep.* 7; *Or. c. Ar.* 2.14; 3.14.

43. Dörries, *Geschichtsquelle,* p. 388.

44. Athanasius *V. Anton.* 70.

45. Ibid., p. 82. J. H. Newman related the prophecy to the events of 356, which are treated in *Apol. de fuga* 6–7 and *H. Ar.* 55–56 (*Vide NPNF,* vol. 4, p. 218, n. 16).

46. Ibid. *Vide* Athanasius *Ep.* 53.

47. Athanasius *V. Anton.* 86. The story is told, in somewhat different form, in *H. Ar.* 14. There the letter is sent to Bishop Gregory and passed on to Balacius, who is bitten not by Nestorius' mount but by his own. The mention of Gregory (d. 345) and the prefecture of Nestorius (345–52, according to the Festal Index), if reliable, fixes the date of the "mishap" in 345. It remains puzzling why the two accounts of the event differ in detail. The more elaborate version in *V. Anton.* may result from receipt of new information about the incident.

48. Athanasius *V. Anton.* 89.

49. Ibid., 91.

50. Ibid., 91–92.

51. Ibid., 89.

52. Alexander *Ep. ad Alex.* (Opitz³, Urk. 14.20, p. 24, lines 9–12).

53. Athanasius *Or. c. Ar.* 3.20 (Bright, pp. 174–75).

54. Ibid., 3.38 (Bright, p. 193).

55. Ibid., 2.76 (Bright, pp. 146 47).

56. Alexander *Ep. ad Alex.* (Opitz³, Urk. 14.13, p. 21, lines 19–22).

57. Athanasius *De Decr.* 6. *Vide* pp. 63–64, chap. 2 *supra.*

58. Athanasius *Or. c. Ar.* 1.5–6 (Bright, pp. 5–6). Athanasius states the counterproposition in 1.9 (*NPNF* translation): "Wherefore He is very God, existing one-in-essence with the very Father; while other beings to whom he said, 'I said ye are Gods,' had this grace from the Father, only by participation of the Word, through the Spirit."

59. *Vide* chap. 1, pp. 28ff. *supra.*

60. Arius *Ep. ad Alex.* (Optiz³, Urk. 6.2, p. 12, line 9).

61. Athanasius *V. Anton.* 7.

62. This description of Satan contains the charge made elsewhere (*Or. c. Ar.* 3.17, 19, 25) by Athanasius against the Arians.

63. Athanasius *V. Anton.* 5. *Vide De Inc.* 50, and also 22, 25, 27, 52.

64. Athanasius *Or. c. Ar.* 3.51 (Bright, p. 204). The theme is not absent from the *Vita Antonii*. Antony proclaims in a sermon to visiting philosophers (chap. 74) that the "Word of God has not changed" but assumed a human body in order that man might "partake in the divine and spiritual nature." *Vide* also *Or. c. Ar.* 1.16; *Ep. ad Adelph.* 4; *Ep. ad Epict.* 6; *Fest. Ep.* 5.5.

65. Athanasius *V. Anton.* 5, 7.

66. Ibid., 10.

67. Ibid.

68. Athanasius *Or. c. Ar.* 3.51 (Bright, p. 204). Athanasius also refers to the sun's withdrawal of its ἀκτῖνας during the passion of Christ (*Or. c. Ar.* 1.7; *Ep. ad Adelph.* 10; *Ep. ad. Maximum* 2).

69. Athanasius *V. Anton.* 7 and 66. *Vide* Athanasius *Or. c. Ar.* 3.49, 52; *Fest. Ep.* 5.5. For an interesting treatment of the importance of Phil. 3:13–14 in patristic writings in the East, *vide* Ronald E. Heine, *Perfection in the Virtuous Life,* Patristic Monograph Series 2 (Cambridge, Mass.: Greeno, Hadden & Co., 1975), app. C, pp. 241ff.

70. Athanasius *V. Anton.* 12–14.

71. The power of the sign of the cross, which comes into play here and in chaps. 23, 35, 78–80, is treated by Athanasius in *C. Gent.* 29 and *De Inc.* 47.

72. *Vide* p. 66 and n. 99 in chap. 2 *supra*. In *V. Anton.* 16, Antony instructs the monks that the reward for ascetic virtue will be received in heaven when "putting off the body which is corruptible, we receive it back incorruptible." Cf. Athanasius *Or. c. Ar.* 2.74 and 3.33.

73. Athanasius *Or. c. Ar.* 3.23 (Bright, p. 178).

74. *Vide* Alexander *Ep. ad Alex.* (Opitz³, Urk. 14.29, p. 24, lines 9–12) and Athanasius *Or. c. Ar.* 1.37 and 2.50.

75. Athanasius *V. Anton.* 58. *Vide* also the healing of Martinian's daughter in chap. 48.

76. Ibid., 39.

77. Ibid., 38.

78. In Athanasius *V. Anton.* 24 and 30, Luke 10:19 is invoked in ways paralleled in *Fest. Epp.* 4 and 7. Luke 10:18 (Satan's "fall like lightning") appears in *V. Anton.* 40, in *De Inc.* 25, and in *Or. c. Ar.* 3.40.

79. Athanasius *V. Anton.* 28, 30, 41. *Vide* also chaps. 44 and 48. In chap. 49, the crowd's enthusiasm for "the things the Lord was doing through him" causes Antony to retreat into the Upper Thebaid for fear that "he might become prideful or someone . . . might think more of him than was warranted." Elsewhere Antony prays for sufferers; he does not boast if the Lord heals them, nor does he murmur if his prayers for healing are not answered. "And the ones who were cured were taught not to give thanks to Antony, but to God alone" (56). Similarly, in chap. 64 a young

man, having been freed of possession by a demon, "embraced the old man, all the while giving thanks to God."

80. Athanasius *V. Anton.* 35, 42, 18, 34.

81. Outside of the *Vita Antonii* Athanasius is fond of using συνεργέω and its noun forms in the sense of "conspirator"—for example, in reference to Meletian and Arian collusion (*Apol. c. Ar.* 17), to Satan and his co-workers *(Sermo major de fide* 19 and 28), and to the Arian Gregory's associate, Philagrius. In *Apol. c. Ar.* 44, however, he speaks of God's grace assisting (συνεργούσης) the emperors in their convening of the Synod of Sardica. For Asterius' view of the Word as God's *under*worker and assistant, *vide* chap. 3, pp. 115–16 *supra.*

82. Athanasius *V. Anton.* 84.

83. Ibid., 55. Cf. Athanasius *Fest Ep.* 2.2.

84. Athanasius *V. Anton.* 19.

85. Ibid., 20. Similar ideas, supported by the same biblical text, are found in *C. Gent.* 30. The specific emphasis on willing is not present in this passage, nor is the treatment of the soul's rectitude κατὰ φύσιν. But for Athanasian views on the purity of the soul, see *C. Gent.* 2ff. Another significant passage concerning the soul occurs in *V. Anton.* 34 and parallels the reference to Elisha's soul (2 Kings 6) employed in *H. Ar.* 40.

86. *Vide Verba Seniorum* 4.1; 7.9.

87. Athanasius *V. Anton.* 7, 20, 70.

88. Note particularly the employment of Phil. 3:13–14 in *V. Anton.* 7 and 66. Parallel use of the idea occurs in *Or. c. Ar.* 3.49 and in *Fest. Ep.* 5.5, with reference to the hope that the faithful "may not eat the Passover unworthily."

89. *Verba Seniorum* 10.5.

90. Alexander *Ep. ad Alex.* (Opitz[3], Urk. 14.34, p. 25, lines 1–3).

91. Ibid. (Opitz[3], Urk. 14.30, p. 24, lines 12–21).

92. Athanasius *V. Anton.* 70.

93. Ibid.

94. *Vide* Acts 5:15 and 19:11–12. Ernst Haenchen writes about the healing efficacy of Peter's shadow in these terms: "This idea of the apostle is so heightened as to be fantastic: Peter need not so much as touch a sick person to cure him—it is enough for his shadow to fall on him. If this is so, however, the apostle can no longer be distinguished from the θεῖος ἄνθρωπος dear to paganism. We see here the danger threatening the popular tradition of the apostolic miracles: it transforms the μάρτυς Ἰησοῦ Χριστοῦ into a man filled to his very shadow with miraculous power, by the aid of which he directly manifests the divine omnipotence" (Ernst Haenchen, *The Acts of the Apostles,* trans. B. Noble and G. Shinn [Oxford: Basil Blackwell, 1971], p. 246).

95. *Vide* Athanasius *V. Anton.* 85.

96. *Verba Seniorum* 17.19.

97. *V. Pach.* 25, Athanassakis, pp. 31, 33.

98. Heb. 2:10 and 12:2. *Vide* the remarks by C. F. D. Moule, "The Christology of Acts," in Leander E. Keck and J. Louis Martyn, ed., *Studies in Luke-Acts* (Philadelphia: Fortress Press, 1980), p. 180.

99. Athanasius *Or. c. Ar.* 3.2 (Bright, p. 156).

5

Divine Will
and Divine Nature as
Christological Options

ARIAN CHRISTOLOGY:
A CHRISTOLOGY OF DIVINE WILL

We have argued that since the opening volleys of the controversy, Arian Christology turned on the necessity of defending a doctrine of the "changeability" of the Son of God. This meant that they gave themselves up to a relentless defense of the freedom of the Son's will to incline to good or to evil. It was, as the orthodox were quick to point out, as possible for the Son to sin as not to sin. The Arians had assented to that theoretical possibility but did so only out of a sure conviction that God foresaw that the Son would not sin. Christ's ministry, both as obedient agent of creation and among humans, was proof of that inclination only to the good.[1] For them Jesus Christ was "predestined" to be Son of God and "firstborn" from the dead. Thus the Arian theologians conceived predestination along the lines of major non-Gnostic Greek Christian thinkers of the second and third centuries: predestination meant "foreseen merit."[2] God foresaw the perfect obedience and hence the meritorious salvation of his servant.

To biblical Platonists like Bishops Alexander and Athanasius such a changeability in the redeemer was unthinkable. Both the nature of divinity as they understood it in late Platonic categories and the exigencies of salvation depended on the ability to distinguish between divine nature which was unchangeable and creaturely nature which was corruptible of substance and mobile of will. Therefore, beginning with Alexander, they distinguished between the unchangeability of the Son because of his divine nature and the changeability of all other creatures because of their need of the Creator.

161

He [Christ] is on the one hand unchangeable, being perfect and sufficient in all respects, while they on the other hand, liable to turning in both directions, stand in need of his assistance (βοήθεια).[3]

At an early stage of the controversy, then, the battle lines were drawn between orthodox and Arian in terms of whether the Son was conceived to have a creaturely nature—and that meant a mutable nature and will—or whether he was thought to be divine by nature and so unchangeable in essence and inclination. This way of formulating the question was guaranteed to raise the most far-reaching controversy in the churches since the Gnostic crisis. We can forgive a scriptural illiterate like the Emperor Constantine for thinking the fight was about "terms" and yet not understanding the significance of that.[4] But Arius and Alexander and their respective supporters labored under no such limitation. The controversy became immediately a controversy about how biblical terminology was to be translated into christological dogma and hence into schemes of salvation for all believers.

Both sides realized that the person of the earthly Christ modeled our salvation.[5] Each side would construct its own anthropology and the salvation brought according to its own theological hermeneutics. For the earlier Arians the Bible was a book, as we have implied in previous chapters, about a God whose *nature* was unknowable but whose *ways* were made known in the revelation of his will for creatures. The long string of "alones" applied adjectivally to God underscored the Arian sense of divine sovereignty and freedom. Nothing in creation was the result of an outworking of the necessities of divine nature. All—creation and salvation—was the result of the divine will. It was a sovereign and free will which had created creatures through the agency of a freely obedient servant. It was therefore a divine will which destined creatures for a freely obedient sonship.[6] Christ then as preexistent servant and as earthly redeemer models such a scheme of salvation as is founded in a theology of divine will. The redeemer's free obedience in the performance of virtuous acts is what wins him the divine approval; and hence his "promotion" *(beltiōsis)* to the glories and dignities which the scriptures ascribe to the only begotten Son.[7] Thus the Son is rewarded for his obedience, even as other believers shall be rewarded for theirs, not by becoming the "only begotten Son" but by becoming sons and daughters of God—that is, children of the Father's deifying will.

162

It is a scheme of salvation built from first to last on the sovereign, initiating will of God and the responding will of believers. And that is why the awarding of titles and rewards figures so prominently in the Arian christological perspective.

Since the days of Justin Martyr the church had acknowledged the logical connection which existed between free choice and virtue and, hence, rewards. Right-thinking people knew there were rewards or punishments for one's conduct. Such a truism was listed as one of the *probabilia* by the pagan Cicero in his rhetorical manual.[8] But the role free will played in such conduct and its attendant deserts was disputed depending upon one's philosophical school or whether cosmology or ethics were being discussed. Against Stoic doctrines of a limited free will and deterministic notions of fate, which seemed to cancel out human choice in the service of metaphysical necessity, Justin wrote:

> Indeed, every creature is capable by nature of vice and of virtue. Nor would any action of theirs be worthy of praise unless they had the power to incline to either.[9]

With the defense of the creaturehood of the Son, the Arians therefore picked up the defense of the "inclination to either," to echo Justin's phrase. For the Arians, Christ's rewards for meritorious conduct were predicated on just such a necessity as the proper exercise of free will.

The behavioral model for such a Christology was that of a learner obeying a wise teacher. The orthodox took their stand on the philosophical and soteriological implications of the essential properties of divinity, but the Arians conceived of a God who was σοφός and who taught wisdom to his disciples. Thus Arius insisted in his *Thalia,*

> God is *sophos,* because he is teacher of wisdom.[10]

And he described Christ's earthly ministry as a gradual growth in wisdom.

But the teacher-learner model for the relation of Father to Son was also used to describe the preexistent state of the Son. Asterius employed the analogy of the teacher and learner to explain the Son's demiurgic activity:

> On the one hand he [Christ] is a creature and of creation; but he learned to create as from a teacher (διδάσκαλος) or a craftsman (τεχνίτης).[11]

The imagery of the teacher-learner as a christological metaphor had, we maintained, soteriological implications for the rest of humanity. Therefore we ought not to be surprised that Arius' *Thalia* opened with his claim to have *learned* theology from those who were partakers of wisdom, good men who were taught by God.[12] Nor should it seem curious that Arius goes on to claim to have learned wisdom from God and so to "know."[13] The early Arian movement, epitomized in its three central figures—Arius, Asterius the Sophist, Eusebius of Nicomedia—comprised a circle of exegetical theologians in which wise teachers learned wisdom and obedience from God and shared among themselves the salvific turning to the path of virtue with its attendant rewards.

The "Wisdom" of which they spoke had, of course, roots in the philosophical ethics of late antiquity. Yet those roots had been long since appropriated into the church's perspective on the ethical progress of believers, as we have suggested previously. But it was also a biblical perspective on wisdom which these Arians upheld, in which the gift of the Holy Spirit figured prominently[14] and in which they (as their Lord) shared in the divine "accidentally" rather than "essentially."[15] The early Arian theologians constituted a circle of learners of wisdom and "wise" teachers. Thus Asterius the "Sacrificer's" comment about what may be his own lapse into apostasy during the persecution credits both divine aid and "wise teachers" for the restoration to resistance:

> When I came into Christ's vineyard, I was prevented from laboring by bodily weakness but by the zeal of the Great Husbandman and *wise teachers* was aroused to tread the winepress [emphasis added].[16]

Just exactly what persons or factors crystallized such a circle must remain a mystery for the present. Lucian of Antioch has been frequently invoked as the teacher of both Arius and Eusebius of Nicomedia on the basis of Arius' calling Eusebius his "co-Lucianist."[17] The thorough research on the matter of Lucian's influence on the Arians by G. Bardy has produced evidence of a "school" but not of a master. There is nothing to tie Lucian to the early Arians except their adherence to a creedal summary of what they claimed at the Synod of Antioch of 341 was Lucian's faith[18] and, of course, Arius' phrase "co-Lucianist." Their contemporary enemies, Alexander and Athanasius, preferred to invoke the accursed name of Paul of Samosata.[19] Athanasius clearly did not believe that the Arians were really Paul's successors, but by a process of guilt by association he associated Paul, the Arians, and his own anti-Semitic New Testament picture of Jewish views of the Christ.[20] Athanasius' reticence to indicate Arius' dependence on Paul of

Samosata in any straightforward and nonrhetorical manner was probably due to his knowledge of the Arian stress on the preexistence of the Son and attendant cosmology. Paul, as the researches of Robert Sample have shown, had no place for either preexistence or cosmology in his theology.[21]

Alexander was more certain about Arianism's pedigree than was Athanasius: Ebion, Artemon, Paul of Samosata.[22] The brief list occurs in a section of his letter to Alexander immediately after a long discussion in which he has been combating the Arian notion of the progress and improvement of the Son and has been contending for the crucial orthodox distinction between Christ's sonship and ours.[23] In Alexander's mind it seems to have been the notion of a redeemer who advances which linked Arianism to these earlier heresies. What substance is there for such a charge?

While we know almost nothing about the heresy of Artemon, we know something about how the Ebionites portrayed the Christ from a fragment in Eusebius of Caesarea's history. The fragment is important because it tells us what one of the interested principals of the early Arian controversy considered a salient feature of Ebionite Christology. Eusebius writes:

> The first Christians gave these the suitable name of Ebionites because they had poor and mean opinions concerning Christ. They held him to be a plain and ordinary man who had achieved righteousness merely *by the progress of his character* (κατὰ προκοπὴν ἤθους) and had been born naturally from Mary and her husband [emphasis added].[24]

It is the progress (προκοπή) of the Christ that interested Eusebius as his leadoff charge, and that same moral *prokopē* probably brought them into Alexander's list of the Arian theological parentage.

The evidence for Paul of Samosata's influence on the Arians is much stronger. Dr. Robert Sample, working from our then unpublished results on the early Arians, has argued convincingly for a Syrian setting for the early Arians and a Samosatene influence.[25] What interests us here is the heavy emphasis Paul put on the ethical progress of the Christ and his scheme of the Christ's promotion to full sonship.[26] It is precisely this *prokopē* which lies at the very base of the Arian Christology whether considered precosmically or in terms of the earthly ministry and postcrucifixion exaltation of the redeemer. It seems safe to assume that when Alexander combats such a view of the redeemer's advancing sonship, he naturally turns to the last heresy to take a similar stance—that of Paul of Samosata.

But the biblical roots of Paul of Samosata seem to have been slightly different than those of the early Arians. Sample has shown what seems to us to be a consistent dependence on christological and soteriological themes and texts drawn from Luke-Acts.[27] The early Arians, however, seem to have developed a Christology and soteriology much more attuned to the Epistle to the Hebrews. This is not to insist that the Book of Hebrews was *their only or even prime source*. Previous chapters have indicated how widespread was their drawing upon the Old and New Testaments for positions and definitions. It is to suggest that the Christology of Hebrews, read from the standpoint of Arian theological presuppositions, *best summarizes* their themes and positions. It is also to suggest that the exegesis of texts from Hebrews played a far more important role in the controversy than previous scholars have noted.

If for example one reads Hebrews from the standpoint of Arian presuppositions, so many themes that we have identified as central to early Arianism leap to the fore; in fact, Heb. 1:1–4 seems almost a creedal summary of Arian thought. The Christ whom God appoints for virtuous service (1:2; 1:9; 3:2) and so has been exalted with honor and glory and an eternal name (1:4; 2:9; 5:6; cf. 5:6 and 7:28 for a "perfected" Son; 5:9–10; 12:2) looms large. In Hebrews we also read of the Son who learns obedience (5:8) and who obeys God (2:16; 5:9) by enduring even death on the cross (2:9; 12:2). Thereby he overcomes death (2:14). He never glorifies himself but awaits God's acclamation (5:6; 5:10). Like a good high priest this redeemer had to become like his brothers (2:14, 16). He shared equally the temptations of life in the flesh (2:18; 4:16) and sympathized with the weakness and ignorance of humans (5:2). Yet he was piously obedient (5:7–8) and without sin (4:15). Such a scheme of perfecting the pioneer (*archēgos*) through suffering has as its goal the bringing of "many sons" to salvation, "for," in the language of Hebrews,

> the one who sanctifies and the ones who are sanctified are out of one stock (ἐξ ἑνὸς πάντες) [2:11].

Throughout his *Orations*, Athanasius insisted that more pious interpretations could be given to texts which point to the joint origins and destinies of redeemer and redeemed; they refer to Christ's sojourn in the body for our salvation, not to his eternal deity in the Athanasian scheme. One has only to pay attention to the scope (*skopos*) of Scripture to realize this.[28] But the

Arian fires could be fueled by the same texts read according to the Arian insistence that Christ was essentially different from God—a creature meritoriously promoted to sonship and glory as first of the perfected creatures.

The question arises, however pervasive we may *suspect* to be the influence of Hebrews on the Arians, exactly and precisely what texts *were actually employed* by them as planks in their scriptural platform. Here the range of allusions to and citations from Hebrews diminishes somewhat, being confined primarily to the first and third chapters of the letter. Surprisingly, extended discussions of ready-made Arian texts like Heb. 2:11, 14 and 5:1–10 are absent from our sources in their transmitted state. But enough survives of the citations of chapters one and three to give the epistle more prominence in Arian exegesis than researchers have recognized.

Heb. 1:1–4 seems to have been an important Arian proof text. Already in his brief early confession of faith addressed to Bishop Alexander, Arius has alluded to Heb. 1:2. The allusion has passed unnoticed in critical editions of the letter and in the secondary literature. Arius writes,

> For the Father, having given him the inheritance (τὴν κληρονομίαν) of all, did not deprive himself of those things which he has ingenerately in himself.[29]

The phrase "the inheritance of all" is an allusion to Heb. 1:2b, in which Arius, citing from memory, has substituted κληρονομία for the κληρονόμος of our Heb. 1:2b.[30] From the context of Arius' letter, it seems he used the text to stress the received (derivative) nature of Christ's existence, in creating whom God deprived himself of none of his essential properties. In his systematic refutation of the Arian exegesis of Hebrews 1, Athanasius does not quote Heb. 1:2b (citing only 1:2a), because he is worried about a far more damaging text to his case, Heb. 1:4.[31]

The Arian usage of Heb. 1:4 was seen as a major difficulty by Athanasius. He begins a systematic refutation of their position in his first *Oration,* and this continues for several chapters.[32] In our earlier chapters we indicated that Arius alludes to this text in his *Thalia.*[33] Athanasius indicates that Arian exegesis stressed the "become better" (κρείττων γενόμενος) of Heb. 1:4. He combats their use of the term "become" applied to the coming into being of the Son,[34] but it seems clear that his real problem lay in their stress on the comparative "better." They had insisted that Christ's being compared to the angels showed that he did not differ from them[35] and so belonged to "things

167

originate."[36] It is precisely this usage of κρείττων that Arius had indicated in his *Thalia* with the words

> One equal to the Son the Superior (ὁ κρείττων) is able to beget, but not one more excellent (διαφορώτερον) or better (κρείττονα) or greater (μείζονα).[37]

Arius emphasizes the similarity of the Son to other possible redeemers that God could have created; at the same time he affirms the perfection of the one God *in fact did create*. There could have been *others* but *none better* than this son. Athanasius will maintain in contrariety that the "better" of Heb. 1:4 refers to a "better" (that is, distinct and unique) nature; and therefore Christ's ministry is better than any before him.[38] And he will marshal other uses of the comparative from Hebrews (7:22; 8:6; 7:19; 9:23) to underscore his understanding that St. Paul was only meaning to contrast divinity with things originate.[39] Whether the Arians actually used the list of texts Athanasius cites to buttress their case on κρείττων is impossible to say. However, they surely and certainly were partial to the Heb. 1:4 text.

The signal importance to the Arians of Heb. 3:1–2a has already been discussed,[40] and it is not our intention to cite every mention or possible usage of the letter by them. What we are indicating here is how easily the Christology and soteriology of Hebrews can be accommodated to Arian hermeneutic perspectives and how central to their thinking were certain key texts drawn from Hebrews. It is precisely this that gives back to the Arians one of the scriptural bases which has been largely passed over by scholars.[41] And it is also this fundamental sympathy to Hebrews that differentiates the Arians from Paul of Samosata, who preferred Luke-Acts.[42] Thus while Arianism in its early stages bears its most striking resemblance to Robert Sample's recovery of Samosatene Christology, an Antiochene "succession" of this Christology is not a simple linear progression.

What exact theological traditions lie at the heart of early Arianism cannot be clearly extracted at this point. New factors and forces have entered into the world of late antiquity which seem to break the continuity with the late third century, as we shall see even more clearly in the case of Athanasian Christology.

Where then can we look for the supporters of the Arian movement in its early stages? What, apart from the somewhat problematic references of the later historians,[43] could constitute the setting in life of early Arianism? C. W. Mönnich, in what we consider to be a landmark essay on Arianism, suggested an ascetic circle (monks, confessors, pneumatics, ones who struggle for perfection) as the likely partisans.[44] And as we have seen, Athanasius' elaborate and concerted attempt to win Antony for Nicene Christology and soteriology suggests the kind of lively appeal that a Christology and soteriology based on progress in doing the will of God unto perfection could have.[45] Such a commitment to *prokopē* in its more classical guise was still alive in Egypt in the late fourth or early fifth centuries in a textile representation of the goddess of the hearth, Hestia Polyolbos. Among the gifts she is offered by flanking putti are *prokopē* and *aretē*.[46] We should perhaps look for a circle or setting in which pagan and Christian/biblical notions of progress in virtue could come together in an emphasis upon the ethical progress and perfectibility of grace-filled persons. That the pagan as well as the Christian tradition allowed a progress in virtue which led one to deification and unchangeability has already been noted.[47] Contemporary pagan, like Christian, theology was ready to note that the deification one achieved by being brought to the divine state through virtue was based on a similarity of virtue between God and creatures and not on a change of natures.[48]

The radical step taken by the Arians was in extending that kind of deity to the redeemer. In this, as we have seen, the Arians were aided and abetted by certain motifs in the Bible. Yet certain pagan traditions may be operative here also. The Pythagorean Sthenidas wrote an interesting passage in his *On Royalty* in which he distinguished between the first God who is king "by nature and essence" (φύσει καὶ [ὠσίᾳ]) and the king (on earth) who is king "by birth and imitation" (γενέσει καὶ μιμάσει).[49] A king is wise (σοφόν) only as an imitator (ἀντίμιμος) and emulator (ζηλωτός) of the first God. The God who rules all possessed wisdom in himself (ἐν αὐτῷ κεκταμένος τὰν σοφίαν), whereas the king who exists in time has knowledge (ὁ δ' ἐν χρόνῳ ἐπιστάμαν).[50] The king will imitate this God if he renders paternal care for his people, for as Sthenidas says,

> It is natural that the first God had been considered as the Father of the gods and the father of men for this reason above all, that he is benevolent to all beings which he has created, which is why one would ever wish him to neglect his rule, because it was not sufficient to have been simply the maker of all beings, but he is still by nature (πέφυκε), for all, indistinctly, the tutor (τροφεύς) and teacher (διδάσκαλος) who teaches all that is good and law-making. . . . The wise and legitimate king will be, then, an imitator (μιμητὰς) and servant (ὑπερέτος) of God (τῷ θεῷ).[51]

169

We can note themes encountered already in Arianism in the entire Sthenidean passage: kingship and wisdom possessed naturally by the first God but by origination (γένεσις) by the king who has these through imitation; the retention of the title διδάσκαλος for that first God; and finally, the king as servant (ὑπερέτος) of the God. The piece shows the influence of first and second God speculation.[52] It was in this very vein that Arians framed the relationship between God and Christ. That Arius or Asterius read Sthenidas can be debated. The central point is more important: to persons familiar with this kind of discussion, the Arian christological scheme would not sound foreign or innovative.

Important also to Arian Christology was the distinction between the acquired titles and glories of the Christ and the God who bestowed them. But again the distinction which reserved natural perfection to Deity and virtues by acquisition to creatures turns up in our quotation from Sthenidas and was not unknown in other ancient writers.[53] It was therefore possible for lines of biblical concepts such as we have examined in Hebrews and late classical notions of deity or rulership by imitation and virtue to meld in Arian circles. Thus the Arians could make their appeal in terms understandable to people schooled into both biblical and late classical notions of progress and virtue—in short, to the very kinds of people with whom Athanasius has to do in his writings.

The Arians' special interest in the wise teacher partaking in wisdom may lead us to circles in Egypt which continued the long interest in wisdom literature.[54] In short, we are suggesting that the setting of Arianism can best be found by researchers who focus on those areas where the redeemer is understood to be a perfected creaturely model for us, where obedience to the will of God and progress in virtue are the operative categories for *both* Christology *and* soteriology, and where biblical and classical notions of wisdom have high currency.

ATHANASIAN CHRISTOLOGY: A CHRISTOLOGY OF DIVINE NATURE

A new interpretation of the early Arians requires at least a brief examination of their greatest opponent's thought. For once the early Arian program comes to the fore, it enables us to view Athanasian theology from a slightly different perspective. And here we come to a theology and a

Christology in which nature language has risen to dramatic prominence in Christian theology to control and interpret the language of divine "will" and "willing." Like his Arian enemies, Athanasius inherited a theological tradition in which both "essentialist" and "voluntarist" languages were used of the Divine Being. If, as we think we have shown, the early Arians concluded that the divine nature communicated nothing—not its essence nor its wisdom—but that all creation depended on divine will, Athanasius inclined sharply toward the opposite pole: the key to both Christology and salvation lay in understanding the implications of the knowable properties (not divine planning and willing) which characterized the Son and undergirded our salvation.

Alexander of Alexandria first raised the storm by insisting on the eternality of "Father" and "Son"[55] in such a way that both persons seemed to Arius to share in the divine nature.[56] As the Arian wags so tartly expressed it, Christ had become God's brother rather than God's Son.[57] Yet this was the course which the Alexandrian bishops of the early fourth century had set for Christology, one founded upon the insistence that the Father-Son relationship was guaranteed by a "natural" rather than a "voluntary" bonding. Having identified two senses of the term "son" in Scripture, one biological (Isaac, son of Jacob) and the other "adoptive" (in which son was a circumlocution for "believer"), Alexander and Athanasius chose the former sense for their Christology and the latter sense for their soteriology. Christ was a son by nature; all others, by adoption.[58]

Such an ontological linkage between Father and Son which made paternity and sonship coeternal was viewed by the Arians as a dangerous promotion of the Son to equality with the Father, as indicated by their "fraternal" quip cited above. The fact of the matter seems to have been that Athanasius continued to regard God the Father as the common source for Persons of the Trinity,[59] but the clear and apparent ontological superiority of God to Christ which Origen preserved in his use of the term $arch\bar{e}$ had certainly been obfuscated if not eliminated.[60]

As we shall see, this "ontological" relationship which existed between Father and Son raised some specific problems for Athanasius' incarnate redeemer, which his Arian opponents were quick to exploit. But here a more general point should be made. Athanasius regarded all language of divine will and willing applied to Christ as suspect of heretical interpretation and potentially destructive of our salvation unless it was controlled and

171

interpreted by notions of what is proper to divine nature. Technically speaking, for Athanasius there is no such thing as "free will" in God,[61] and nowhere is this stance of his more apparent than in his discussion of the Son's generation.

Alexander of Alexandria had introduced all manner of "essential" imagery into the early stages of the Arian debate to counter their stance that Christ was a child of will and hence a son by adoption.[62] But it was Athanasius who expanded, developed, and systematized essentialist thinking into a full Christology and soteriology. The Arians had objected that

> Unless he [Christ] has come to be by will, then God had a Son by necessity and against his good pleasure (μὴ θέλων).

Athanasius' reply to their charge that he had imposed necessity on God shows the principle which undergirds his entire Christology:

> And who is it then who imposes necessity on him . . . for what is contrary to will they see; but what is greater and transcends it has escaped their perception. For as what is beside purpose is contrary to will, so what is according to nature (κατὰ φύσιν) transcends and precedes counseling (τοῦ βουλεύσεσθαι). . . . As far then as the Son transcends the creature, by so much does what is by nature (κατὰ φύσιν) transcend the will (τῆς βουλήσεως).[63]

In this section of the *Orations* Athanasius contrasts the begetting of a son, which is a "natural" (κατὰ φύσιν) process involving essence *(ousia)*, with the planning or designing of a task, represented by such terms as βούλομαι, βούλησις, βούλημα.[64]

Thus the language of divine essence must interpret and control all terminology of willing or purposing, for it is the superior and prior category for understanding characteristics of the divine. Essences are prior to "terms," and being is prior to counseling or willing, Athanasius argues,[65] but this never implies an *un*willing generation of the Son by the Father. Nor can language of divine willing imply a subsequency in time;[66] for there is no interval (διάστημα) in the commanding and willing of Deity.[67] Thus God's will (βουλή) cannot be likened to human counsel which can come and go, but must be considered a "living will" (ἡ ζῶσα βουλή).[68] And Christ *is* that living will.[69] The numerous scriptural terms to which the Arians could point which seemed to indicate voluntary desire on God's part to create the Son and all other creatures (θέλειν and its cognates) or decisive intentionality (βούλεσθαι and its cognates) to create (and even save) were interpreted and controlled by the ontologically prior and morally preeminent category of "essence."[70] Thus while the Arians might think themselves justified in emphasizing again and again God's free decision to create the Son and the Son's free decision to obey the divine will, no option is shut tighter by Athanasius than the voluntaristic relationship between Father and Son. Divine willing—both desiring (θέλειν and so forth) and deciding (βούλεσθαι and so forth)—means to Athanasius a fundamental instability and capriciousness in the order of creation and the process of salvation. What is willed can be *un*willed at any moment. What God creates by will, he can *un*create. The problem with will is that it has to be situationally and momentarily free and therefore cannot be eternally fixed or predictable. *Will* implies an inclination which can shift rather than constancy of purpose and action. Thus he writes:

> For to say "He was begotten by will" (ἐκ βουλήσεως) means first that he was not; but second, also it signifies he [God] has an inclination either way, as was said; so that someone could suppose that he was able not even to will the Son. But to say regarding the Son, "He was able even not to exist" is an impious and rash conclusion (τόλημα) reaching to the essence of the Father; as if what is properly his essence was not to exist. For it is like saying, "The Father was able not to be good (ἀγαθός)." But just as the Father is always and by nature good, so he is always generative (γεννητικός) by nature.[71]

Thus decision and intentionality are removed from the sphere of the generation of the Son. God does not will to create the Son; rather the Deity is, as in the quote above, "generative" (γεννητικός) or "fruitful" (καρπογόνος).[72]

The relationship between Father and Son is, of course, one of mutuality; they love each other and will the same things.[73] But their prior and more secure relationship is ontological and not transactional. Thus the Arian way of construing the Son's being "in" the Father as based on mutuality of wills is vigorously opposed by Athanasius. The preposition "in" signifies an ontological relationship. Thus when one speaks of the Father's will (βούλημα) being "in him," or of our salvation as being founded "in the Lord," or of the Son's being "in the Father" or "in himself" (God),[74] such phrases signify an ontological reality. The transactional model of will that runs in Arian thought from the creation of the Son through that of the redeemed can play no role in Athanasius' system.[75] Counseling (βούλησις) is external (ἔξωθεν) to a nature or secondary to it; and therefore the more transcendent (and hence more pious) category by which to understand the Father-Son relationship is "nature" (τὸ κατὰ φύσιν).[76]

Nowhere does the Athanasian desire to exclude the "will" as the operative category of understanding the Father-Son relationship come out more clearly than when he describes how God could be enclosed in a body. In a curious passage in his *De Incarnatione,* he writes:

> For indeed he was not circumscribed (περικεκλεισμένος), nor was he in the body but not present elsewhere. Nor while he moved (ἐκίνειν) the body was the universe emptied of his power (ἐνεργείας) and providence; but most marvelous (τὸ παραδοξότατον), being Logos, he was not enclosed (συνείχατο) by anything, but rather he himself enclosed all things.

> . . . just as while present in the whole of creation, he is on the one hand outside of all according to essence (κατ᾽ οὐσίαν), but he is in all (ἐν πᾶσι) with respect to his own power (ταῖς ἑαυτοῦ δυνάμεσι), ordering the whole (τὰ πάντα), and spreading his own providence everywhere over all, and vivifying at the same time each and every thing, enclosing the whole and not being enclosed (περιέχων τὰ ὅλα καὶ μὴ περιεχόμενος), but being wholly in every regard in his Father alone. Just so [that is, as in his presence in creation] existing in the human body, and himself vivifying it, likewise he also vivifies the whole and he was in all things (ἐγίνετο), and he was outside of the whole.[77]

The quotation contains the important commonplace "enclosing (περιέχειν) but not enclosed" used by earlier authors to distinguish divine being which could not be enclosed (and hence controlled or understood) from divine activity which could be encompassed. William R. Schoedel's superlative history of this commonplace (and its sister term, "containing not contained") has shown its importance and meaning for earlier authors.[78] In line with this usage of the commonplace, but now applied to the incarnate one, Athanasius makes the standard points: if we are speaking about the divine nature (κατ᾽ οὐσίαν), this cannot be enclosed by the cosmos or the body; if we are describing the powers of the Logos (ἐν ἑαυτοῦ δυνάμεσι), these are "in all things" (ἐν πᾶσι).[79] This same kind of distinction appears in Philo, Irenaeus, and the Coptic *Teachings of Silvanus* (even applied to the incarnation).[80] Clement of Alexandria expresses a similar sentiment when considering the Son from the standpoint of his nature:

> From his own point of view the Son of God is never displaced; not being divided, not severed, not passing from place to place; being always everywhere, and being enclosed (περιεχόμενος) nowhere.[81]

Origen, in his *De Principiis,* speaks out of both sides of his mouth. We are encouraged to think of the Logos or Sophia of God circumscribed (at least for a time) by the body.[82] The discouragement comes in a very problematic section of *De Principiis* Book IV in which we may perceive the traces of Rufinus' tampering, but it is not impossible that Origen was in sympathy with the text as we have it.[83]

Thus there are some Alexandrian precedents for Athanasius' use of the commonplace both of the Second Person of the Trinity and for the incarnation; the precedents appear particularly in those writers sensitive to the problems of speaking about the divine nature qua nature. It is what is *missing* in the Athanasian usage that is fascinating. The commonplace "enclosing, not enclosed" was developed by Philo in its antithetical form to show a sharp antithesis between God and lower gods and, in a less sharp form, in the philosophical tradition to contrast "higher and lower dignity."[84] Clement of Alexandria uses the notion of enclosure precisely in this sense, as does *Silvanus,*[85] and perhaps Origen also. But in all these writers it is clear that the Second Person of the Trinity is subordinated to God the Father either with respect to his being or in that he is the servant of the Father's will. Origen's subordination of the Logos to the Father's "being" and "willing" is well-known.[86]

In Athanasius' Christology both are notoriously absent. For Athanasius, to be "in the Father" while being "in the body" implies no clear subordination of natures and no dependence on divine will. His Son was a Son "by nature," and therefore the attributes of the nature (φύσις, οὐσία) of true divinity belonged *by nature* to the Son. The begraced mediator of the early Arians could be said to be "in the Father" in the same way as all others, for "in him we live and move and possess our being" (Acts 17:28).[87]

Athanasius will quote Acts 17:28 only to describe the Logos' presence in the body (that is, explanatory of the divine ubiquity but never of the relationship of the Son to the Father).[88] Athanasius will speak an older christological language in which God creates the world *through* the Son or administers providence through him or gives us grace through the Son,[89] but the controlling concept is that in the Son there is no diminution of the divine nature and no externality to the Father represented by any dependency on will. The Son is the exact expression of the Father's nature. It is precisely the Arians who, because of their distinction of divine natures and dependency of the redeemer on the will of God, will raise the question of an incarnation conceived along Athanasian lines:

> How can this one be contained (χωρεῖν) in that one, and that one in this one? Or how is the Father at all able, being greater (μείζων), to be contained (χωρεῖν) in the Son who is lesser (ἐλλάτονι)?[90]

Two groups of opponents more exactly suited to each other could hardly have been found. Athanasius rests secure on the identity in essence of Father and Son (though not their numerical unity)[91] while the Arians rank the natures. But more important for our purposes here is the way Athanasius' theology shies away from the linchpin of early Arian Christology and soteriology—the will of God. He rejects the Son's generation by, and hence his dependency on, the will of God because it could mean that conceivably the Son could not have existed. A Son by will, as we have seen, means a Son who might *not* have existed as well as one who did. But more interesting still is Athanasius' tendency to extend the divine nature's natural fruitfulness to God's desire to create the creaturely universe. With Plato, Athanasius can say the God of all is good by nature and that goodness "cannot even grudge existence but desires all to exist as objects of his loving-kindness."[92] It is not that God needs anything.[93] It is that Athanasius does not want to emphasize too much creation as an act of divine choice or inclination, for then the divine being could change its mind or alter its purpose. Plotinus took this same position for the same reason in his second *Ennead*.[94] Athanasius' God operates not simply by conviction or commitment but out of essential goodness or philanthropy.[95] This control of the potential instability of divine will can be seen in his Christology. Athanasius asserts, the Logos is not generated by an act of will, nor can it be so terminated; the incarnate Logos cannot increase in virtue except in his human aspects, because that way the Son cannot *decrease* in virtue;[96] the divine Son is by nature secure and stable in his goodness.

It is this Athanasian confidence in the stability of divine nature over and against his fears for the instability of human nature which constitutes the very heart of both his Christology and his soteriology. It is the instability of rational natures—the fact that the will can change and shift—which leads him to oppose the Arians and to downplay the role of will in the incarnate Christ and its role in Christ's work of salvation. Athanasius' theology is a theology of divine nature's perfection controlling and stabilizing a shifting universe.

ATHANASIAN SOTERIOLOGY

"Essentialist" thinking constitutes the basis of Athanasius' soteriology. We can see this most clearly by realizing that Athanasius founds his soteriology and Christology in a description of the characteristics of human *nature* rather than the human "situation." That is to say, what we predicate about human nature, qua physical beings, is the key to salvation's necessity and content. For example, the dominant problem which necessitates the physical incarnation of the redeemer is not the disobedience of human creatures. People disobeyed beginning with Adam and continuing with great persistence and no little inventiveness in that venture. But since the Fall and its perdurance, something radical has happened. Athanasius speaks of it in a variety of ways; but anthropologically, it means that death, mortality, and *corruption* are no longer *external* to human nature but an essential part of it.[97] Therefore repentance, while important to a proper Christian attitude, is simply irrelevant to the initial reversing of the human condition:

> Now if there were merely a misdemeanor in question, and not a consequent corruption (φθορά), repentance were well enough. But if, when transgression had once gained a start, men became involved in that corruption which was their nature, and were deprived of the grace which they had, being in the image of God, what further step was needed? Or what was required for such grace and such recall, but the Word of God, . . .?[98]

What we have after repentance (which means turning and willing what God wills) is an obedient creature who is dying, fading, rotting away—in short, penitent corpses! However, there *are* those mortals who now by the grace of the incarnation have escaped the consequences of their natures and who anticipate the benefits of the resurrection.[99] And in the *Life of Antony* Athanasius has given us a portrait of one—we notice at points in the tract that Antony does not age or change in physical appearance.[100] Antony shows by anticipation the properties of that grace which in the resurrection life will reverse mortal characteristics, even as the representative body of the Logos itself experienced no decay. Certainly the deep Egyptian preoccupation with physical preservation of the corpse has had its influence here. Christians continued not only mummification in Athanasius' day and beyond, but also the practice of displaying the mummy of the departed one in the parlor for long periods after death, a practice which the blessed

Antony inveighs against.[101] Moreover, Athanasius describes our human plight in the *De Incarnatione* in terms of the fading funeral portrait.[102] The picture of the afterlife is considerably different in Athanasian and Egyptian pagan thought-circles.[103] All we wish to emphasize here is the mutuality of concern for the natural instability of creaturely life. Here the Athanasian concern goes well beyond patristic commonplaces which view death neutrally as the "debt we all owe nature," or even beyond the usual consequence of death as punishment for sin against God. It is not just death but continuing corruption even after death which is the real problem.[104]

Athanasius' Logos becomes incarnate because the cosmos is dissolving (διαλύειν).[105] It is ontologically linked to "that which is not" and therefore abides in death, not simply in the sense that we die, but in the sense that we are disintegrating (διαλύειν).[106] It is the perishing creation, this dissolving cosmos, this world on the brink of utter dissolution, that is offensive to God's goodness. It is bad publicity for God because it is effacing God's works.[107] It is not a consequence of the divine nature that the Son takes a body but a requisite of stabilizing a universe about to give God its Creator a very bad name indeed.

When therefore Athanasius comes to describe the incarnation, he says that Christ did not simply will (ἠθέλησεν) to become incarnate or to appear (ἤθελε φανῆναι), for this could be accomplished by a θεοφάνεια.[108] But out of *philanthropia* he takes a body which condescends to our nature.[109] In fact, the state of creation is now such that no mere act of divine will (θέλων) or fiat (νεῦμα) could save it.[110] For because of Adam's fall, corruption (φθορά) was not external (ἔξωθεν) to the body but had become attached to it; therefore the Logos had to be fused (συμπλακῆναι) to the body to reverse that death and corruption.[111]

In the light of what has been said, it should come as no surprise to us to discover how Athanasius deals with the agony and struggle of Gethsemane. All the marks of Jesus' indecision and turmoil (that is, mutability and instability) are ascribed to the flesh; but it is "God himself doing the willing."[112] What God wills in this case is to be in a suffering body for our salvation; and although Athanasius says that Christ could lay his life down and take it up again when he willed,[113] he has in mind here not just the power of deity to do all kinds of things but the sure conviction that God redeemed his creation in accordance with what was necessary for our salvation. In short, the will of the redeemer is the essential extension not of divine choice but of divine nature. The agony of alternative decision making tortures the flesh, not the Logos who acts in all things in accordance with his essential properties.

This brings us to the very heart of the import of Christ's work for humanity and, thus, of the Athanasian soteriology. Christ has given to us a physical nature redeemed from corruption by making available to human nature a grace that is irreversible. We have seen already that the problem with the will, as Athanasius conceives it, is precisely that it can incline to good or evil. So the soul stays in perpetual motion; if it is not involved in good, it is turning to evil.[114] Hence while God and his Word are unchangeable, creatures are not. The Arians had insisted that Christ possessed free will and hence a changeable nature.[115] But the Athanasian soteriology turns on the elimination of the changeable nature of the redeemer and the provision of an irreversible grace to humankind. Adam's nature was changeable, and Christ came to overcome and eliminate precisely this changeability, thus giving the flesh freedom not to sin.[116] Athanasius responds to the Arian exegesis of Psalm 44:7 (LXX):

> But the statement "you have loved righteousness and hated iniquity" set forth in the psalm does not show, as you think, the nature of the Logos to be "changeable" (τρεπτήν), but rather it even signifies from this his unchangeability. For since the nature of originate creatures is changeable, and some on the one hand transgressed but others disobeyed, just as was said; and their actions are not steadfast (βεβαία), but often it is possible that one good man presently is changed afterward and becomes another, so that the man now righteous (δίκαιον) is found shortly to be unrighteous; therefore there was need of an unchangeable (ἄτρεπτος) one, in order that men might have as an image (εἰκόνα) and type (τύπον) for virtue that immutability (ἀμετάβλητον) of the righteousness of the Logos.[117]

For Athanasius precisely the problem of this changeable nature is that it indicates a corruptible nature. That is why he fights changeability in the Christ and why his soteriology is geared to moving us from the realm of changeability to unchangeability. For this, our nature must be brought into contact with the divine nature; hence the Logos is wedded to the body in such a way that it will not be external to it. But we should not miss the result of the incarnation: it has brought to human nature a grace unlike Adam's, which was external. Christ has brought a grace which is secure and irreversible. It is this grace which enables us to escape our natural state by participation in Christ and to abide (μένειν, διαμένειν) in him.[118] Thus the

Spirit is securely received by us.[119] This is the reason why the Athanasian Christ speaks the words of John 17:21, "As thou, Father, art in me, and I in thee, that they may be one in us." Athanasius writes,

> . . . and if He should use the expression "as we," again this is nothing other than that such a grace of the Spirit as is appointed for disciples may be infallible (ἀδιάπτωτος) and irrevocable (ἀμεταμέλητος [lit., "unrepented"]).[120]

It is, then, a world of change and corruption, which means in spiritual terms a world of the receiving and the losing of grace, that Athanasius' soteriology is geared to overcome:

> For when a mere man "receives," he has also the possibility to be deprived; and this was demonstrated with respect to Adam; for "receiving," he lost. But in order that grace might be inseparable (ἀναφαίρετος) and be kept secure (βεβαία) by men, on account of this he appropriates to himself (ἰδιοποιεῖται) the gift, and he is said to have received ἐξουσία as man, which he always has as God.[121]

Thus also because the Word has united himself to our nature, we are able to remain free from sin, to have permanent power over the demons and permanence in the resurrection life.[122] For Athanasius rational creatures are not going to continue to sin either in this life or in the resurrection life, so that now one may look securely to life in Christ rather than to a series of present or future worlds in which sin might occur again, as in Origen's scheme.

Humankind then experiences an advance that takes place—a προκοπή in its very fleshly nature which will abide (διαμένειν) infallibly (ἄπτωτος) because the Logos is not external (ἔξωθεν) to the flesh.[123]

> But [Athanasius writes, alluding to the phrase of Prov. 8:22] if he was not created for us, we are not created "in him" (ἐν αὐτῷ); and not having been created in him, we do not have him in ourselves (ἐν ἑαυτοῖς) but we possess [him] externally (ἔξωθεν), as if we have received instruction (τὴν μάθησιν) from him as from a teacher. And thus is our condition—once more (πάλιν) the sin of the flesh, abiding in [us] (ἐμμένουσα), reigned just as much, not having been cast out of the flesh.[124]

The Athanasian Christology was founded in a theology of the differences between divine and human nature. By linking the Christ essentially and eternally to God, Athanasius insures that the incarnation will bring the divine nature into contact with human nature. Human nature is lost in a disintegrating world in which changeability shows itself as corruptibility of flesh and instability of mind and will. God is always, but man and the cosmos are about to be dissolved into nonexistence. To rectify this, the God who operates out of his nature sends the Son by nature to renew our nature. By our participation in him and through the flesh which he has renewed, *grace has been made irreversibly available to the cosmos and to human persons. In short, the universe and the life in grace have become stabilized in the very structure of things.*

A new doctrine of grace for a stabilized order of redemption has come to the fore. It was a way of expressing the possibility of Christian perseverance to the end, a problem that Augustine must wrestle with two generations later in the West. The East could never have formulated the gift of perseverance in terms of the bondage of the individual will. That would have violated its own commitment to the importance of choice and free will. Foreknowledge of God, by which was meant "foreseen merit," was as close to predestination as an Easterner could come. But Athanasius provided the very "next best thing"—an unchangeable type of virtue and an irreversible grace in the order of things available to human persons who were enabled to participate in this through Christ's redemptive work.

All of his mature life Athanasius fought against the changeability of the kind of redeemer who lived according to the will of God. The reasons for this we have already seen. Will implies changeability in two directions—toward vice or toward virtue. And changeability itself implies a receiving of grace and a losing of it. Few ages would know these facts better than that of Athanasius. A phrase from canon 12 of Nicaea catches up the horror at such an action:

> Those who have been called by grace, and have at first displayed their ardor, but afterwards have run like "dogs to their own vomit" [Prov. 26:11] . . . [125]

It is a canon about bribery to buy back military office. But it sounds the themes that pepper Athanasius' writings and haunt the Nicene canons—love and betrayal, grace and backsliding.[126] When persecution arises, when a person is one thing and then turns to become another, what advance is there by Christians, and how can we be assured of such advance? Adam and the devil with their changeable natures changed their allegiances.[127] Saul persecuted David.[128] The Christ is torn from God by Arians, and Meletians rend the church.[129] Love and betrayal—the Judas theme—flits in and around orthodox writings. For example, Judas appears in Athanasius' Easter letter of A.D. 331, eating of the Passover with Jesus while plotting.[130] A

181

preoccupation with deceit, "feigned" grace, the fall from grace, the "few who are chosen" haunts his letters. The devil is restless to bring us down. Meletians form a living proof that Christian people betray Christ and each other. So much hangs on an emperor whose theological inclinations are capricious. Persecution by tax collector and petty ecclesiastic is the given of daily life for orthodox or Meletian.[131]

So acute is the problem of betrayal and backsliding that the fourth century will need to construct a history of those who did not backslide or betray and march them out as heroes and saints of the faith: Moses, David, above all Job, concerning whom there are extant a number of commentaries.[132] Athanasius has the standard catalog of heroes. But his are founded in a doctrine of grace peculiarly his own. It is the unchangeable savior, eternally and essentially one with the Father, whose grace has weakened the demons and saved us from the consequences of our nature. The Athanasian Antony is a figure who testifies to that every time he gets an audience. Thus he is also the figure who testifies to a resolve to reach his goal without falling:

> Let this especially be the common aim (σπουδή) of all, neither to give way having once begun, nor to faint in trouble, nor to say: We have lived in the discipline (ἐν τῇ ἀσκήσει) a long time; but rather as making a beginning daily let us increase our earnestness (τὴν προθυμίαν).[133]

Thus Antony abides firm (ἐπιμένειν) in his daily discipline and cannot be turned from his purpose (προαίρεσις)[134] or his resolve (πρόθεσις, προθυμία).[135] Even when devils disguise themselves as monks in order to trouble them about the efficacy of the solitary life,[136] monks do not need to listen to them; for, as Antony is made to explain,

> . . . it is unseemly, since we possess the Holy Scriptures and the freedom (ἐλευθερίαν) which comes from the Savior, to be taught by the devil, who has not observed (τηρήσαντος) his own order (τὴν ἰδίον τάξιν) [that is, of evil], but whose resolves go from one thing to another (ἀλλ᾽ ἕτερα ἀνθ᾽ ἑτέρων φρονήσαντος).[137]

By the "grace given by the savior," monks like Antony have power to tread on serpents. And Antony, mouthpiece for Athanasius, can trot out the famous unchangeability text from Rom. 8:35 and say, "Nothing shall separate us from the love of Christ."[138]

The monks thus fortified by rejoicing in Christ will therefore be like Job rather than Judas.[139] The Christ who cannot change, who by nature has stabilized an unstable cosmos, has brought to his saints the unchanging virtue, the secure and stable grace.

The nature of Athanasius' objections to the teaching of the Arians can now be seen in so much sharper relief. Their insistence that the sovereignly free divine will ran throughout the orders of creation and redemption could only horrify him. To insist upon the transactional model of free divine initiative and free creaturely response, so that even the Christ advanced in virtue as all other creatures had to do, would only, in Athanasius' view, enshrine capriciousness and reversibility in the very heart of Christian existence. The older anti-Gnostic Origenistic universe which could encompass a tremendous leeway of possibility and reversibility in the order of redemption was dying in the East. Athanasius sounds its death knell in his controversy with the early Arians. That more flexible universe, if preserved, seemed to him and his successors in the Alexandrian episcopal chair to enshrine a darker possibility: that we could career about in a spiritual world in which those whom we know should be lost (like Satan) could turn and be saved; and those whom we know are saved (like the saints) could turn and fall again. It is a permanence for human salvation that the new East seeks through its ontology. Athanasius is its spokesman, and his concept of the incarnate Logos is its guarantor:

> for in him [Christ] it was the flesh which advanced and his is it called . . . that man's advance might abide (διαμένειν) infallibly (ἄπτωτος), because of the Word which is with it.[140]

NOTES

1. *Vide* end chap. 1 *supra*.
2. Cf. chap. 1, n. 121.
3. Alexander *Ep. ad Alex.* (Opitz³, Urk. 14.29).
4. *Ep. ad Alex. et Ar.* 17.10 (Opitz³, p. 32).
5. Cf. Maurice Wiles, "Soteriological Arguments in the Fathers," *Studia Patristica* 9, TU 49 (Berlin: Akademie Verlag, 1966), p. 324.
6. *Vide* n. 70 *infra* for the terminology of *will* and *willing* in the controversy.
7. For the meanings of *monogenēs* in the controversy, *vide* Gregg and Groh, pp. 277–78.
8. Cicero *De Inventione* I.29.46 (Loeb Classical Library, p. 87).
9. Justin Martyr 2 *Apol.* 7, *Fathers of the Church: A New Translation*, trans. Thomas B. Falls (New York: Christian Heritage, 1949).
10. *De Syn.* 15.3 (Opitz², p. 242, line 18). Cf. chap. 1 *supra* at nn. 44 and 77.

11. Frg. IX (= Athanasius *Or. c. Ar.* 2.28) (Bardy, *Lucien,* p. 345). Cf. Athanasius' objections to a concept of the Son learning virtue (*Or. c. Ar.* 2.28–29).

12. Athanasius *Or. c. Ar.* 1.5 (Bright, p. 5): ". . . , τὰδε ἔμαθον ἔγωγε ὑπὸ τῶν σοφίας μετεχόντων, ἀστείων, θεοδιδάκτων, κατὰ πάντα σοφῶν τε." For μετέχειν as denoting accidental rather than essential participation, *vide* chap. 3 *supra.*

13. Athanasius *Or. c Ar.* 1.5 (Bright, p. 5): ". . . ,'ὑπο τε θεοῦ μαθὼν σοφίαν καὶ γνῶσιν ἐγὼ ἔγνων.' "

14. Cf. the Arian emphasis on the assistance of the Spirit in the ministry of Jesus (chap. 1 *supra* at nn. 32, 153–61) and Arius' phrase in the preface to his *Thalia* (*Or. c. Ar.* 1.5, Bright, p. 5): "ἅγιον θεοῦ πνεῦμα λαβόντων."

15. *Supra,* n. 12.

16. *In Ps.* VIII, *Hom.* 4, ed. M. Richard, p. 123; translation from John Barnes and Henry Chadwick, "A Letter Ascribed to Peter of Alexandria," *JThS* 24 (1973), p. 447, n. 1. *Vide* ibid., p. 446, for Asterius' lapse. The imagery of the husbandman, drawn from John 15, was apparently applied to God by Dionysius of Alexandria, who claimed he had not employed the imagery of the plant divisively of the Father and the Son: Athanasius *De Sent. Dionys.* 10.3 (Opitz², p. 53).

17. É. Boularand's speculation on a period of study at Antioch as a fellow pupil of Lucian remains sheer speculation, as he himself recognizes: "Les débuts d'Arius," *Bulletin de littérature ecclésiastique* 65 (1964): 178–79.

18. Sozomen *H.E.* 3.5; cf. G. Bardy, *Recherches sur Saint Lucien d'Antioch et son école* (Paris: Gabriel Beauchesne et ses fils, 1936), pp. 9, 107–8.

19. Alexander *Ep. ad Alex.* (Opitz³, Urk. 14.35, p. 25, line 11); Athanasius *De Decr.* 10 and 24; *Or. c. Ar.* 2.13.

20. *H. Ar.* 71; *De Decr.* 10 (Paul of Samosata and the Sadducees); 24 (Caiaphas and the Samosatene).

21. Robert L. Sample, "The Messiah as Prophet: The Christology of Paul of Samosata" (Ph.D. diss., Northwestern University, 1977), pp. 103–4, 109.

22. *Ep. ad Alex.* (Opitz³, Urk. 14.35, p. 25, lines 10–11).

23. Ibid., 14.30–34.

24. *H.E.* 3.27.1–2. Translation is by Kirsopp Lake in *Eusebius, The Ecclesiastical History,* vol. 1, Loeb Classical Library (London: Wm. Heinemann; Cambridge, Mass.: Harvard University Press, 1959), p. 261.

25. Sample, "Messiah as Prophet," pp. 164–69, 170–86.

26. Ibid., pp. 109–10.

27. Ibid., pp. 156ff.; *vide* also n. 42 *infra.*

28. *Or. c. Ar.* 3.29. *Vide* T. E. Pollard, *Johannine Christology and the Early Church,* Society for New Testament Studies, Monograph Series 13 (Cambridge: Cambridge University Press, 1970), pp. 186–87; Hermann Joseph Sieben, "Herméneutique d' l'exégèse dogmatique d'Athanase," in *Politique et théologie chez Athanase d' Alexandrie,* ed. Charles Kannengiesser (Paris: Beauchesne, 1974), pp. 195–214.

29. Opitz³, Urk. 6.4, p. 13, lines 6–7.

30. Arius may have inserted the κληρονομία from Heb. 9:15 or Heb. 11:8, or he may have cited it from Eph. 1:18.

31. *Or. c. Ar.* 1.58.

32. *Or. c. Ar.* 1.53–59. But the comparative "better" of Hebrews continues to be discussed throughout chaps. 60–64. At first glance Heb. 1:4 appears to be the third Arian text to be systematically exegeted by Athanasius, being preceded by Phil. 2:9–10 and Ps. 44:7–8 (LXX). But the latter key Arian text (*vide* Gregg and Groh, pp. 275 and 278) is quoted in Heb. 1:8–9. Thus material from the first chapter of Hebrews becomes Athanasius' *second* exegetical item, after Phil. 2:9–11.

33. Chap. 1 *supra* at nn. 111–12. Alluded to in the *Thalia,* Athanasius *De Syn.* 15.3 (Opitz²); for Athanasius' testimony to direct Arian citation of the text to establish the Son's creaturehood *vide Or. c. Ar.* 2.18. The *Thalia* (Opitz², p. 243, lines 7–8) carries in a list of "scriptural" names of the Christ the term ἀπαύγασμα, which appears in Wisd. of Sol. 7:26 but also in Heb. 1:3. The Heb. 1:4 allusion follows immediately upon these two lines. Heb. 1:3 was cited at the beginning of the controversy by Alexander in his deposition of Arius (Urk. 4b.13, Opitz³, p. 9, lines 3–4).

34. *Or. c. Ar.* 1.56, 58.

35. Ibid., 1.57; R. Greer, *Captain of Our Salvation,* (Tübingen: J. C. B. Mohr, 1973) pp. 89–90, treats Athanasius' exegesis of the passage.

36. *Or. c. Ar.* 1.59.

37. Athanasius *De Syn.* 15.3 (Opitz², p. 243, lines 9–10).

38. I.e., *Or. c. Ar.* 1.59, 62.

39. Ibid., 1.59.

40. Chap. 1 (*supra*) at nn. 113ff. *Vide* Greer, *Captain of Our Salvation,* pp. 94–95.

41. The most recent attempt to reconstruct the original *Thalia* mentions Heb. 1:4 but does not appear to accent the direct allusion to the text by Arius: G. C. Stead, "The *Thalia* of Arius and the Testimony of Athanasius," *JThS* 29 (1978), p. 28, and p. 31, n. 3 (but cf. p. 30). Greer, *Captain of Our Salvation,* p. 88, lists the key Hebrews proof texts and discusses them well; but his reliance on Alexander and Athanasius results in Arius' theology retaining its traditional (and erroneous) simplicity (e.g., pp. 68–70).

42. *Vide* Sample, "Messiah as Prophet," pp. 224–66 (for the edition of Paul's fragments), and n. 27 *supra.*

43. For example, Socrates' insistence that Arianism spread on the wings of "dialectic" may ultimately derive from his Platonic bias: cf. Glenn F. Chesnut, *The First Christian Histories: Eusebius, Socrates, Sozomen, Theodoret and Evagrius,* Théologie historique 46 (Paris: Éditions Beauchesne, 1977), pp. 173–76.

44. C. W. Mönnich, "De Achtergrond van de Arianse Christologie," *Nederlande Theologisch Tijdschrift* 4 (1950): 394–95.

45. *Vide* chap. 4 *supra.*

46. Currently in the Dumbarton Oaks Collection: W. Fritz Volbach, *Early Decorative Textiles* (London: Paul Hamlyn, 1969), fig. 32. Peter Brown, *The World of Late Antiquity A.D. 150–750* (New York: Harcourt Brace Jovanovich, 1971), p. 79, fig. 57, also reproduces this figure but dates it to the sixth century. Volbach's dating is to be preferred.

47. *Vide* chap. 1 *supra* pp. 17ff.

48. Pagan: cf. Porphyry, chap. 1 *supra,* at n. 106. For Christian deification and the more materialistic twist given to it by Athanasius (though a divinized creature never ceases to be a creature), *vide* J. Roldanus, *Le Christ et l'homme dans la théologie d'Athanase d'Alexandrie* (Leiden: Brill, 1968), pp. 165 and 195.

49. Sthenidas, *Peri Basileias* VII. 63, p. 45, ed. Louis Delatte, *Les Traites de la royauté d'Ecphante, Diotogène et Sthenidas,* Bibliothèque de la Facultè de Philosophie et Lettres de l'Université de Liège XCVII (Paris: Librairie E. Droz, 1942). Our thanks to Gerald S. Vigna for calling our attention to this text.

50. Ibid., p. 46.

51. Ibid.; trans. from the French translation of Delatte (p. 56).

52. Ibid., p. 274. *Vide* pp. 275–76 for first and second God speculation.

53. Cf. ibid., p. 277.

54. Cf. the influence (and juxtaposition) of wisdom literature models and that of the Hellenistic diatribe in the *Teaching of Silvanus:* William R. Schoedel, "Jewish Wisdom and the Formation of the Christian Ascetic," in *Aspects of Wisdom in Judaism and Early Christianity,* ed. Robert L. Wilken (Notre Dame; University of Notre Dame Press, 1975), pp. 169–99, and Wilken's own fine essay in this volume on the *sophos* and *sophia* in the *Sentences of Sextus,* "Wisdom and Philosophy in Early Christianity," pp. 143–68.

55. Socrates, *H.E.* I.5: Arius *Ep. ad Eus.* (Opitz³, Urk. 1.2); Alexander *Ep. Encycl.* (Opitz³, Urk. 4b.7, p. 7, line 19), *Ep. ad Alex.* (Opitz³, Urk. 14.26, p. 23, lines 29–31); Athanasius *De Decretis* 3.6 (Opitz², 6.1, p. 5, lines 23–26).

56. Cf. Arius *Ep. ad Eus.* (Opitz³, Urk. 1.5, p. 3, lines 5–6); Alexander *Ep. ad Alex.* (Opitz³, Urk. 4b.7, p. 7, lines 19–20); Arius *Ep. ad Alex.* (Opitz³, Urk. 6.3).

57. Athanasius *Or. c. Ar.* 1.14 (Bright, p. 15).

58. Athanasius *De Decretis* 3.6 (Opitz², 6). *Vide* Gregg and Groh, p. 271. For the Nicene fathers' use of *homoousios* in this regard *vide* G. Christopher Stead, *Divine Substance* (Oxford: Oxford University Press, 1977), pp. 248 and 250.

59. Ibid., pp. 250 and 256.

60. Cf. E. P. Meijering, "Athanasius, On the Father and the Son," in *God Being History: Studies in Patristic Philosophy* (Amsterdam: North Holland Publishing Co., 1975), pp. [91]–[98].

61. E. P. Meijering, *Orthodoxy and Platonism in Athanasius: Synthesis or Antithesis?* (Leiden: E. J. Brill, 1974), pp. 76–77.

62. *Ep. ad Alex.* (Opitz³, Urk. 14.26, 28, 47). *Vide* his comments on Arius' points at ibid. 14.46.

63. *Or. c. Ar.* 3.62 (Bright, p. 215); *NPNF* translation, altered.

64. Cf. *Or. c. Ar.* 3.59–62.

65. *Or. c. Ar.* 2.3. Athanasius maintains that will is secondary or external to a nature (*Or. c. Ar.* 2.2; 3.62). The mobility of counseling (τὸ βουλεύεσθαι) or choosing (τὸ προαιρεῖσθαι) indicates that such an activity is an "accident" (πάθος) of a rational nature rather than an essential property (cf. *Or. c. Ar.* 3.62).

66. *Or. c. Ar.* 3.66.

67. Cf. *C. Gent.* 42.3–4, Migne PG 25, 83A: The creature's beginning (ἀρχή) differs from the Son's (John 1:1) in that created beings have a διαστηματική ἀρχή (*Or. c. Ar.* 2.57, Bright, p. 127).

68. *Or. c. Ar.* 3.63; 3.65; 2.2.

69. *Or. c. Ar.* 2.31; Eusebius of Nicomedia explicitly rejects such a hypostasizing of will: *Ep. ad Paulin.* 8.7–8 (Opitz³, p. 17).

70. The synonyms and antonyms employed in *Or. c. Ar.* 3.66 indicate how βούλομαι and related words connote voluntary planning, decision, or counseling on God's part while θέλειν and related terms primarily connote voluntary desire. But Athanasius also mixes up and interchanges counseling and desiring terminology (as at *Or. c. Ar.* 2.29; cf. 2.30) depending on the scriptural texts he is citing and the particular point of contention with the Arians. The scriptures, which could speak both of the εὐδοκία of God's will (θέλημα) and the βουλή of God's will (θέλημα) (Eph. 1:5 and 11), did not always lend themselves to precision in the attempt to distinguish between planning and desiring. The Arians seem to have insisted on the Son being begotten "at his [God's] will (τὸ βούλημα) and pleasure (τὸ θέλημα)" (*Or.* 3.59); and here we can see that θέλημα is a synonym of εὐδοκία (so Athanasius at *Or.* 3.64, Bright, p. 217; cf. 3.62, Bright, p. 215, where μὴ θέλων equals "unwillingly" or "against good pleasure") (cf. *Ad Afros* 7). Arius himself seems to have employed the nouns θέλησις (Athanasius *De Syn.* 15, Opitz², p. 243, lines 3, 5, 11, 19) and θέλημα (Opitz³, Urk. 1, p. 3, line 1: here in parallelism with βουλή; Opitz³, Urk. 6, p. 12, line 9; p. 13, line 4), but without discernible precision. Eusebius of Nicomedia used the term βούλημα (Opitz³, Urk. 8, p. 17, lines 4–5) to exclude any generation by God that would imply a compromise of his freedom or a sharing of his *physis/ousia;* and this seems to have been Arius' prime concern, though his vocabulary differed slightly from Eusebius'. Asterius employed the noun βούλησις to underscore this same point (frg. VI, Bardy, *Lucien*, p. 344). But he seems to have been the Arian theologian who most clearly differentiated between "choosing/purposing" language and "desiring" language in concepts of "willing" (frgs. IIb, VIII, XIV, XV: Bardy, *Lucien*, pp. 343, 344, 346). Thus Asterius is probably the primary target for Athanasius' attack against βούλομαι and related terms in *Or. c. Ar.* 3.59–64 (cf. 2.29). *Vide* n. 65 *supra* for Athanasius' objection to the Son's being begotten by divine choice or purpose. But applied to the redeemer, the terminology of choosing and loving/desiring was for the Arians closely related (cf. p. 14 *supra* and Athanasius' discussion at *Or. c. Ar.* 3.66).

71. *Or. c. Ar.* 3.66 (Bright, pp. 219–20).

72. *Or. c. Ar.* 2.2.

73. *Or. c. Ar.* 3.66.

74. *Or. c. Ar.* 2.76, 2.77, 3.67, 2.30, respectively.

75. Cf. Asterius in Athanasius *De Syn.* 19 (Migne PG 26, 716C): "If the willing (θέλειν) of God had passed through all creatures successively, clearly the Son also, being a creature, was begotten and made by willing (βούλησις)." See chap. 1 *supra* for the transactional quality of willing.

76. *Or. c. Ar.* 3.62.

77. *De Inc.* 17.1 (SC, vol. 18, p. 324).

78. William R. Schoedel, " 'Topological' Theology and Some Monistic Tendencies in Gnosticism," in *Essays on the Nag Hammadi Texts in Honor of Alexander Böhlig,* ed. Martin Krause (Leiden: E. J. Brill, 1972), pp. 88–108.

79. Schoedel, " 'Topological' Theology," p. 98, makes this same point from the *De Decr.* 11.

80. Ibid., pp. 95 and 105.

81. *Strom.* VII.2, *ANF* translation, vol. 2, p. 524, altered (GCS 5.4–5).

82. *De Princ.* 2.6.2 (GCS, p. 140); 2.11.6 (GCS, pp. 190–91).

83. Ibid., 4.4.1 (GCS 28); 4.4.2 (GCS 29); 4.4.3 (GCS 30).

84. Schoedel, " 'Topological' Theology," pp. 94–95.

85. Ibid., p. 103: *Teachings of Silvanus* 113.9–11 (Schoedel translation). In Clement of Alexandria *Strom.* VII, the Son's nature is described as "the greatest excellence" (ἡ μεγίστη ὑπεροχή: GCS 5.4) which "arranges (διατάσσεται) all things according to the Father's will" (κατὰ τὸ θέλημα τοῦ πατρός). The Son is the "Lord of all" but the best one serving (ἐξυπηρετῶν) the will of the all-ruling Father (GCS 7.1). *Vide* also GCS 8.5. Irenaeus of Lyons had refused rather clearly to subordinate the Son to the Father; but he just as resolutely refused to speculate on the precise ontological relation of Father to Son in the face of the Gnostic threat; *vide* Pollard, *Johannine Christology,* p. 47 and n. 1. To the passages of Irenaeus that Schoedel cited should be added *Haer.* 2.30.9 and 4.6.2.

86. *De Prin.* 1.3.5.

87. Athanasius *De Decr.* 3.20; *Or. c. Ar.* 3.1.

88. Cf. *De Inc.* 17.4; *Or. c. Ar.* 3.1.

89. God is the Creator of the universe (*C. Gent.* 40.1–2) who creates *ex nihilo* by his Word (*De Inc.* 3.3) and who orders and administers the universe through him (*C. Gent.* 47.4). The giving of grace to creatures proceeds on the principle that what the Father gives, he gives through the Son (*Or. c. Ar.* 1.45); and the Son is said to give what the Father gives (ibid., 3.12). Therefore the grace is one (ibid., 3.13). *Vide* also *Or. c. Ar.* 3.32–33 for this; A. Grillmeier, *Christ in Christian Tradition,* vol. 1, 2nd rev. ed. (London: A. R. Mowbray & Co.; Atlanta: John Knox Press, 1975), p. 313, for his realization that more is involved in Athanasius' concept of Christ than *communicatio idiomatum.*

90. *Or. c. Ar.* 3.1 (Bright, p. 154).

91. Cf. Stead, *Divine Substance,* pp. 250 and 266. Athanasius was not overly burdened with precision in his use of the terms *ousia* and *physis.* He seems to have

used *ousia* in connection with Christ's generation to designate the divine essence and origin vaguely contrasted to the human (Stead, *Divine Substance,* p. 238). He employed *physis* in this same general sense of a contrast between divine and human natures; but the term can specify a characteristic of essence, such as God's immateriality and incorruptibility or human materiality and corruptibility (Roldanus, *Le Christ et l'homme,* pp. 35–37).

92. *C. Gent.* 41.2, quoting Plato *Timaeus* 29E (quoted also at *De Inc.* 3.3).

93. He quotes the old commonplace at *C. Gent.* 22.3, 28.1.

94. *Vide Ennead* II.9.8.

95. *Philanthropia* is one of Athanasius' favorite terms for describing the motive for God's approach to persons in the *De Inc.:* 1.3, 8.1, 8.4, 12.6.

96. Cf. *Or. C. Ar.* 3.51–52 in the light of this suggestion and the question put to the early Arians reported in Alexander *Ep. Encycl.* (Opitz³, Urk. 4b.10).

97. Cf. *De Inc.* 3.4–5; 5.1. In *Or. c. Ar.* 2.68, Athanasius indicated that Adam's grace was external (ἔξωθεν) to his body before the Fall. If this is not in conflict with the statements in the *De Inc.,* it must mean that an external grace would have sufficed for Adam, since before the Fall corruption also was external to his nature. But after the Fall and through practice in sinning, corruption is now joined to the body; thus the Word must be joined to the body in the incarnation (*De Inc.* 44.4). Hence the Word is not external to the body (*Or. c. Ar.* 1.45). In *De Inc.* 5.1, Athanasius indicates that the propinquity of the Word kept the first person's natural corruption away from him (citing Wisd. of Sol. 2:23–24). Cf. Roldanus, *Le Christ et l'homme,* p. 112.

98. *De Inc.* 7.4, Library of Christian Classics translation; 44.4. Cf. *De Inc.* 7.1–3. *Or. c. Ar.* 2.68 makes the point that people would continue to sin and be worsted by the flesh.

99. *C. Gent.* 2.1.

100. *V. Anton.* 14 and 93. Roldanus has suggested that the absence of a true doctrine of original sin made it possible for Athanasius to allow for specific individuals who did not sin (*Le Christ et l'homme,* p. 71). *Vide* also n. 132 *infra* and chap. 1, n. 114 *supra.*

101. *V. Anton.* 91; cf. Philip David Scott-Moncrieff, *Paganism and Christianity in Egypt* (Cambridge: Cambridge University Press, 1913), pp. 105 and 206.

102. *De Inc.* 14, noted by Robert Hardy, Library of Christian Classics, vol. 3, p. 46. Scott-Moncrieff, *Paganism and Christianity,* p. 27, thought the practice of painting portraits of the deceased on boards ended shortly after the Hadrianic era. But cf. the early fourth-century portraits cataloged at nos. 5 and 6 in *Pagan and Christian Egypt: Egyptian Art from the First to the Tenth Century A.D.* (Brooklyn Museum: Brooklyn Institute of Arts and Sciences, 1941 [2d reprint 1974]), p. 16.

103. Cf. Scott-Moncrieff, *Paganism and Christianity,* pp. 100–101.

104. For Athanasius it takes the incarnate work of Christ to repay that debt (cf. *De Inc.* 20) and to return us to a state of "natural" dying (ibid., 21), in which state we await the grace of the resurrection. Roldanus, *Le Christ et l'homme,* p. 63, has shown

that Athanasius indicates that φθορά continues beyond θάνατος and represents the more serious problem.

105. *C. Gent.* 41, Migne PG 25, 84A: "ὁρῶν οὖν τὴν γενητὴν πασᾶν φύσιν, . . . ῥευστήν οὖσαν καὶ διαλυμένην· "

106. *De Inc.* 4.5; cf. *C. Gent.* 4.4 and *De Inc.* 3.4.

107. *De Inc.* 6.1.

108. Ibid., 8.3.

109. Ibid., 8.1.

110. Ibid., 44.1.

111. Ibid., 44.4–5. Thus the Logos is "in" the body rather than external (ἔξω) to it (ibid., 44.5).

112. *Or. c. Ar.* 3.57: ". . . ἵνα δείξῃ ὅτι θεὸς ἦν θέλων μὲν αὐτός."

113. Ibid.

114. *C. Gent.* 4.3; cf. *V. Anton.* 74.

115. *Or. c. Ar.* 1.22; cf. *Or.* 2.18 and texts cited *supra* at chap. 1, pp. 13ff.

116. *Or. c. Ar.* 1.51.

117. Ibid. (Bright, p. 53); ibid., 3.20. Both texts cited in chap. 1, n. 67.

118. *Or. c. Ar.* 2.61; 3.58; cf. *De Inc.* 5.1. *Vide* Roldanus, *Le Christ et l'homme,* p. 60, for the importance of "participation" in this process.

119. *Or. c. Ar.* 1.50. While it is true that everything, including sanctification, is predicated on the incarnation (Roldanus, *Le Christ et l'homme,* pp. 154–55), the Spirit actualizes the possibility of salvation in each single individual (ibid., p. 149).

120. *Or. c. Ar.* 3.25 (Bright, p. 179). The quote from John 17:21 is the *NPNF* translation.

121. *Or. c. Ar.* 3.38 (Bright, p. 193).

122. Ibid., 2.69 and 3.40.

123. Ibid., 3.53. For the permanence and stability of grace under this arrangement, *vide* also Roldanus, *Le Christ et l'homme,* pp. 195–97.

124. *Or. c. Ar.* 2.56 (Bright, p. 125).

125. James Stevenson, ed., *A New Eusebius: Documents Illustrative of the History of the Church to A.D. 337* (London: S.P.C.K., 1960), p. 361; Joannes Dominicus Mansi, *Sacra Conciliorum Nova et Amplissima Collectio* (Graz: Akademische Druck- und Verlagsanstalt, 1960), vol. 2, pp. 673–74. For the Eastern Origenist historians' commitment to free will in contrast to Augustinian views of fall and history, see the incisive comments of Chesnut, *The First Christian Histories,* pp. 87–88, 93, 117–20, 243–44. For predestination as "foreseen merit": chap. 1, n. 121 *supra.*

126. Cf. canons 3 (on clergy living with women), 8 (on readmittance of the Novatianist clergy), 10 (ordained "lapsed"), 11 (falling away in time of persecution), 17 (usury practiced by clergy), 19 (rebaptism of Paulinists). Cf. also canon 12 (*supra,* p. 181).

127. Cf. the texts cited at n. 121 *supra* and n. 137 *infra* and chap. 2, n. 67 *supra.*

128. *Ep.* 10.4: Esau also persecutes Jacob, and Joseph is sold into slavery.

129. *Ep.* 10.9; 6.6. Cf. *V. Anton.* 89.

130. *Ep.* 6.11 and 7.9. Note in the latter reference the concern for those who have been sanctified and then are defiled—what can be termed the "many are called but few are chosen" theme. Cf. also the "bread of deceit" theme in *Ep.* 7.5 and the preoccupation with those who fall from grace (*Ep.* 3.3–4; 10.4; 11.4) or who feign grace (*Ep.* 11.8). To these must be added the general problem of the larger public pressing in numbers into the "church of the saints" (*Ep.* 7.4).

131. If Athanasius' writings give us a picture of *his* persecution by his enemies, the Meletian documents published by H. Idris Bell, *Jews and Christians in Egypt: The Jewish Troubles in Egypt and the Athanasian Controversy* (London: British Museum, 1924), show us how military officials could be pressed into service against the Meletians (and innocent villagers who had dealings with them) by the partisans of Athanasius: *vide* P 1914, pp. 58–71.

132. Two of the commentaries are Arian. For the Latin *Anon. In Iob, vide* Migne PG 17, 371–522, and the critical comments in Michel Meslin, *Les Ariens d'Occident 335–430* (Paris: Éditions du Seuil, 1967), pp. 201–26. For the Greek Arian commentary on Job, *vide* Dieter Hagedorn, ed., *Der Hiobkommentar des Arianers Julian* (Berlin and New York: Walter de Gruyter, 1973). Athanasius has had to address the general problem of heroes and saints due to Arian pressure (cf. *Or. c. Ar.* 3.10), and so he preserves lists of those scriptural figures capable of advance (cf. *Or. c. Ar.* 3.52, for Enoch, Moses, Isaac); but he also has a list of figures who endured in time of persecution—for example, David and Jacob—who appear in the *Ap. de Fuga* 20 and *Or. c. Ar.* 3.52 (cf. *Ep.* 10.4). Job is cited as an example at *Ep.* 14.3 (A.D. 342), 10.4 (A.D. 338), 13.2 (A.D. 341), and at *V. Anton.* 29 and 51 (here Job 5:23 is applied to Antony).

133. *V. Anton.* 16, Migne PG 26, 868A, *NPNF* translation.

134. Ibid., 7, Migne PG 26, 853A.

135. Πρόθεσις: *V. Anton.* 5, Migne PG 26, 845C; 12, Migne PG 26, 861A. Προθυμία: *V. Anton.* 11 (Migne PG 26, 861A) and 7 (Migne PG 26, 853A).

136. *V. Anton.* 25.

137. *V. Anton.* 26, Migne PG 26, 881C.

138. *V. Anton.* 40. The Athanasian Antony here quotes Rom. 8:35 of the unchangeability of affection granted to believers. Athanasius would distinguish this kind of unchangeability from that of the Son of God; precisely this distinction came out in the debate over this text at Nicaea: Gregg and Groh, pp. 267–68, and chap. 2, p. 68 *supra*.

139. *V. Anton.* 42.

140. *Or. c. Ar.* 3.53 (Bright, p. 206); *NPNF* translation, altered.

Epilogue

The outbreak of the Arian controversy heralded a new era in the history of Christianity in late antiquity. The most usual way of assessing the contribution of the controversy to changes in both Christianity and the life of late antique people has led historians to chronicle the subtleties and shifts of councils and policies (both secular and ecclesiastical) as they originated from various warring factions. And in fact, the Arian controversy had represented a dramatic means of demonstrating the new place held by Christian controversy on the center stage of late antiquity. This central position was a watershed that separated fourth-century ecclesiastics from their forebears.

But politics is not the only measure of the new situation of Christianity in this period. We have tried to examine another signal change. With the outbreak of the controversy, competing notions of salvation—and thus competing models of "holiness" and "perfection"—were offered for consideration and adoption to a vast Eastern constituency. Ecclesiastics were confronted with the choice between an orthodoxy in which grace had come to be the entry into a stabilized order of redeemed creation and an Arianism in which grace empowered people for moral advance in a transactional universe. Both options had predecessors in early Christianity, but no direct and easily traceable links run from earlier Christian thinkers directly into either orthodox or Arian camps. This is not to say there were no direct lines of influence from third-century theologians; in fact, we have tried to show such where they seemed germane and could inform the controversy. But we do want to emphasize the accumulating evidence that Athanasius' brand of Christology, soteriology, and biblical exegesis, no less than that of the Arians, sounded numerous new notes that would have made him, as well as his enemies, a curiosity rather than a hero in the East of previous decades.

Christian theologians since the Gnostic crisis had thought in both ontological and covenantal categories. They had lived with the language of being and essence and the language of willing and electing. By the opening volleys of the Arian controversy these categories had become competing options for Christology, soteriology, and in fact, ecclesiastical parties. It was not that either side refused utterly to employ one of the two languages. But each turned to the wider East to demand which of the categories—being and essence or will and willing—would rule and interpret the other in Christian discourse, exegesis, and Symbol.

Research needs to proceed with the problem of how and why this tension came to focus at this precise point in history and what its effect was on the next generation of "Nicene" and Arian thinkers. Here work must continue to examine the theological consequences of the late third-century Origenist controversy, even as new research has begun into the impact of the Synod of Antioch of A.D. 268. Social and historical factors must be taken into account in assessing the new kind of orthodoxy represented by Athanasius and the aggressive soteriology of the Arians and the implications of both for future generations.

However scholars finally assess the roots and consequences of the controversy, this book has attempted to set a new agenda for discussion, one embracing such questions as, what salvation does the redeemer model, what relationship exists between the redeemer and the redeemed, what is the path toward perfection or holiness, and what consequences does this have for an understanding of the interrelation of human action and divine initiative? Our research on such kinds of questions suggests we are approaching one of the last great battles in the East between humanistic and theistic tendencies in Christian theology and, hence, the opening stages of the final transformation of the classical world which will constitute the Byzantine Age in the East. If so, both Arians and orthodox deserve their fair share of the credit for helping to produce the new world of late antiquity.

194

Index of Subjects and Modern Authors

Sample, Robert L., 2, 31, 39–40, 165, 168, 184–85

Sanctification, 52–53, 55, 59, 67, 73, 107, 124, 132, 134, 144, 146, 153, 166, 190

Sardica, Synod of, 129, 158

Satan, devil, 29, 46, 64, 131, 133, 141, 145, 148, 158, 181–83. *See also* Demons

Saul, 181

Savior, 1–2, 4, 8, 12–13, 22–24, 27, 47, 49–51, 54, 58–60, 61–63, 65, 67, 69, 79, 92, 104, 108–9, 117, 142–51, 182. *See also* Redeemer; Salvation; Soteriology

Schoedel, William R., 174, 186, 188

Scott-Moncrief, Philip David, 189

Scripture, use of—Old Testament, 9, 11, 14–15, 19–21, 25, 32, 34, 38, 41, 48, 53, 57, 59, 61, 63–64, 66, 68–69, 74–76, 84–85, 93, 95, 98–99, 104, 107–9, 111–12, 123, 126–27, 158, 179–80, 185

Scripture, use of—Gospels and Acts, 3–7, 9–10, 18, 20–22, 24, 26–28, 36, 38–39, 48, 54–55, 59–62, 64, 68–70, 75–76, 84, 89–90, 104, 107, 109, 115, 117, 123, 129, 148–49, 157–58, 166, 168, 175, 180, 184, 187

Scripture, use of—Pauline Epistles, 2, 11, 20, 24, 39, 46–47, 51, 55, 59, 61, 68–69, 72, 74, 84, 89, 103, 123, 127, 140, 146, 148, 157–58, 182, 185

Scripture, use of—Hebrews, 11, 13, 21, 38, 53, 57, 60, 67, 69, 73, 104, 107–8, 112, 119, 122, 126–27, 152, 159, 166–68, 170, 185

Scripture, use of—other Epistles, 11, 23, 47, 58, 89–91, 117, 185

Seeing, of God by Son, 7, 9–11, 13, 62–63, 90, 100, 105, 109, 115. *See also* Knowledge, Son's of Father; Limitations, Son's

Serapion, 141

Servant, Son as, 11, 24–25, 28, 79, 95, 115, 117, 161–62, 166, 169–70, 175. *See also* Ministry, Jesus'

Sieben, Hermann Joseph, 184

Similarity, Son to God, 5, 50, 100, 103. *See also* Likeness, Son to God

Simonetti, Manlio, 31

Sin, 17, 29, 39, 66, 69, 132, 161, 166, 177–80

Singularity of deity. *See* Monotheism

Solomon, 55

Son. *See* Adoption, Sonship by; Anointed, Christ as; Appointed, Son as; Beget, begotten; Beloved, Son as; Brother, Christ as; "Certain One"; Chosen, Christ as; Commonality, Father and Son, Son and believers; Conformity, Father and Son; Consubstantial; Covenantal, Sonship as; Creation, Son as agent of; Creature, Son as; Creaturehood, Son and believers; Dependence, Son's; Derivative, Son's powers and status as; Distinctness, Son from Father, Son from creatures; Election, Sonship by; Equality, Father and Son, Son and creatures; Eternal, Son as; Existence, Son's; Faith, fidelity (Son's); First-born, Son as; Flesh, Son's; Formed, Son as; Generation, of Son; Glory, Son's; Human characteristics, Son's; Identity, Son with divine nature; Ignorance, Son's; Image, Son as God's; Incarnation; Instrument, Son as; Jesus of history; Knowledge, Son's of Father; Likeness, believer to Son, Son to God; Limitations, Son's; Mediator, Christ as; Merit, Sonship by; Ministry, Jesus'; Obedient, Son as; Offspring; Only-begotten; Originate being, Son as; Participation (Sonship by); Power, Son's; Preeminence, Son's among creatures; Preexistence;

Unbegotten, 33, 45, 50, 80–82, 88–89, 92, 97–99, 103, 110, 117, 123, 126
Unbegun, 23, 61, 77, 82, 88–89, 96, 98
Unchangeability, 1, 13–14, 19, 21, 25, 31, 50, 58, 63–64, 67–68, 70, 74, 86, 88–89, 91, 95, 99–100, 107, 112, 143, 149, 152, 161–62, 169, 179, 181–83. *See also* Changeability
Underworker, 24–25, 116
Unity, believers and God, Son, 28, 48, 60, 147
Unity, Father and Son, 2, 26–28, 34, 48, 54, 60, 69, 107, 117, 129, 147, 182. *See also* Identity, Son with divine nature

Vice, 111, 127, 163, 181
Victory, victorious, 14, 22, 68, 133, 145, 148, 166
Virtue, x, 14, 17–25, 28, 51–52, 58–60, 67, 69–70, 73–74, 86, 92, 96, 101, 111–12, 114, 117–18, 124, 127, 132, 134, 139, 141–46, 148–49, 151–53, 157, 162–64, 166, 169–70, 176, 179, 181, 183. *See also* Advance, moral or ethical; Ethical conduct
Volbach, W. Fritz, 186
Voluntarist, Father-Son relationship as, 26, 57, 92, 94, 97, 115, 152, 171–73, 187. *See also* Will

Wentzel, A., 72
Wiles, Maurice, 31, 38, 118
Wilken, Robert L., 186
Will, x, 5–12, 14–15, 17–19, 24–29, 31, 36, 38, 43, 50, 52, 54, 57–58, 60–64, 67–70, 78, 80, 82, 85, 91–92, 94–99,

101, 103–6, 111, 113–14, 116–17, 125, 132, 145, 147, 149, 152, 161–63, 169–79, 181, 183, 187, 194. *See also* Pleasure; Purpose
Wisdom, as title or attribute, 1, 9–10, 13, 20, 24, 28–29, 44, 51, 54, 56–58, 63, 65, 70, 73, 96, 103–8, 111, 113–15, 123, 127, 140, 146, 164, 175
Wisdom, God's, 88, 104–5, 115, 163, 169–71
Wisdom, Son's, 19, 59, 69, 105, 111, 144
Wisdom, wise, 15–16, 36, 62, 163–64, 170
Wisdoms, 25, 102, 104, 114, 123
Wise man (sage), 15–16, 18, 33, 36, 101, 132
Wolfson, H. A., 35–36, 118
Wonders. *See* Miracles
Word (Logos), 1, 4–7, 9–15, 18, 23–26, 28–30, 41, 44, 46, 48, 50–60, 62–66, 69, 72–74, 77–79, 83, 86, 88, 92–93, 95–99, 101–10, 112–13, 115–16, 123, 125, 127–28, 135, 140, 143, 146–47, 150, 153, 156–57, 174–80, 183, 188–90
Words (Logoi), 25–26, 56, 70, 85, 102, 111, 114
Work, Christ as, 1, 44, 46, 49, 62, 78, 91, 93, 97
Work, Son's, 22, 25–26, 28–29, 51, 61, 67, 97, 144, 147–48, 181
Works, 20–21, 23, 27, 38, 57, 59, 61–62, 83, 85, 91, 96, 104, 106, 114, 117, 144–45, 147–53, 162, 178
Worship, 49, 80, 124, 137–38, 140

Zeno, 33, 35

Index of Ancient Authors

Alexander of Alexandria, *Ep. ad Alexandrum,* 2, 3, 8, 19, 30, 33, 37, 41, 47, 50, 53, 55, 57–58, 63, 70–76, 82, 85, 119–23, 125–26, 129, 143, 156–57, 162, 183–84, 186

Alexander of Alexandria, *Ep. Encycl.,* 7, 14, 32–34, 70–71, 73, 80, 83, 103, 105, 119–22, 124–26, 186, 189

(Anonymous) Arian Homily, 30, 39, 41

(Anonymous) *In Iob,* 191

Antony (?) (Letter reproduced by Ammon and attributed to Antony), 132, 154

Aristotle, *Metaphysics,* 125

Aristotle, *Rhetoric,* 70

Arius, *Ep. ad Alexandrum,* 32, 39, 70, 82, 88, 104, 119–24, 126, 128, 156, 167, 185–86

Arius, *Ep. ad Eusebium,* 32, 37, 71, 82–83, 100, 119–22, 124–26, 186

Arius, *Fragments,* 26–27, 41

Arius, *Thalia,* 7, 21–23, 30, 32–33, 38–39, 41–42, 44, 56–58, 61, 65–66, 69, 73, 75, 80, 83–84, 90, 96, 98, 100, 102, 106, 113, 115, 118, 120, 121, 124, 163, 167–68, 183–85

Asterius the Sophist, *Fragments,* 32, 38–41, 85, 93–95, 103–4, 113, 115, 117, 121, 123–25, 128–29, 163, 184, 187

Asterius the Sophist, *In Ps. Hom.,* 164, 184

Athanasius, *Ad Episc. Aegypti,* 75, 155–56

Athanasius, *Apol. c. Ar.,* 154, 156

Athanasius, *Apol. ad Constantium,* 154

Athanasius, *Apol. de fuga,* 154–56, 191

Athanasius, *C. Gent.,* 157, 176, 187–90

Athanasius, *De Decretis,* 7, 23, 25, 30, 33, 35–41, 51–52, 56, 61, 70–76, 83, 86, 119, 121, 123, 128, 144–45, 156, 184, 186, 188

Athanasius, *De Incarnatione,* 75, 148, 157, 174, 177–78, 188–90

Athanasius, *De sententia Dionysii,* 46, 56, 71, 73, 119, 122, 184

Athanasius, *De Synodis,* 7, 10, 21, 23, 30, 32–35, 37–39, 41–42, 56, 70–71, 73, 75, 80, 82, 90, 98, 119–22, 124–26, 128–29, 168, 183, 185, 187–88

Athanasius, *Or. c. Ar.,* 2–6, 9, 11, 13–14, 20–28, 30–42, 47–48, 50, 53–55, 57–62, 65, 70–76, 83, 85, 92, 96, 99, 105–7, 112, 116, 119–26, 128–29, 141, 145–47, 153–57, 159, 163, 166–67, 172–73, 176, 179–80, 183–91

Athanasius, *Ep. ad Adelph.,* 157

Athanasius, *Ep. ad Afros,* 39, 58, 74, 119, 128, 187

Athanasius, *Ep. ad Dracontium,* 155

Athanasius, *Ep. ad Epict.,* 157

Athanasius, *Ep. ad Maximum,* 157

Athanasius, *Ep. Fest.,* 46, 71, 154–57, 191

Athanasius, *Historia Arianoram ad Monachos,* 137–38, 154–56, 184

Athanasius, *Hom. in Luc,* 70, 74

Athanasius, *Hom. in Mt.,* 121–22

207